Chinese Food and Foodways in Southeast Asia and Beyond

Chinese Food and Foodways in Southeast Asia and Beyond

Edited by
Tan Chee-Beng

NUS PRESS
SINGAPORE

© 2011 Tan Chee-Beng

Published by:

NUS Press
National University of Singapore
AS3-01-02, 3 Arts Link
Singapore 117569

Fax: (65) 6774-0652
E-mail: nusbooks@nus.edu.sg
Website: http://www.nus.edu.sg/nuspress

ISBN 978-9971-69-548-4 (Paper)

All rights reserved. This book, or parts thereof, may not be reproduced in any form or by any means, electronic or mechanical, including photocopying, recording or any information storage and retrieval system now known or to be invented, without written permission from the Publisher.

National Library Board, Singapore Cataloguing-in-Publication Data

Chinese food and foodways in Southeast Asia and beyond / edited by
Tan Chee-Beng. – Singapore: NUS Press, c2011.
p. cm.
Includes index.
ISBN: 978-9971-69-548-4 (pbk.)

1. Chinese – Food – Southeast Asia. 2. Chinese – Food – Social aspects – Southeast Asia. 3. Cooking, Chinese. 4. Cooking, Chinese – Social aspects – Southeast Asia. 5. Southeast Asia – Social life and customs. I. Tan, Chee Beng.

GT2853
394.12089951059 -- dc22   OCN713737562

Typeset by: International Typesetters Pte Ltd
Printed by: Mainland Press Pte Ltd

Contents

Illustrations	vii
Acknowledgements	ix
Introduction	1

PART I • Overview and Chinese Food in Diaspora

1. Cultural Reproduction, Local Invention and Globalization of Southeast Asian Chinese Food   23
   Tan Chee-Beng

2. Gastronomic Influences on the Pacific from China and Southeast Asia   47
   Nancy J. Pollock

3. Global Encounter of Diasporic Chinese Restaurant Food   75
   David Y.H. Wu

PART II • Chinese Food and Foodways in Southeast Asia

4. The Dragon's Trail in Chinese Indonesian Foodways   107
   Myra Sidharta

5. Acculturation, Localization and Chinese Foodways in the Philippines   124
   Carmelea Ang See

v

6. The Chinese Foodways in Mandalay: Ethnic Interaction, 141
Localization and Identity
Duan Ying

7. *Banh Cuon* and *Cheung Fan*: Searching for the Identity of 156
the "Steamed Rice-flour Roll"
Chan Yuk Wah

PART III • Beyond Southeast Asia

8. Transnational Cuisine: Southeast Asian Chinese Food in 175
Las Vegas
Jiemin Bao

9. Four Dances of the Sea: Cooking "Asian" As Embedded 192
Australian Cosmopolitanism
Jean Duruz

10. Southeast Asian Chinese Food in Tea Café and Noodle 218
Shops in Hong Kong
Veronica Mak Sau Wa

Contributors 236

Index 239

Illustrations

A Chinese Cambodian woman in Phnom Penh frying spring rolls	27
Lunbnia served in a restaurant in Quanzhou during Qingming	27
A Hainanese Chicken Rice stall in Kuala Lumpur	37
Laksa House at the Central Market in Adelaide	38
A Malaysian restaurant in New York Chinatown	38
Lap-lap in Vanuatu made from taro or other roots, baked in leaves with coconut cream	52
David Wu eating *Ganchao Niuruo Hefen* (Fried Beef Flat Rice Noodle) and *Cuipiji* (Crispy Chicken) in a Chinese restaurant in Honolulu, Hawaii	82
Variety of dishes around the cut-up *lontong* (rice roll cooked in banana leaves) to make it into *lontong capgomeh*	114
Stir fried bean sprouts with salted fish	116
Mie Belitung without gravy	119
Lumpiang sariwa	131
Pancit canton	134

Wedding banquet at the Yunnanese Association in Mandalay	146
Qingming rite at the Cantonese Association in Mandalay	148
A woman in Ho Chi Minh City making *banh cuon*	160
A *banh cuon* dish	160
Selling Vietnamese rice noodle and cakes in Hanoi	166
A Chinese Thai Restaurant in Las Vegas with names in English, Thai and Chinese	184
Chef Cheong Liew	193
A Chinese Singaporean food restaurant in Hong Kong	227
A Chinese Malaysian food restaurant in Hong Kong	228

Acknowledgements

We are grateful to Chiang Ching-kuo Foundation for International Scholarly Exchange for funding participants of the conference project "Chinese Foodways in Multicultural Southeast Asia" which was coordinated by the editor of this book. The project participants presented their papers at The 10th Symposium on Chinese Dietary Culture, which was co-organized by the Foundation of Chinese Dietary Culture and the Department of Anthropology, The Chinese University of Hong Kong, and was held in Penang on 12–14 November 2007. We thank the Foundation, in particular its Chairman Mr. George C.S. Wong and its Director Ms. May Chang, for the support and co-operation. The editor wishes to thank all participants of the conference project. Special thanks to Prof. Sidney W. Mintz who gave the keynote speech "Diffusion, Diaspora and Fusion: Evolving Chinese Foodways" at the conference, and who has been very supportive of this book project. The conference papers are printed in *The 10th Symposium on Chinese Dietary Culture* (Foundation of Chinese Dietary Culture, 2008). The papers selected for this book have all been substantially revised. We wish to also thank the two anonymous reviewers for their detailed comments which were useful for our final revision. Finally, we are grateful to Paul H. Kratoska and Lena Qua of NUS Press for bringing this book to publication.

Introduction

Tan Chee-Beng

Chinese Migration and Chinese Food

In writing about Chinese food in southern China, E.N. Anderson and Marja Anderson (1977: 319) write: "The food of contemporary southern China is, in the opinion of many, the finest in the world. It combines quality, variety, and a nutritional effectiveness that allows it to sustain more people per acre than any other diet on earth except modern laboratory creations that demand a major industrial input." The Chinese in Southeast Asia and in Taiwan are predominantly people whose migrant ancestors came from South China, who brought the food traditions from Fujian and Guangdong (then including Hainan Island) to these regions. The diverse Chinese foods in Southeast Asia — the Minnan (Southern Fujian) food, Fuzhou food, Chaozhou food, Cantonese food, Hakka food, Hainanese food, and others — and their influence in the region had their origin in Chinese migration. And the culinary inventions of the Chinese in different Southeast Asian countries have added to the rich heritage of the Chinese food.

Chinese cookbook writers often classify Chinese regional food into eight main types (*ba da caixi*), namely, Lucai (Shandong cuisine), Sucai (Suzhou cuisine), Chuancai (Sichuan cuisine), Yuecai (Guangdong cuisine), Zhecai (Zhejiang cuisine), Mincai (Fujian cuisine), Xiangcai (Hunan cuisine), and Huicai, also called Wancai (Anhui cuisine). Each of these eight major cuisines actually comprises various regional cuisines in the respective province. For example, Sucai comprises Nanjing cuisine, Yangzhou cuisine, Suzhou City cuisine and others, while the Chaozhou food of Guangdong cuisine is actually closer to that of the Minnan of Fujian cuisine. In addition there are eight well-known cuisines, namely Jingcai (Beijing cuisine), Hucai (Shanghai cuisine), Qincai (Shaanxi cuisine), Ecai (Hubei cuisine), Yucai (Henan cuisine), Jincai (Tianjing cuisine), Dongbeicai (Northeast cuisine covering liaoning, Heilongjiang and Jilin) and Diancai (Yunnan cuisine). Of these Beijing, Shanghai, and increasingly Yunnan cuisines are known to most Chinese.[1] The detailed classification of regional cuisines is actually quite recent since the Qing dynasty. For a long time in Chinese history the culinary distinction had been between the north and the south, and as Sabban (2000: 201) points out, it was during the development of the urban civilization in the Song dynasty that local food traditions became "systematized and recognized as constitutive elements of a genuine culinary style."

Simoons (1991: 44–57), like some other writers on Chinese food in English, classifies Chinese regional cuisines into "northern" (Beijing, Shandong, Henan, Hebei, Shanxi and Shaanxi), "eastern" (Jiangsu, Anhui, Jiangxi, Zhejiang and Fujian), "western" (Sichuan, Yunnan, Hunan, Hubei and Guizhou) and "southern" (Guangdong and Guangxi). Newman (2004) classifies the regional Chinese cuisines into Cantonese and Other Southern Foods; Beijing, Shandong and Other Northern Foods; Sichuan, Hunan and Other Western Foods; Shanghai and Other Eastern Cuisines; and Lesser-Known Culinary Styles. Actually the lesser-known styles may be quite known, too. For example, the Hakka cuisine is well known in Malaysia, Taiwan and Hong Kong. Even when the regional classification is comprehensive, we must remember that each locality in a particular region in China may have its own famous tradition. For example, Shunde cuisine is quite well known in Hong Kong, this being the cuisine from Shunde in Guangdong, known for its fresh water fish cuisine and the use of milk for cooking. While Chinese foods in Southeast Asia are mainly derived from Fujian and Guangdong regional cuisines, those from other parts of China can also be found in established restaurants, especially

Introduction 3

since the 1990s with the greater globalization of Chinese food due to the migration or hiring of chefs from China.

Migration involves carrying along cultural traditions and adaptation. Migrants can reterritorialize many if not most of their food traditions, but the lack of some traditional ingredients or the change in taste as a result of localization mean that reproduction of food heritage also involves reinvention; and the use of local ingredients as well as exposure to new culinary knowledge facilitate innovation and the acquisition of new cuisine. The Chinese migrants in Southeast Asia were also exposed to the cuisines of the Chinese from different parts of China. Chinese food heritage in Southeast Asia is thus enriched by both diverse Chinese regional cuisines as well as locally developed Chinese cuisines. It has also influenced indigenous Southeast Asian cuisines.

Anderson (1988: 258) observes that "Chinese overseas retain their diet longer and more faithfully than do many immigrant groups." This is especially so in Southeast Asia, where there are relatively more Chinese outside the Chinese land than in other parts of the world. Southeast Asia is also the crossroads of many civilizations, Chinese, Indian and European in particular, and so the Chinese in the region have developed their distinct Chinese cuisines that may be described as Chinese Malaysian and Singaporean cuisine, Chinese Indonesian cuisine, Chinese Filipino cuisine, and so on. With re-migration to other parts of the world, especially America, Europe and Australasia, and also "back" to Hong Kong, Macao, mainland China and Taiwan, the Chinese cuisines from Southeast Asia have also spread and globalized.

The book is an attempt to examine the diversity and contribution of the Chinese culinary heritage in Southeast Asia as a result of migration from China and localization in Southeast Asia. It also describes the globalization of Chinese food beyond China and Southeast Asia, in particular that which has been reinvented or innovated in Southeast Asia. While we are not able to cover all the countries in Southeast Asia — it will be nice, for instance, to have chapters on the Chinese food and foodways in Cambodia and Laos — nevertheless this volume highlights the culinary contribution of the Chinese in diaspora, Southeast Asia in particular. The proportional greater number of Chinese in Malaysia and Singapore has resulted in the development of a great many local Chinese foods for the local Chinese populations, and these have also become significant nowadays for tourism and globalization. Also significant is the spread of Southeast Asian Chinese foods via Thai, Indonesian, Malaysian

4   *Tan Chee-Beng*

and other Southeast Asian restaurants. Of the indigenous Southeast Asian food, Thai food is perhaps the most globalized cuisine from Southeast Asia. There are in fact around 20,000 Thai restaurants outside Thailand (see Van Esterik 2008: 92). And in the Netherlands, as anyone who has been there soon learn, many Chinese restaurants in fact serve Indonesian Chinese food.

I shall now introduce the chapters in this book, and then I will discuss a few themes that run throughout it.

Chapters in this Book

The papers in this volume are revised versions of the papers of the conference project "Chinese Foodways in Multicultural Southeast Asia," of which I was the principal investigator, and the project was sponsored by the Chiang Ching-kuo Foundation for International Scholarly Exchange. The papers were presented at The 10th Symposium on Chinese Dietary Culture: Chinese Food in Southeast Asia, organized by the Foundation of Chinese Dietary Culture and the Department of Anthropology, The Chinese University of Hong Kong, and held in Penang, Malaysia, on 12–14 November 2007. The symposium papers, including eight of the chapters in this book, can be found in *The 10th Symposium on Chinese Dietary Culture* (2008). I have invited Dr Jiemin Bao and Dr Jean Duruz to write about their study in Las Vegas and Adelaide, respectively, and I believe they add to the strength of the book.

This book is divided into three parts. Part 1 is Overview and Chinese Food in Diaspora. The three chapters give an overview of Chinese food in Southeast Asia and its globalization, as well as the diffusion of food from China and the accessibility of Chinese food in restaurants worldwide. In Chapter 1, Tan Chee-Beng uses the examples of Chinese Malayan food — Chinese foods in Malaysia and Singapore — to describe Chinese diasporic food as developed from culinary reproduction, localization and local culinary invention. The chapter also discusses the globalization of Chinese foods from Southeast Asia. It gives various examples of the diasporic Chinese food, some of which are referred to by a number of contributors in this book. Tan points out that the development of a great variety of local Chinese foods in Southeast Asia is made possible by the existence of "an internal market that facilitates the commercialization and innovation of Chinese foods to cater to the taste of the local Chinese population."

Introduction 5

Chapter 2 on "Gastronomic Influences on the Pacific from China and Southeast Asia" by Nancy Pollock compares Chinese foodways with that of the Pacific. The author describes the historical background of food in China and its diffusion to the rest of the world. This appropriately provides a background to readers of this book. The author is a well-known anthropologist who studies food and foodways in the Oceania. Thus her chapter also gives the readers an enlightening glimpse of "Chinese gastronomic globalization across Oceania." Thus far the Chinese significant gastronomic contribution is via the market gardens which produce vegetables and the restaurants that cater to "different types of Pacific feasting and sharing." Nancy Pollock points out that "Chinese food in the Pacific is seen as cheap, filling, tasty, and cosmopolitan." The chapter provides a wider perspective for the understanding of the globalization of Chinese food.

In Chapter 3 entitled "Global Encounter of Diaspora Chinese Restaurant Food," David Wu uses his life-long experiences from research and travels, especially in East and Southeast Asia, Papua New Guinea and USA to discuss the complexity of Chinese cuisines in the context of global cultural influences. In particular, he describes Chinese food and foodways in Papua New Guinea and Chinese restaurants in USA. Ethnicity, global capitalism and mass media "have played an important role in shaping new developments in the diasporic Chinese cuisines." There are "authentic" Chinese cuisines, and there are localized Chinese cuisines as well as fusion Chinese cuisines. His experiences reveal "complicated stories of food as cultural commodities that routinely undergo a process of globalization, adaptation, heterogeneity, hybridization, internationalization and complete transformation."

The four chapters in Part 2 describe Chinese food and foodways in Southeast Asia. In Chapter 4 Myra Sidharta writes about Chinese food and foodways in Indonesia, which has some similar characteristics with Malaysia in that Indonesia is also predominantly Muslim and uses Malay as national language. However the size as well as the ecological and cultural diversities of Indonesia offer more diversified environments in which Chinese migrants have adapted to. There is also much more culinary interaction between the populations in Indonesia, and as Myra Sidharta has pointed out, the influence of the Chinese foodways is evident everywhere in Indonesia; and the Chinese Indonesian cuisine is "a hybrid menu with the style of Chinese cuisine and the taste of the native Indonesian foodways." At the same time the opening of many new Chinese restaurants continue to introduce "genuine" Chinese food.

In Chapter 5 Carmelea Ang See, who is a Chinese Filipino very familiar with the food scene in the Philippines, provides us with interesting examples of localization and innovation of Chinese foods in the country. Like most Chinese in Indonesia, Malaysia and Singapore, most Chinese in the Philippines are Hokkiens, i.e., they are Minnan people, descendants of migrants from southern Fujian. Yet they have developed different localized Chinese foods while passing on similar food from southern Fujian. This only shows that cultural interaction enriches culinary heritage. At the same time, the Chinese Filipino food and food-ways have "influenced and is enhanced" by Filipino cuisines. Compared to Malaysia and Indonesia, Chinese Filipino foods are most localized and integrated into the local cuisines; and in fact the Filipinos, who are mainly Catholics, have adopted many aspects of Chinese foods and foodways. Of the three countries, Malays in Malaysia have a stricter observation of culinary boundary between the Chinese and themselves who are Muslims, and it is only since the 1980s that some items of Chinese cooked food are adopted by the Malays, and there remain rather few *halal* Chinese restaurants.[2] Of course food ingredients like bean curd and soy sauce have long been adopted by the Malays, as do the other populations in Southeast Asia.

Chapter 6 on "The Chinese Foodways in Mandalay" is written by Duan Ying who had conducted his doctoral research in Burma. The Chinese in the Burmese city are mostly Yunnanese. The chapter informs us about a different kind of Chinese cuisine than those found elsewhere in Southeast Asia. Like the Chinese elsewhere in Southeast Asia, the Yunnanese in Mandalay have also innovated local Chinese dishes. Duan Ying, who is from Kunming, Yunnan, finds that the Yunnanese there like a sour and spicy soup which they claim is Yunnanese but he has not seen this dish in Yunnan. The Yunnanese have also inherited many dishes which are similar to those in Yunnan. Duan Ying shows the significance of foods in relation to regional Chinese identities in year-round rituals. At the same time the popular teashops are important venues where the people exchange information, including sharing views about their common fate in a country dictated by a military regime.

In the case of the southern Chinese and the Vietnamese, historically they share so much not only in Confucian traditions but also in food. Chan Yuk Wah in Chapter 7 uses the examples of the popular Cantonese and Vietnamese breakfast called *cheung fan* in Cantonese and *banh cuon* in Vietnamese, to show how originally a similar dish of rice-flour rolls is

Introduction 7

today influenced by national boundaries and nationalism to become distinct national traditions, being Cantonese/Chinese or Vietnamese. She argues that there are in fact two local traditions of one dish type. Using her analysis of the rice-flour rolls, she points out the problem of lining cultural boundaries with geographical boundaries. "Cultures do not stop at border crossings," Chan Yuk Wah puts it very well.

In Part 3: Beyond Southeast Asia, we have three chapters. Jiemin Bao, who has done research among the Chinese Thais in Thailand and USA, writes about Southeast Asian Chinese food in Las Vegas. She emphasizes the agency of restaurants and chefs in the making and remaking of Southeast Asian Chinese foods. Jiemin Bao points out that Southeast Asian Chinese food in Las Vegas has gone through "de/reterritorialization" twice, once in Southeast Asia and again in USA. Like Chan Yuk Wah, Bao emphasizes that "cuisine is neither bounded by ethnicity nor national boundaries," and so she prefers not to describe the Southeast Asian Chinese food in Las Vegas as "ethnic." Instead of "ethnic food" Jiemin Bao introduces the term "transnational cuisine."

By describing a famous chef of Malaysian Chinese origin in Adelaide, Jean Duruz in Chapter 9 discusses the "embedding and fusing of foods," in particular how Chinese food, Southeast Asian elements included, is implicated in the production of hybrid forms of "Asian-Australian culinary citizenship." Chef Cheong Liew's nostalgic memory of food and foodways in Malaysia is part of his experience as chef in Australia. Another part of this experience is Cheong Liew's connection to local sites, such as Adelaide's Central market. Through descriptions of the chef's market visits — his purchases, interactions, rituals and attachments — we are given a picture of the foods and life there. Foods, of course, include Southeast Asian food, such as Laksa, that is so popular in Malaysia and Singapore, and indeed in Adelaide, too.

Laksa is becoming popular in Hong Kong, too. In Chapter 10 Veronica Mak describes the popularity of Southeast Asian Chinese food in tea café and noodle shops in Hong Kong. She describes the diffusion of Southeast Asian foods to Hong Kong and how these have been transformed to suit Hong Kong taste as well as the need of convenience and easy preparation in cafés and noodle shops. The spicy taste is kept to the minimum and this is helped by the use of more coconut milk to curry dishes. The media also play a major role in popularizing Southeast Asian foods. She concludes that Southeast Asian Chinese food provides a novel taste, at the same time its underlying culinary culture is still Chinese, and such foods like

Laksa, Fried Kway Teow and Curry Mee are becoming part of the Hong Kong food scene.

Migration, Localization and Innovation

A prominent theme that runs throughout this book is the localization of food. The concept of localization is most relevant to the discussion of migration, local adaptation and cultural production. Localization may be understood as "the process of becoming local, which involves cultural adjustment to a local geographical and social environment, and identifying with the locality" (Tan 1997: 103, see also Tan 2004: 23). In the case of culinary localization, this involves change in cooking to suit the changing taste of the migrants and their descendants as a result of their localization to the local living (such as the acquisition of spicy taste) or to suit the taste of the non-Chinese local population, as in the evolution of Chinese food in America to cater to the taste of the majority non-Chinese population. Localization may involve borrowing culinary ideas from the local population as well as the innovative use of local ingredients for the cooking of Chinese food. All these inevitably involve re-creation and creation of new dishes. We thus find in this book many examples of distinctive Malaysian, Indonesian, Filipino, and other Southeast Asian Chinese foods. Indeed Carmelea Ang See makes a very appropriate comment about Chinese Filipino food: "Everyone knows that the noodles are Chinese in origin, however, everyone also acknowledges that these food items are also truly Filipino." Indeed noodles can be cooked in different ways to produce distinctive noodle dishes, and even in China people in different regions make their distinctive style of local noodle dishes. Chinese migrants in Southeast Asia further created their own style of noodle dishes, taking advantage of local culinary knowledge, the use of local ingredients as well as the culinary styles of the other Chinese populations. The well-known Penang Hokkien Mee (*mee* is the Malaysian English version of the Hokkien word *mi* for noodle) is an example. Also called *hemi* or "prawn noodle," this is a Chinese Malaysian invention that uses prawn-based soup and prawns.

Such adaptation and transformation of cuisines is common of migrants, as Bao also notes in her study of Southeast Asian Chinese food in Las Vegas. Migration and re-migration not only contribute to the diffusion and globalization of cuisines, they also contribute to the re-creation of cuisines. Myra Sidharta in this book mentions about the re-migration of

Introduction 9

Chinese Indonesians to the Netherlands and Europe, North America and Australia and the diffusion of Chinese Indonesian food in those countries. What is even more interesting is the re-migration of Chinese Indonesians "back" to China, where they reproduce their distinctive Chinese Indonesian food (Tan 2010). Veronica Mak in this volume describes the adoption and localization of some Southeast Asian foods such as Fried Kway Teow, Curry Mee (both Chinese Malaysian and Singaporean noodles) and Beef Satay as foods served in the Hong Kong style café called *cha chaan teng*.

As the Chinese in Southeast Asia are mostly migrants or descendants of migrants from South China, we can still find similar foods between them, even though there may be some differences in re-invention. Of course we find tofu (bean curd) throughout Southeast Asia and in many parts of the world; and in Southeast Asia this is well adopted by the majority indigenous populations. In fact the Malay word for tofu is *tauhu* which is based on Hokkien (i.e., Minnan) pronunciation.[3] The chapters by Myra Sidharta, Carmelea Ang See and Jiemin Bao mention the Chinese spring roll called *lumpia* in Indonesia, the Philippines and in Southeast Asian restaurants in Las Vegas. It is also popular in Vietnam and Cambodia and of course in Malaysia, Singapore and Thailand where it is known as Poh Pia (see Tan Chee-Beng's description in Chapter 1). In addition Carmelea Ang See writes about *hopia* in the Philippines. The similar kind of biscuit with mung bean filling is called in Hokkien *daosa bnia* (popularly written as Tao Sar Pia) in Malaysia and Singapore, where different towns have their own famed variety. The origin of this bean-paste biscuit is in Southern Fujian, where it is still commonly available, and a brand from Xiamen is available at Xiamen Airport.

The Chinese in Southeast Asia live in multi-ethnic environment where they have also been exposed to European influences since the colonial days. It is in this multi-ethnic, historical and global setting that they have reproduced and re-invented Chinese foods as well as incorporating local and global influences into their cuisines. They are used to crossing ethnic boundaries in their daily eating, and have in fact also included some non-Chinese style of cooking at home. However, as Duan Ying points out in the case of Burma where the Chinese are used to the curry dishes of the Burmese, they still "prefer eating Chinese food even though Burmese diets are also common in their daily diets." In fact Chinese in different Southeast Asian countries prefer not just Chinese cuisine but their Southeast Asian regional Chinese cuisine, which may be described as Chinese Malaysian cuisine, Chinese Filipino cuisine, and so on.

Agency

Another common theme in this book is the agency of the chefs, in particular their creativity in reproducing and inventing dishes. As Jiemin Bao concludes in her paper, the chefs are "key players in facilitating cultural and dietary diversification." A chef's experiences influence his or her style of cooking as well as the transmission of a particular kind of food heritage; this transmission is of course not static but is shaped by the chef's local and global cultural encounter. Jean Duruz describes the famous chef Cheong Liew in Adelaide. She writes, "Remembered traces of Chinese heritage, of childhood and family life in Malaysia, of migration and re-settlement in Australia are ever-present in Cheong's gastronomy." Restaurants where chefs cook are thus important establishments which not only reproduce a particular style of cuisine but also re-define and invent dishes. The institutionalization of chopsuey as a Chinese American food has to do with Chinese restaurants in America creating and popularizing this food (see Lee 2008 and the chapter by David Wu in this book). Mass media and food critics, as the chapter by Veronica Mak shows, also play important roles in introducing and popularizing certain Southeast Asian foods. The acceptance and popularity of some Southeast Asian Chinese cuisines in Hong Kong owes much to the media reports and the food critics' writing and endorsement as well as their presentation on television.

Ordinary cooks, who may not be professionally trained, as well as ordinary people who cook at home all play their part in the reproduction and innovation of a diasporic population's food as well as borrowing culinary ideas from the local and the global. The historical role of the Hainanese cooks in Malaysia and Singapore is an example. In Malaysia many migrants from Hainan worked as cooks for the well-off people as well as making food for sale, and indeed many coffee shops in then Malaya and Singapore were owned by the Hainanese. Hainanese cooks no doubt played an important role in the re-invention of Hainanese Chicken Rice (*hainan jifan*), which has now become a globalized Chinese Malaysian and Chinese Singaporean food. This is actually a delicious Chinese fast food using ingredients common in Chinese cooking although eaten with a special chilli dip.[4] The dish is a Southeast Asian Hainanese re-invention of the famed Wenchang Chicken Rice from Wenchang in Hainan Island.[5]

Many Chinese in Southeast Asia hire indigenous domestic helpers (generally called maids in local English),[6] and they also contribute to the introduction of local cuisines. Duan Ying in his chapter on the Chinese

Introduction 11

in Burma mentions that Burmese domestic helpers hired by the Chinese are trained to cook Chinese food but they also introduce Burmese food to these families, and most Chinese women can cook Burmese dishes. Overall each Chinese diasporic family, through their own localization experience as well as through the introduction of domestic helpers, incorporate some local styles of cooking and cuisines into their daily diet. It is significant that we pay attention to the roles of domestic helpers and hired cooks. In the case of the localized Straits Chinese in Penang, Malacca and Singapore, popularly known as Babas (see Chapter 1), the well off among them, up to around the 1950s, hired Hainanese cooks and Cantonese domestic helpers called "Ah Sum" who usually wore white cotton blouse and black pants.[7] They must have influences on cooking traditional Chinese foods, even though they had been taught to cook Nyonya food, too.

Authenticity

The reproduction of a food tradition in restaurants and in the diaspora often raises the question of authenticity. The discourse of authenticity with regards to food assumes that food has an essentialized style and taste. This is especially so with tourists and migrants moving to a new place and desire eating their familiar food; they expect to have the same kind of presentation and taste as they are used to before migration. From their point of view, whether a food is authentic or not is a real issue, that is, whether the food is cooked according to the style and taste available in the original place of production. Such a discourse on authenticity involves comparison with one version treated as the standard. For example, people who have eaten Peking Duck in Beijing will use such an experience and knowledge to judge the Peking Duck prepared in a restaurant in New York or, for that matter, in Hong Kong. Perhaps it is not authentic because it is too oily compared to the one in Beijing or the way of eating is not the same. It is in this sense that David Wu in this book writes of authenticity, comparing to the foods he was familiar with in Taiwan and Beijing.

However, migrants often acquire new taste and readjust their "traditional" food to their new taste, such as the Chinese in Malaysia generally like spicy food even though the earliest migrants from Fujian and Guangdong generally did not consume chilli. Thus when a food is reterritorialized in another land, like migrants themselves, they may become localized or re-invented. Chinese Malaysians may not like the kind of Laksa served in the food courts or most of the restaurants in Hong

Kong but the hardly spicy and creamy Laksa seems to be well accepted by the people in Hong Kong. Authenticity after all is very much a personal taste and personal nostalgia. The authenticity of food is based on personal experience, and there is really no authentic "authentic food." To the extent that food is claimed to be ethnic, such as being Chinese (and specifically Cantonese, Chinese Malaysian, etc.) or Thai, people generally do expect to find certain features associated with such food, and so the discourse on authenticity is not one that can be just brushed aside.

Traditional Chinese foods are best preserved in festivals and banquets. Chinese restaurants catering wedding banquets generally have certain standard Chinese dishes (such as Shark's Fin Soup) even though the Chinese restaurants in different countries also provide local Chinese foods and tastes preferred by the local Chinese. Duan Ying points out that most restaurants in Mandalay are Yunnanese and foods provided at Chinese banquets reflect the diversity of Chinese foods in the city. With the hiring of chefs from China since the opening up of China, new regional Chinese foods are introduced to Southeast Asia, adding to the diversity of the region's Chinese foods, as Myra Sidharta has also observed in Jakarta.

Social Status and Identity

The perception of authenticity has implication on the status of a food. Both David Wu and Nancy Pollock mention of Chinese food as cheap in America and the Pacific. This has to do with the easy availability of simple and cheap Chinese food in many Chinese food outlets. As a result the general public perception in America is that Chinese food is of low status. But there are of course expensive Chinese restaurants serving *haute* cuisine. David Wu suggests that this has also to do with the attitude of the larger society about ethnic food. He points out that when non-Chinese operate "Chinese" restaurants according to Western standard, "they would be accepted as high-class restaurants serving high cuisine." In Southeast Asia, the popular perception is that the best local Chinese cuisine is to be found in coffee shops and popular local restaurants rather than at expensive hotels. Interestingly the inclusion of Southeast Asian dishes as international food in restaurants outside Southeast Asia, as Veronica Mak shows in her description of the food in Hong Kong, provides a cosmopolitan identity.

Food conveys identity. Nyonya food, for example, is very much associated with Baba identity (see discussion by Tan Chee-Beng in Chapter 1). Among the diverse Chinese populations, certain foods are associated with

Introduction 13

specific Chinese speech groups (see Chapter 1). It is common knowledge among the Chinese in Southeast Asia that *niang tofu* (tofu stuffed with minced meat) is associated with the Hakka, so is *meicai kourou* (braised pork with salted dry vegetable). It is interesting to note that the food of the largest Chinese speech group in Malaysia, Singapore and the Philippines, namely the Hokkien (referring to the Chinese of Southern Fujian or Minnan people), is not so much projected as distinctive, rather it is taken for granted. On the other hand we have Teochiu porridge sold in restaurants and there are Teochiu restaurants in Malaysia and Singapore. In a trip to Semarang in Indonesia in August 2007, I noticed that there were a number of Teochiu restaurants advertising prominently "*masakan Tio-ciu*" or "Teochiu food." We had dinner at one such restaurant and the owner was from Kalimantan.[8] In Hong Kong, Teochiu (and Hakka) restaurants are also very distinctive, so is the Cantonese cuisine from Shunde. This is not surprising since the majority takes the presence of their food for granted; it is the presence of minorities that are perceived as distinctive. Similarly in USA, for instance, ethnic foods really refer to the food of the *other*, the minorities.

Crossing Boundary and Globalization

The description in the various chapters in this book shows that there is much crossing border as well as globalization. Chan Yuk Wah in her chapter on steamed rice-flour rolls shows that it is pointless to say whether this food dish, called *banh cuon* in Vietnam and *cheung fan* in Cantonese, is Chinese or Vietnamese in origin. In the first place Guangdong in South China borders Vietnam and both were seen by the ancient Chinese as belonging to the "Southern Barbarians (*nanman*)," and historically both shared many cultural features. In the case of the Chinese in Cambodia, their Chinese foods are much influenced by the migrants from Vietnam (Chinese and Vietnamese), as I had found in my trip to Phnom Penh in August 2009.[9]

Even in the case of such popular Southeast Asian Chinese food as *kway teow*, one cannot say it is definitely invented by the Chinese in Malaysia or the Chinese in Thailand. The term *kway teow* is not a Cantonese or Minnan term as it is not used in Fujian, Taiwan, or the Cantonese-speakers in Hong Kong and Guangdong. Thus in both Hong Kong and Taiwan *kway teow* is used as a loanword from Southeast Asia, written as 貴刁 (*guidiao* in Mandarin) in Hong Kong. Actually the rice-flour noodle is known to the Cantonese-speakers in China as *hohfan* but the dish of fried rice noodle with eggs and shrimps is Southeast Asian in origin and hence the loanword. Perhaps the Teochius in Malaysia and Thailand introduced this dish which is known in Teochiu by that name and written as 粿条 (*guotiao* in Mandarin). And *kway teow*, both in soup form or fried, has really crossed border even in Southeast Asia, most commonly found in Malaysia, Singapore and Thailand, and now business people from Singapore and Malaysia have brought them to many other countries. Migrants and chefs from this region have helped to globalize this form of rice-noodle dish worldwide, and the Penang-style fried *kway teow* known as Penang Fried Kway Teow is especially well known. Anyway *kway teow* as a dish is a local creation by the Chinese in Southeast Asia and it has been crossing border in the region before being globalized to the rest of the world. However, as Veronica Mak points out, the fried *kway teow* in Hong Kong is really a localized version characterized with the use of roasted pork. It tastes very different from that in Malaysia and Singapore.

As food can be associated with identity and be used in the politics of identity, boundaries may be drawn. This is especially interesting in the case of Malaysia and Singapore. Historically, the Chinese in Malaya (today's West Malaysia) and Singapore did not draw a clear boundary between them, and the local Chinese food such as Hainanese Chicken Rice, Fried Kway Teow, Curry Laksa, and others are the common heritage of the Chinese in both Malaysia and Singapore. Today with Malaysia and Singapore as separate sovereign states, some politicians and communal leaders of the two countries dispute with one another about the national identity of these foods. Singapore, being more aggressive in promoting its foods for tourism, understandably has promoted them as Singaporean, and so some Chinese politicians and community leaders in Malaysia seek to reclaim these foods as Malaysian. The Federation of Hainanese Associations (Hainan Huiguan Lianhehui) in Malaysia has even introduced certification of Hainanese Chicken Rice to certify that the food sold in the outlets concerned is authentic (see *Xingzhou Ribao*, 6 Dec. 2009, p. 6). In reality, these food created by the Chinese migrants in Malaya and Singapore cannot be separated by the present-day state boundary.

In fact such Malaysian and Singaporean dishes like Hainanese Chicken Rice and Laksa have become globalized, and are available in Malaysian and Singaporean Chinese restaurants in many cities around the world, where there are significant number of Chinese migrants from these

Introduction 15

countries, from Adelaide to New York City, for instance. The globalization of Chinese food from Southeast Asia is the globalization of a diasporic Chinese cuisine, unlike the direct globalization from China to the West that Roberts (2002) has written about. Of all the cities outside Southeast Asia, the Southeast Asian Chinese cuisine is most accepted and even integrated into the Hong Kong Chinese foodways. The Southeast Asian Chinese foods are not only available in "ethnic restaurants" (i.e., Malaysian, Indonesian, Baba etc.), some of them have actually become part and parcel of the uniquely Hong Kong *cha chaan teng* café cuisine (see chapter by Veronica Mak).

Conclusion

The development of Southeast Asian Chinese food is closely linked to the cultural reproduction and culinary invention of the Chinese. The cultural change, in food and foodways, is influenced by interethnic interaction, localization, as well as interacting with the global. In fact the formation of the respective Southeast Asian Chinese food heritage forms the cultural heritage by which the Chinese in the respective Southeast Asian countries relate to themselves and to others. It expresses their local identity. The development of the Southeast Asian Chinese culinary cultures shows that culture is enriched by cross-cultural interaction. Chinese Malaysian food culture, for example, develops in the multi-ethnic environments where the Chinese learn from other ethnic cuisines at the same time it is shaped by the presence of different Chinese speech groups and flourishes in the "coffee-shop market" which encourages the innovation of dishes. It is not high-class Chinese restaurants that contribute to the development of the rich varieties of Chinese Malaysian food, it is the so-called informal market of the hawkers that fosters the development of so many delicious local Chinese dishes.

The spread and localization of Chinese foods in Southeast Asia perpetuate and diversify Chinese foods and at the same time creates new foods. All these add to the culinary diversity of the Chinese in global distribution and enrich the already rich varieties of Chinese food in the world. The migration and re-migration of the Chinese as well as globalization bring some items of Southeast Asian Chinese food to different parts of the world, including to China.[10] As Southeast Asian Chinese foods reterritorialize in these new lands, the whole dynamics of culinary reproduction, localization and invention operate again, creating even more new Chinese foods that are the results of more than one cycle of migration and culinary reproduction. There is also the overall contemporary globalization that continues to influence the production of food and foodways.

Food is very much associated with identity. The non-China origin aspects of the Southeast Asian Chinese food distinguish it from the Chinese food in China. Among the Chinese in Southeast Asia, the different levels of food localization are associated with categories of Chinese having different levels of acculturation. The more Malay or Javanese acculturated Chinese Peranakans have more localized foods, some of which like the Nyonya Cuisine (see Chapter 1) in Malaysia and Singapore have become commercially popular. Indeed Chinese in Southeast Asia are very multi-ethnic in their eating of food, but at home they generally eat their traditional Chinese and local Chinese foods. The culturally more localized Babas, for example, eat more localized Chinese foods (i.e., Nyonya food) than the less acculturated Chinese who stick to more "traditional" Chinese foods. The Chinese in Penang, due to Baba influence, generally cook many items of localized Chinese food at home, as is obvious in the items of foods cooked at home listed in Yeap (1990: 106–7).

Viewing food and foodways as cultural heritage, the study of Southeast Asian Chinese food and foodways adds to our knowledge of Chinese culinary heritage. Chinese cuisines have been associated with regional cuisines in China, and there are many Chinese restaurants all over the world which seek to provide "authentic" Chinese food. Authentic or not, the ever culinary reproduction, localization and innovation of Chinese food continuously enrich the culinary heritage of the Chinese of different nationalities. Increasingly many people in the world are not only influenced by the Chinese food from China but also food developed by the Chinese in different parts of the world. The great varieties of diasporic Chinese foods from all over the world are good to eat and to study.

Notes

1. Beijing and Shanghai cuisines have been well known, and with the opening of Yunnanese restaurants since the 1980s in many Chinese cities outside Yunnan as well as in Hong Kong, more and more Chinese have tasted Yunnanese cuisine of one type or another.
2. But see Tan's political economy argument in Chapter 1, that the lack of more *halal* restaurants selling Chinese food is really because there is a relatively large Chinese population that Chinese food sellers can rely on.

Introduction 17

3. A number of Hokkien food terms have entered Malay and other indigenous people's vocabularies. Other than *tauhu*, the Malay word *tauge* for bean sprouts is also derived from Hokkien. In Javanese, *suikei* refers to the frog dish, and the origin of the word is Hokkien for frogs which the Javanese called *kodok*.

4. The special features of the Hainanese Chicken Rice are the boiled chicken and the chicken-flavoured rice. The dish is actually not difficult to make. The recipe from Cheong (2009: 139) is as follows: Put a piece of crushed ginger into a chicken's stomach and use 80° centigrade lukewarm water covering the whole chicken to cook for 15 minutes over high heat. Turn off the heat and soak for 10 minutes. Remove the chicken and keep the broth. Heat up 1tbsp oil and stir fry 1 tsp minced garlic until fragrant, add rice which has been washed and drained. Put the rice into a rice cooker and add sufficient chicken broth to cook. The chicken is chopped into pieces and served with the cooked rice. For the chilli sauce, use 150g long red chilli, 75g small chilli (called *cili padi* in Malay and *zhitianjiao* in Mandarin), 75g garlic, 75g ginger, blend these ingredients in a blender, take out and add 2tsp salt, and squeeze lime juice into the sauce when serving.

5. I visited Wenchang in July 2009 mainly to taste the Wenchang Chicken Rice (*wencang jifan*) which is popular there. Asked any person from Hainan Island and he or she is most likely to be able to talk about Wenchang chicken and the chicken rice. Traditionally the chicken used were free range chicken but today they are likely to be partially free-ranged only, while Hainanese Chicken Rice in Malaysia and Singapore nowadays, or for that matter anywhere else, use farmed chicken. A woman in Haikou, capital of Hainan, told me that when she visited Hong Kong in 1937 when she was a small girl, she had seen food sellers selling cooked Wenchang chicken from door to door, carrying the chicken on a big plate. In her second trip to Hong Kong immediately after the war, in 1946, there was no such door-to-door sale, instead Wenchang chicken was sold at small restaurants and cafes. This shows that migrants from Wenchang had brought along their style of cooking chicken to Hong Kong. It is likely those in Malaysia and Singapore used the Wenchang style to reinvent a "new" dish now known as Hainanese Chicken Rice. For migrants it was relevant to use the term "Hainan," while in Hainan, to this day, it is only relevant to refer to the specific place of origin, namely, Wenchang. I thank my M.Phil. student from Hainan, Wu Huanyu, who helped to get details about her grandmother's account of her trips to Hong Kong described here.

6. In Malaysia and Singapore, these domestic helpers are mostly from Indonesia and the Philippines.

7. For a description of the Ah Sums among the Babas, see Gwee (2010).

8. In 8–17 August 2007, Myra Sidharta accompanied me and my wife to various towns and cities in Java and Madura to visit Chinese temples. We are grateful to Myra's hospitality and sharing of her knowledge on the Chinese in Indonesia.

9. During my brief trip to Phnom Penh in August 2009 to look into the Chinese food scene, I found that many localized Chinese Cambodians were from families or individuals who had re-migrated from Vietnam, and the migration from Vietnam continues to this day. Thus the foodways of the localized Chinese in Cambodia are influenced not only by the Khmer foodways but also by the Vietnamese and Chinese Vietnamese foodways. With the influx of Chinese business people from China and countries in Southeast Asia, there are restaurants which introduce Chinese foods from different origins. I found two inexpensive but good restaurants which sold Chinese foods from Malaysia and Singapore; one owned by a Malaysian Chinese and the other by a Singaporean Chinese, and both hired Vietnamese waitresses. All these, including restaurants run by Chinese from mainland China, Hong Kong and Taiwan, no doubt influence the Chinese food and foodways in Cambodia. I thank Dr Ngin Chanrith and his wife Channy for their hospitality while I was in Phnom Penh.

10. Hainanese Chicken Rice is now served in the cafe of many major hotels in China, and it may become another regional Chinese food in China as not many people there know its Southeast Asian origin and simply associate it with Hainan Island.

References

Anderson, E.N. 1988. *The Food of China*. New Haven and London: Yale University Press.

Anderson, E.N., Jr. and Marja L. Anderson. 1977. "Modern China: South." In *Food in Chinese Culture: Anthropological and Historical Perspectives*, ed. K.C. Chang. New Haven and London: Yale University Press, pp. 317–82.

Cheong, Patsie. 2009. *Reminiscing Local Dialect Cuisines*. Kuala Lumpur: Seashore Publishing (M) Sdn Bhd.

Gwee, William. 2010. "Remembering the Ah Sums." *The Peranakan*, no. 3 (2010): 12–4.

Lee, Jennifer 8. 2008. *The Fortune Cookie: Adventures in the World of Chinese Food*. New York: Twelve.

Newman, Jacqueline M. 2004. *Food Culture in China*. Westport, Conn.: Greenwood Press.

Roberts, J.A.G. 2002. *China to Chinatown: Chinese Food in the West*. London: Reaktion Books.

Simoons, Frederick J. 1991. *Food in China: A Cultural and Historical Inquiry*. Boca Raton, FL: CRC Press.

Sabban, Françoise. 2000. "Chinese Regional Cuisine: The Genesis of a Concept." In *The 6th Symposium on Chinese Dietary Culture*. Taipei: Foundation of Chinese Dietary Culture, pp. 195–207.

Introduction 19

Tan, Chee-Beng. 1997. "Chinese Identities in Malaysia." *Southeast Asian Journal of Social Science* 25 (2): 103–16.

———. 2004. *Chinese Overseas: Comparative Cultural Issues.* Hong Kong: Hong Kong University Press.

———. 2010. "Reterritorialization of a Balinese Chinese Community in Quanzhou, Fujian." *Modern Asian Studies* 44 (3): 547–66.

Van Esterik, Penny. 2008. *Food Culture in Southeast Asia.* Westport, Conn.: Greenwood Press.

PART I

Overview and Chinese Food in Diaspora

CHAPTER

1

Cultural Reproduction, Local Invention and Globalization of Southeast Asian Chinese Food

Tan Chee-Beng

Introduction[1]

Migration and the reproduction as well as invention of cuisines deserve serious academic attention. Much has been written about migration and migrants' adaptation to the host societies. Since the 1990s, scholars influenced by post-modern rhetoric have rephrased this as migration and deterritorialization, emphasizing detachment and fragmentation, and in the words of James Clifford (1997: 244), "experiences of displacement." The focus has been on diasporic discourses and transnationalism, and Ong and Nonini (1997) bring this into focus in the study of Chinese overseas. Migration of course involves leaving a territory and people have been migrating within their country and abroad, and they carry with them knowledge and experiences which they try to rebuild in the new environment. In this perspective the concept of reterritorialization helps to rectify the view of deterritorialization, that there is the "process of reinscribing culture in new time-space contexts" (Inda and Rosaldo 2002: 10). This is an important process of migrants adapting to a new environment, rebuilding their cultural life after migration. The term "reinscribing culture" is a good way of conceptualizing the reproduction of culture away from an original homeland.

Migrants also reinscribe their culinary culture; they reproduce their familiar food and taste. But they may be limited by the lack of certain ingredients, thus influencing the making of familiar food. At the same time they have access to new ingredients and the culinary knowledge of the local people as well as historical and global influences in their part of the world. Thus migrants and their descendants not only reproduce their traditional foods, they also re-invent and in fact invent new foods. The Chinese in Malaysia and Singapore, because of their relative population size[2] and living in the cross-roads of major civilizations and global interaction, have a huge variety of Chinese foods that include traditional and localized Chinese foods. Because of remigration of Chinese Malaysians and Chinese Singaporeans as well as globalization, many of these Chinese Malayan foods (see below) can be found in Malaysian and Singaporean restaurants in many major cities around the world. In fact, Chinese Malaysian and Chinese Singaporean food along with Thai food, Vietnamese food and Indonesian food are the most globalized foods from Southeast Asia.

This chapter uses the examples of Chinese Malayan food to highlight the development of diasporic Chinese food, a term which I use for convenience to refer to the Chinese food outside the Chinese culinary homeland in China. It provides examples of Chinese food in Southeast Asia, Malaysia and Singapore in particular. Some Chinese Malayan foods are mentioned by a number of authors in this book because of its regional presence, too, in the rest of Southeast Asia, and so the description in this chapter serves to provide some familiarity to some of these foods. I will introduce these foods according to the three main processes of their development in the Southeast Asian multi-cultural context, namely culinary reproduction, localization and invention, and globalization. In other words, the study of food is really the study of the cultural dynamics of constant negotiation between continuity and transformation, and the three major processes of cultural reproduction, local inventions and globalization are really the lens to understanding migration and cuisines, and for that matter, understanding any culinary heritage.

Chinese Malayan food refers to food that is not just Chinese but is also distinctive of Chinese Malaysians and Chinese Singaporeans. For convenience I use Chinese Malayan food instead of Chinese Malaysian and Chinese Singaporean food. Singapore left Malaysia to form an independent country in 1965. Historically Singapore was part of the Johor sultanate before it came under British colonial rule in 1819. The Chinese in the island and the Malayan mainland called Malaya shared much of the historical development, and they reproduced and invented their Chinese food without any culinary border between them. They have shared similar food heritage although nowadays the nationalist state differentiation has led some people in the two countries to regard the common food heritage separately as Singaporean or Malaysian.[3]

Reproduction of Chinese Food

Chinese migrants to different parts of the world passed down "traditional Chinese food" or "standard Chinese food." The terms are used loosely to refer to food cooked in the style assumed to be originally brought from China or are perceived as standard Chinese food that is reproduced by Chinese in and outside China and in Chinese restaurants. One can, for example, order *yangzhou chaofan* or Yangzhou Fried Rice in Chinese restaurants in Hong Kong, Singapore, New York or Auckland although the details may vary between them. Similarly the Sichuan tofu dish *mapo doufu* (Spicy Sichuan Tofu) is available in many Chinese restaurants worldwide, although it may not be *ma* or as *ma* (numbing spicy because of the use of Sichuan pepper) or as spicy as in Sichuan.[4] Major Chinese restaurants, while also serving localized food, generally sell "standard" Chinese foods, i.e., foods perceived to be representative of a regional cuisine in China, and so function to perpetuate, introduce and spread Chinese food. In trying to conform to known recipes, they standardize Chinese foods, while each chef also modifies the ingredients according to his or her experience and initiative. Overall, Chinese foods in global distribution are reproduced from a core food heritage that had developed in different regions in China,[5] and to this is added foods that are locally innovated or are adopted from the local people.

Understanding the food heritage in China is thus relevant to understanding the Chinese food and foodways worldwide, and for Southeast Asia, the food and foodways in different regions of South China are most relevant. Comparison between similar foods in China and in the Chinese diaspora is a useful area of research that will inform us much about the changing continuity, symbolism and localization of "traditional" Chinese food items. It has much to tell us about the dynamics of a culture. For example, the Chinese in China and worldwide still share certain similar items of food as well as the concept of *bu* (health-enhancing) and the general principle of cooling and heating food. This is for instance, emphasized in the food for the postpartum women. The idea of *bu* and the cooling/heating principle can easily be applied to adopted or locally innovated foods, and so overall the confinement food of the Chinese in different parts of the world really comprises both traditional Chinese and localized Chinese foods.[6]

Traditional Chinese food is also perpetuated in daily meals and especially in food prepared for festivities and special occasions. Despite the consumption of bread for breakfast or pizza at restaurants, rice remains the basic staple. The combination of rice, meat and vegetables at each main meal remains the basic principle of preparing daily meals or ordering food in Chinese restaurants. Some of the traditional food items reflect speech-group identity.[7] The Teochiu and the Hokkien are Min-speakers (although of different dialects) and they in fact also share some common dishes. For example, the popular Malaysian and Singaporean hawker food Oh Chian (H: *ozian* 蠔煎, "oyster omelette") is found in both southern Fujian and in Chaozhou, homeland of the Teochiu in China. However, in Southeast Asia, this dish has more fried egg than oysters which are smaller in size. This is an example of "traditional" Chinese or China-origin food not exactly the same as in China.

Another example is the popular Poh Pia (H: *bohbnia* 薄餅, fresh spring roll, literally thin snack referring to the thin flour skin) in Malaysia and Singapore. This has cooked vegetarian food and some pork or seafood (usually prawns and crabmeat) put in a sheet of plain flour "skin" (Poh Pia skin), which is rolled up before serving.[8] The vegetarian ingredients always include jicama (called *shage* 沙葛 in Mandarin, *bangguang* in Malaysian Hokkien and *guazu* in Quanzhou Minnan language) and firm tofu. In Quanzhou, Fujian, the similar item of food is much larger in size with different vegetarian ingredients and does not include jicama, and it is called *lunbnia* (润饼), not Poh Pia. The terms differ only in the reference, in Minnan language, to the flour skin as thin (*boh*) or soft (*lun*), hence *bohbnia* (Poh Pia in Malaysian Hokkien transcription) or *lunbnia*. While the fresh spring roll is the popular type in Quanzhou, Malaysia and Singapore, it can also be fried. The fried spring roll is called Poh Pia Zni (Fried Poh Pia) in Malaysia and Singapore. The smaller fried spring roll is popular all over Southeast Asia, and is known as *lumpia* in Indonesia and the Philippines (see the chapters by Myra Sidharta and Carmelea Ang See); obviously the term is derived from the Minnan term *lunbnia*. In Mandarin

A Chinese Cambodian woman in Phnom Penh frying spring rolls. (Photograph by Tan Chee-Beng, August 2010)

Lunbnia served in a restaurant in Quanzhou during Qingming. Diners use the thin rice sheets to make the fresh spring rolls. (Photograph by Wu Ruirong, April 2010)

28   *Tan Chee-Beng*

this fried spring roll is called *chunquan*. The spring roll is popular, too, in Vietnam and Cambodia, and the best spring roll which I have eaten was actually made by a localized Chinese woman in Phnom Penh.[9] It seems to me that the fresh spring roll (i.e., not fried) is the original form, and the fried type is a later development, most probably popularized in Southeast Asia. In fact in Indonesia, there is a distinction between *lumpia kering* (literally dry *lumpia*), the fried spring roll and *lumpia basah* (literally wet *lumpia*), the fresh spring roll.[10] In Thailand the spring roll, including the fried one, is called Poh Pia,[11] as in Malaysia and Singapore.

Different speech groups do have their distinctive festive food.[12] In the case of the Hokkien, for example, "red tortoise cake" (H: *ang ku kueh* 紅龜粿) is an essential item for the celebration of a child's first month after birth.[13] This is made of rice flour with mung bean paste filling with the image of a tortoise on the top-side of the red "skin," hence the name. Tortoise of course symbolizes long life in Chinese culture. The Minnan people in Taiwan (generally called Taiwanese) also make this for the same occasion, showing the common Minnan culture. The reproduction of traditional food is most evident in foods prepared for religious celebration and for festivals. The Chinese in Southeast Asia observe the major Chinese festivals, in particular, the Chinese New Year, Qingming (when the Chinese visit graveyards around 5 April), Duanwu Festival (which falls on the 5th day of the Chinese 5th moon, associated with dragon boat race and the making of the Chinese rice dumplings called *zongzi* [see below]), Zhongyuan Festival (popularly known in English as the Hungry Ghost Festival which falls in the 7th moon of the Chinese calendar), Zhongqiu or Mid-Autumn Festival (which falls on the 15th of the Chinese 8th moon), and Dongzhi or Winter Solstice Festival (which falls on 22 December or 23 December). These festivals are also observed by the Chinese in Taiwan, Hong Kong, Macao and mainland China, as well as by many Chinese around the world. Unlike in Hong Kong, Chongyang (the 9th day of the 9th moon), when the Hong Kong people visit their ancestors' graves, is generally not observed by the Chinese in Southeast Asia. Each festival is associated with certain foods or when foods are offered to deities. Thus Chinese of different nationalities eat *zongzi* during Duanwu and give mooncakes to relatives and friends to celebrate the Mid-autumn Festival.

Traditional does not mean unchanging as the application of culinary knowledge is influenced by individual liking and innovation and by local circumstances. For example, the Malay (and English)-speaking Babas in

Southeast Asian Chinese Food   29

Malacca, like the other Chinese, make the Chinese-style dumpling called *zongzi* or *chang* in Hokkien for the Duanwu Festival. As described in Tan (2007), the dumplings made by the Babas and the non-Baba Chinese may appear similar, but there are some differences in the ways of making them. For example, the Baba meat dumpling differs from the usual Hokkien meat dumpling. In the case of the Baba, the pork is finely chopped and fried and the dumpling is sweet, unlike the non-Baba type which is slightly salty and the meat is not finely chopped. Of course some items of traditional/standard Chinese food appear to be "unchanging." *Shaoji* or roasted crisp chicken appears to be similar whether made in Penang or Hong Kong, but the taste reflects the cook's individual use of ingredients and in Malaysia, this is popularly eaten with chilli dip. However, to give another example, in the case of Ban Chian Ke (peanut crumpets) (see Yeap 1990: 91), I find that it is the same in Malaysia and in Quanzhou. This is also popular in Taiwan where it is known as *banziandeh* (板煎嗲) (Huang 2004: 26–7).

With the end of the Cold War and the global movement of people from and to China, and the emergence of China as an economic power house, we find that since the 1980s, more and more restaurants in Southeast Asia have employed cooks from China. *Lanzhou lamian* (Lanzhou hand-made noodle), for example, is now easily available in Singapore whereas as recent as in the 1980s this was not a common dish in Southeast Asia. Chinese restaurants serve to perpetuate "standard" Chinese food as well as globalize Chinese food that originated from different regions of China. The hiring of cooks from China introduces new Chinese foods and this also reinforces the reproduction of Chinese cuisine among the Chinese in Southeast Asia and elsewhere in the world as well as introducing Chinese cuisines from different parts of China. There is thus increasing Chinese culinary globalization. Hong Kong and Taiwanese cuisines have of course been also influencing the Chinese food in Southeast Asia. The Chinese roast meat in Malaysia and Singapore, for example, is often associated with Hong Kong and even advertised as Hong Kong roast meat (*xianggang shaola*). The Taiwanese culinary impact has been more recent since the 1980s, especially with the introduction of tea shops serving Taiwanese tea and snacks and the opening of outlets selling various kinds of tea (such as *zhenzhu naicha*[14]) and tea-flavoured drinks and food such as beef noodle. Thus in the midst of localization, there is constant forces of culinary reproduction through the Chinese cooking at home, preparation of food for festivals, and the sale of "authentic" Chinese food in restaurants as

30 *Tan Chee-Beng*

well as the introduction of "new" food from mainland China, Hong Kong and Taiwan.

Localization and Innovation

The Chinese in Southeast Asia have experienced culinary localization not only in the kinds of food eaten but in certain foodways, so much so that the Chinese of each country can be culinary distinguished, such as between the Chinese of the Philippines and the Chinese in Malaysia or the Chinese of Burma, as the Chinese food and foodways of each country reflects the foods and foodways of the respective country. This also makes them different from the regions of China where their ancestors migrated from. The Hokkien Malaysians' love of chilli is very distinct from the Chinese in the parts of southern Fujian where their ancestors came from. My research in Yongchun in southern Fujian, where my grandfather migrated from, shows that the people there generally do not eat chilli; the small number of chilli plants are planted by the Hunan woman married into the community in recent years. In the city of Quanzhou, there are some changes as more Sichuan restaurants are established by the migrants from Sichuan, and some local Minnan people are beginning to eat hot dishes. But overall, the Minnan people in China do not consume chilli hot dishes.

In various parts of Southeast Asia, there are Chinese (such as the Malacca Baba) who have been so acculturated that many of them even eat with their fingers as do the indigenous people, although today this practice is usually confined to the domestic sphere rather than in restaurants. In the public arena, the general Southeast Asia way of using spoon (handled by the right hand) and fork (handled by the left hand) is adopted by the Chinese, too. Indeed, not all Chinese in Southeast Asia use chopsticks or are comfortable with handling them. The common use of fork and spoon and eating out of a plate is markedly distinctive when a Southeast Asian Chinese meets a Chinese from China, who expects to have chopsticks even when rice is served on a plate, otherwise they will ask, "How do I eat this?", that is, if chopsticks are not available. There are other differences in Chinese foodways between the Chinese in China and the Chinese in Southeast Asia. In Yongchun, Fujian, the villagers eat rice porridge (*zhou*) for breakfast and dinner, and rice (i.e., *fan*) for lunch, since this is more filling for farmers who work in the field during the day (see Tan 2003). The Chinese in Southeast Asia, including those of Yongchun descent, will find this rather weird, for *fan* rather than porridge is eaten at the main

Southeast Asian Chinese Food

meals, although rice porridge is occasionally cooked. This is especially so among the culturally more localized Chinese who share the same view with the local non-Chinese (such as the Malays) that rice porridge is generally for babies and the sick.

Most fascinating is the localization of Chinese in Southeast Asia and their invention of local Chinese food as well as the adoption of local non-Chinese food (see also Tan 2001). There are two main types of such food, namely the innovation based on existing Chinese culinary knowledge and innovation derived from local culinary knowledge combined with Chinese culinary knowledge. The rich varieties of Chinese hawker food in Southeast Asia owe much to the many items of locally innovated Chinese food. There are, for example, various kinds of noodles that the Chinese in Southeast Asia have innovated. There is the famous Penang Fried Kway Teow. This is actually fried broad rice noodle, called *hofan* (*hefen* in Mandarin) in Cantonese, but the Malaysian fried noodle with egg, cockles and prawns is unique, and in Hong Kong this Malaysian Chinese style of rice noodle is transcribed in Chinese characters according to how it is pronounced by the Hokkiens in Malaysia and Singapore as *gwaitiow* 貴条 (*guitiao* in Mandarin), even though the characters used in Southeast Asia are *guotiao* 粿条. As shown in the paper by Veronica Mak in this book, the one in Hong Kong is very much Hong Kong localized.

In Malaysia, Singapore and Thailand, there is another *hofan* dish, namely the wet-fried broad rice noodle cooked with prawns, egg white, pork or seafood and vegetables and some gravy. This noodle dish is simply called *hofan*,[15] although in Hong Kong this is qualified as *sap chaau* or "wet fried." There is also the broad rice noodle cooked in soup with shredded chicken, and in Malaysia the style from the city of Ipoh is most famous. Called Ipoh Hofan (怡保河粉), this is also available in some Malaysian Chinese restaurants overseas, such as in Australia.

Another famous Chinese Malayan food is Bah Kut Teh (*bahgutde* 肉骨茶), and the one associated with the town of Klang (not far from Kuala Lumpur) is most well known.[16] This is pork cooked in Chinese herbs together with puffy tofu, and eaten with rice. Visitors to Malaysia may end up being treated Bah Kut Teh by different Chinese hosts for every breakfast, unless he or she is not shy to say that he/she has had enough of it already! There are other examples, not only from Malaysia, but also other Southeast Asian countries. Suffice to say that the production of such varieties of Chinese innovated food in Southeast Asia must have to do with market competition among the sellers who try to come up with their versions of delicious food that is easy to prepare. In Malaysia and Singapore, the Chinese population is relatively big and so Chinese food sellers can concentrate on innovating and selling cooked food to Chinese and non-Muslim clients only. There are rather few Chinese restaurants in these countries selling halal Chinese food, and so it is not surprising that the Chinese cuisine is not as integrated into the indigenous cuisines as in Indonesia and the Philippines. It is actually the larger political economy rather than simply the stricter observation of Islamic dietary rules which account for this.

The other category of locally innovated food involves the use of local ingredients or adoption of non-Chinese culinary knowledge. This is especially so among the more localized Chinese, Chinese who are more locally acculturated, such as the Babas in Malaysia and Singapore, and the localized Chinese in Indonesia called Chinese Peranakan in contrast to the Totok, the "pure" Chinese. In Malaysia and Singapore the Baba cuisine, often referred to as Nyonya food, is well known. The Baba are acculturated Chinese in Malacca who generally speak a creolized Malay (Baba Malay) and English among themselves, although those in Singapore nowadays generally speak English. In terms of gender differentiation, the men are called "Baba" and the women "Nyonya." Since traditionally women cook at home, the food of the Baba is often referred to as Nyonya food. Like the acculturated Chinese in Indonesia, the Malacca and Singapore Babas also identify themselves as "Peranakan."[17] The Straits-born Chinese in Penang were also known as Baba although they speak a localized Hokkien dialect (rather than Malay) and English among themselves. Their localized cuisine shares a lot of similarities with that of the Babas in Malacca and Singapore.

The culinary localization by using local ingredients and local culinary knowledge can be as simple as just adding chilli paste (called *sambal* in Malay) or shrimp paste (*belacan*) and chilli, as in the cooking of *kangkong*, called *tong-choi* in Cantonese or *wengcai* (also *kongxin cai*) in Mandarin. Such a dish of *kangkong* cooked with *belacan* and chilli is also available in Chinese restaurants in Malaysia and Singapore, under the beautiful name *malai fengguang* or "Malay Scenery." *Kangkong* (*Ipomoea reptans*) is of course a very common and important vegetable throughout Southeast Asia and South China. A simple way of eating in Vietnam is to boil the vegetable and eat with a sauce dip. In Malaysia, there is a delicious Chinese hawker food that uses *kangkong*. This is, in Hokkien, *liuhi yingcai*, or *kangkong* with cuttlefish salad flavoured with prawn sauce.

Southeast Asian Chinese Food 33

The adoption of *sambal* allows the Baba to have many *sambal* dishes such as *sambal udang petai* (prawn *sambal* with *petai*) and *sambal bendi* (okra *sambal*) which the Malays also eat, but also pork *sambal* which is forbidden to Muslims. Even fern shoots cooked with *sambal* is available in many Chinese restaurants in Malaysia. Both the fern shoots (*paku* in Malay) and the *petai* (a kind of "stinking" legume harvested from Parkia speciosa tree) are originally indigenous non-Chinese food associated with the Malays and other indigenous minorities. In China fern shoots are locally available and eaten in Yunnan, Guizhou and Hainan. However, the Chinese migrants in Southeast Asia, other than the Yunnanese in Burma and Thailand, were predominantly from Fujian and Guangdong.

Cooking in curry is common in Southeast Asia and the Chinese have adopted as well as innovated curry dishes. A famous curry dish is Fish Head Curry, which is especially delicious when the meaty red snapper head is used. Most of the innovation of Chinese dishes that are derived from local knowledge have to do with the innovative use of ingredients that are commonly used in Southeast Asia, such as palm sugar, galangal (*lengkuas* in Malay), lemon grass (*serai* in Malay), turmeric (*kunyit* in Malay, both the tuber and the leaf), lime, kaffir lime leaf, coriander seeds, and many other local plants and herbs, and of course chilli and *belacan*. Unlike the traditional Chinese way of cooking, cooking Southeast Asian dishes involves the preparation and mixing of spices into a spice mix called *rempah* in Malay. A very well known and delicious dish is Asam Fish Head or Tamarind Fish Head. Tamarind fish dishes in spicy and sour gravy are popular Nyonya dishes (see Lee 1974; Tan, Cecilia 1983).

The famed Nyonya food (Baba food) comprises both traditional Chinese food and many items of locally innovated food that involves the preparation of *rempah* (mixture of spices for a dish), which is especially essential for the cooking of *gulai* dishes, i.e., dishes in gravy. In terms of cooking and preparation, *sambal* dishes, *gulai* dishes, and curry dishes are three categories of dishes that appear least traditionally Chinese. There are of course other categories such as the *acar* (pickles) dishes which are quite distinct from the traditional Chinese types, and in Penang and Kelantan *kerabu* dishes (see below) form another important category. I have classified the Nyonya food in Malaysia and Singapore into the Northern Nyonya Tradition (Penang Nyonya food) and the Southern Nyonya Tradition (Malacca and Singapore Nyonya food) (Tan 2007: 171). They share common dishes but are also distinct. For example, Penang Laksa, also called Assam Laksa (coarse rice vermicelli in hot and sour fish gravy), belongs to the Northern tradition while in Malacca, Johor and Singapore, Laksa is generally understood as Curry Laksa (rice vermicelli in curry soup).

There are also foods that are borrowed from the local non-Chinese peoples, especially those of the Malays in the case of Malaysia, such as *nasi lemak* and *tapai*. The former is rice cooked with coconut milk, traditionally wrapped in banana leaves, together with the chilli paste called *sambal*, some cucumber slices, a slice of egg, some fried anchovy (called *ikan bilis* in Malay) and often some fried peanuts, too. Today *nasi lemak* is really the food of all Malaysians in West Malaysia, and it is available in many restaurants selling Malaysian and Indonesian foods. There are different variations including serving with meat cooked in the Malay style such as *rendang* chicken or *rendang* beef.[18] The Chinese, especially the Babas, have also innovated their own style of *nasi lemak*, which has become a part of their cultural tradition.

The Babas have adopted the fermented rice called *tapai* (pronounced *tapɛ* in Baba Malay), including the taboos that are observed in its making, so that sweet rather than sour *tapai* is produced. There are also regional Malay dishes adopted by the Chinese of different regions. In Kelantan, the Chinese foods include the *kerabu* dishes (spicy salad mixed with minced fish) of the local Malays and Thais, but the Chinese claim to make their own style too. The Thai influence on Penang Chinese food is most visible in the making of *kerabu* dishes, which are generally not known to most Chinese in the southern part of the peninsula, such as in Johor and Singapore. In *Nyonya Flavors: A Complete Guide to Penang Straits Chinese Cuisine* (Wong 2003), there is a section on *kerabu* dishes and these include Chicken Feet Kerabu and Pork Skin Kerabu which reflect distinct Chinese taste. Wong (2003: 61) points out that the preference for *sambal belacan* "thinned down with a little lime juice" distinguishes the Penang Nyonya *kerabu* from the Thai *kerabu* which uses fish sauce, small chilli and lime juice. Overall the extent of localization of Chinese food in Southeast Asia reflects the extent of acculturation, as the more acculturated Chinese such as the Babas in Malacca or the "Peranakanized" Chinese in Kelantan and Terengganu have more localized foods and are more familiar with the Malay foods. The least acculturated Chinese eat more "traditional" Chinese food at home.

Localization and invention are very evident in the Southeast Asian Chinese adoption of some local cakes and pastries which are better expressed by the Hokkien term *ge* or the Malay term *kuih*.[19] For the

Chinese New Year, for instance, the Chinese in Malaysia not only make various kinds of traditional Chinese *ge*, they also make some Malay *kuih* such as *kuih bangkit*.[20] The Babas have the most varieties of *kuih* of Chinese origin, Malay origin, Javanese origin and those that they have innovated. This is true of the Chinese in Indonesia, too. Even the Indonesian Chinese returnees in China continue to make Indonesian *kuih*. In fact the first time I ate Sumba *kuih* was in Yongchun in Southern Fujian, when in February 2006 I visited a Chinese family who had migrated from Sumba. It was Chinese New Year and I was served Indonesian coffee and various kinds of Sumba *kuih* which the wife had made. I have not been to the Indonesian island Sumba, and it was exciting to eat the *kuih* that has its origin from there, of all the places, in China.

In discussing localization and Chinese food in Malaysia, I have mentioned mainly Chinese and Malay cultural interaction; in fact there are influences from other ethnic groups, too. The Penang Nyonya-style Indian Salad called Cheh Hu (H: *cnihi* 青魚, literally green fish) or Bosomboh is obviously of Indian origin (see Cecilia Tan 1983: 18; Wong 2003: 48). Colonial rule also left its mark, especially in the making of some cakes and pastries. There are some examples from Penang. The preferred use of Worcestershire sauce for some food items is an example, such as for the cooking of the special Penang fried chicken called Inchee Kabin (for recipes, see Yeap 1990: 19). Other examples are Kuih Pie Tee (also called Top Hats, being shredded bamboo shoots in piecrust cases)[21] and pineapple tarts. These should also be considered as part of the localization in Southeast Asia, in contrast to the more contemporary influences of globalization. Anyway the Kuih Pie Tee and pineapple tarts are really Chinese innovation in the multi-ethnic environment of Malaysia that includes cultural influences from the West.

The great varieties of Chinese food, especially the local Chinese food, together with Chinese restaurants and Chinese coffee shops (called *kopitiam* in Malaysia and Singapore, from the Hokkien word for coffee shops) as well as hawker centres make up the major foodscape in Southeast Asia, Malaysia and Singapore in particular. Most Chinese coffee shops in Malaysia are also sites of selling hawker foods, where a great variety of delicious local Chinese, Indian and Malay foods are available at inexpensive prices. The hawker centres where there are many hawker stalls selling all kinds of street foods are especially popular in the evening, where many people go for *xiaoye*, a Chinese practice of having after dinner evening snacks.[22]

Globalization of Southeast Asian Chinese Food

As Chinese from Southeast Asian countries migrate overseas they bring along their knowledge of Southeast Asian Chinese food which is "reterritorialized" in other lands. This is especially so with the establishment of Southeast Asian Chinese restaurants beyond Southeast Asia to cater to Southeast Asian Chinese migrants and introduce the food to the local people. Take Malaysia for example, the rich varieties of Chinese Malaysian food is well known and some restaurants catering to some of these foods is found in other Southeast Asian countries and beyond Southeast Asia. For example, Penang Chinese food is sold in some Penang restaurants in Jakarta.[23] There is also a Penang Chinese restaurant in Semarang, another major city in Indonesia.

In Hong Kong, which is a very cosmopolitan city, there are restaurants that serve many kinds of food from different parts of the world. Southeast Asian Chinese food is quite predominant, and some items like Hainanese Chicken Rice, Bah Kut Teh, Satay, and even Laksa have become familiar items to the Hong Kong people, even though Malaysians and Singaporeans may feel that they are not as authentic as in Malaysia and Singapore. Even in restaurants in prestigious hotels serving buffet, when selecting noodle to be cooked, there is often the choice of Laksa soup or other kinds of soup (for example, chicken soup). There are even Baba restaurants, although generally small, run by Malaysians or Singaporeans and even local Hong Kong people. For example, in Mercer Street, Sheung Wan, there is Katong Laksa · Prawn Mee Restaurant and Malaymama Restaurant serving the Penang-style Prawn Noodle Soup (Hokkien Mee), Laksa, and other popular "Baba" dishes, even Tow Suan (split mung bean sweet soup)[24] and *roti kaya*, which is "egg jam on toast;" the egg jam is popular in Malaysia and Singapore. The spicy rice noodle dish called Mee Siam, which uses quite a lot of soybean paste (see Lee 1974: 49 for a recipe), is available in some Malaysian and Singaporean restaurants. Even the Penang style *laksa asam* is available in a small Malaysian Chinese restaurant run by a Chinese family from Penang.[25]

Most striking in Hong Kong is the many Indonesian restaurants run by Indonesian Chinese, serving many types of Indonesian Chinese and Indonesian dishes, but also some popular dishes from Malaysia and Singapore, such as Laksa, Otak-Otak (appropriately described as spicy fish custard in Wong [2003: 142]),[26] Malaysian-style Rojak (Malaysian salad with sweet prawn paste), Bubur Chacha (this is a desert containing

Southeast Asian Chinese Food

A Hainanese Chicken Rice stall in Kuala Lumpur. (Photograph by Tan Chee-Beng, April 1996)

medley of sweet potato, taro, sago and others in coconut milk, etc.),[27] and of course there are many kinds of *kuih*. The marked presence of Indonesian Chinese (Chinese returnees to China who came to Hong Kong mostly in the 1970s) and Indonesian domestic workers create a market for such restaurants and many small Indonesia sundry shops, also run by Indonesian Chinese. My research on Indonesian Chinese in Hong Kong has led me to meet Mr. Jiang in June 2007, who together with another Indonesian Chinese Mr. Chen, established the first Indonesian restaurant in Hong Kong in 1968. His three restaurants are thus named IR 1968, i.e., Indonesian Restaurant 1968, although Mr. Chen had since operated his own restaurant called Indonesia Restaurant.[28]

Laksa House at the Central Market in Adelaide. (Photograph by Tan Chee-Beng, December 2008)

A Malaysian restaurant in New York Chinatown. (Photograph by Tan Chee-Beng, July 2009)

Taking the example of Chinese Malaysians further, we know that countries like the United Kingdom, Australia, New Zealand and North America have been popular destinations where many Chinese from Southeast Asia migrate or go there to study. In these countries there are Southeast Asian Chinese restaurants of one kind or another. Jean Duruz (2007) has written about the Laksa in Australia. Indeed one can get quite good Chinese Malayan food in Australia and New Zealand as Chinese from Malaysia and Singapore have a long history of migration to these Australasia countries. I was pleasantly surprised to have very good Hainanese Chicken Rice in a hotel restaurant in Auckland when I visited the city in July 2009.[29] In April 2009 in New York I had lunch at New Malaysia Restaurant at the Chinatown Arcade. I tried Fried Kway Teow (spelled in the menu as Chow Kueh Teow). Its taste was satisfactory but not convincingly authentic compared to the taste in Malaysia. It seemed to me the Malaysian Chinese food in the restaurant was closer to the Hong Kong localized version.

While Australia, New Zealand, United Kingdom, United States of America and Canada have been popular destinations of Chinese migrants from Malaysia and Singapore, in recent years Chinese Malaysians have also migrated to other destinations, such as Papua New Guinea, where the Chinese migrants there were from Guangdong and Hong Kong (Wu 1982). Here there is now a marked presence of Chinese from Malaysia because of, unfortunately, the involvement by some Malaysian Chinese business people logging there. Many have stayed behind and opened Chinese restaurants selling Chinese foods including Malaysian foods such as Satay, *nasi lemak*, Laksa, Hainanese Chicken Rice, Bah Kut Teh, and others, while supermarkets run by Malaysian Chinese also sell Southeast Asian food ingredients (Ichikawa 2004: 105). Thus as Chinese from Southeast Asia migrate, they also bring along the culinary traditions of their original Southeast Asian countries as well as Chinese food that they have innovated and re-invented in those countries, adding to the ever increasing Southeast Asian and Chinese cuisines all over the world.

Conclusion

The discussion of Chinese foods from Southeast Asia, Chinese Malayan food in particular, shows the culinary reproduction and invention by Chinese migrants and their descendants, as well as the globalization of these foods through migration and diffusion. Chinese food is transmitted in time and space via domestic cooking and the commercial cooking in restaurants. At the same time the cooks at home and the chefs in restaurants and cooking outlets create new local cuisines, contributing towards the rich culinary heritage in Southeast Asia and beyond. To the extent that diasporic Chinese food are created by the Chinese and are seen as such, they may be described as Chinese, even though they have at the same time become larger, also being claimed or perceived as Malaysian, Singaporean, Indonesian or Filipino. Such a distinction is linked to ethnic or national association. In reality all cuisines are part of the human culinary heritage.

The development of a great variety of local Chinese foods in Southeast Asia is made possible by the presence of a large population of Chinese in most cities in the region. There is thus an internal Chinese market that facilitates the commercialization and innovation of Chinese food to cater to the taste of the local Chinese population. This helps to bring about a local cuisine that is Chinese and yet localized. This is unlike in North America which the local Chinese cuisine was initially shaped by the need to sell food to the non-Chinese local population, hence the development of such Americanized Chinese dishes as chopsuey, chow mein and Kung Pao Chicken (see Liu 2010).

In our examination of food heritage in Southeast Asia, there is so much cross-cultural interaction. This is particularly so in the case of food developed by the more localized communities, such as that of the Baba. Influenced by post-modern rhetoric, it is tempting to describe the more localized Nyonya food as hybridized. While I have studied the Babas since the 1970s, I have refrained from using the term hybridization to describe the Baba, whether their culture or their cuisine. Others like Chua and Rajah (2001) have described the Nyonya cuisine as hybridized, with which Anderson (2007) took issue.[30] E.N. Anderson's criticism is based on the understanding that hybridization can only be applied to cultural traditions that are completely alien to each other, and that "Chinese and Southeast Asian cuisines have always been fused" (Anderson 2007: 207). Nevertheless, while different cultural traditions in Southeast Asia have influenced one another, they are also each quite distinct. My objection, rather, is that hybridization oversimplifies the dynamics of cultural change and implies that some cultures are formed by the mere mixing of different cultures. In the case of the Baba, while some of their cultural aspects are highly localized, such as in speaking a creolized Malay dialect, other aspects are still traditional Chinese, such as in the conduct of a funeral. Interestingly, while the Nyonya foods cooked in *sambal* and curry may appear un-Chinese, the Babas keep to the Hokkien traditional preference for pork, and beef hardly appears in Nyonya cuisine.

More significantly, the hybridization rhetoric ignores the agency and creativity of individuals in a population in cultural production and reproduction. Nyonya food is really a product of the Babas (Baba men) and Nyonyas (Baba women), especially the latter, in reproducing Chinese cuisines and creating new cuisines from their knowledge of both Chinese cuisines and local non-Chinese including western cuisines, as well as their innovative use of local ingredients. Nyonya cuisine is not a mere mixing of Chinese and Malay or other indigenous cuisines; it is a cuisine actively produced by the Chinese Peranakan men and especially women in the multi-ethnic and globalized Southeast Asian cultural environments. Furthermore the change in taste, such as acquiring the consumption of chilli and the making of *sambal* very much shape the development of the complex cuisine. It is the acquisition of the local taste, symbolized by the use of chilli, tamarind and lime, which gives the Nyonya food its distinct taste and identity. The study of Southeast Asian Chinese food points to the need to pay attention to the transformation of taste and the development of cuisines.

The Babas are proud of their cuisine, at the same time the cuisine is also seen as Malaysian and Singaporean, more so the latter, where there is official support for the promotion of Baba culture as a local heritage. The commercialization of Nyonya food since the 1980s also contributes to the fame of the cuisine. The same process is happening in Indonesia, where Chinese Peranakan food is increasingly marketed in restaurants, as reported by Myra Sidharta in this book. Is Nyonya cuisine Chinese? Yes, to the extent that the Babas see themselves as Chinese albeit a localized Chinese identity, as symbolized by their cuisine.

Sidney Mintz reminds us that "cuisines are by their nature local, at most regional" (Mintz 2007: 11), and that "cuisines are community based" (Mintz 2007: 12). While for convenience we have used the term Southeast Asian Chinese food, there is really no common Southeast Asian Chinese cuisine, only cuisines produced and consumed by the Chinese communities in different regions of Southeast Asia. Once produced, these cuisines diffuse globally or are brought along by migrants from Southeast Asia. This is the contribution of the Chinese in different regions of Southeast Asia. But as E.N. Anderson points out, "(L)ocal cultures deserve the credit, but through them *humanity* deserves the credit" (2007: 217). The cuisines of the Chinese in Southeast Asia are products of the history of migration and settlement, and they contribute to humankind's culinary heritage.

Notes

1. This is a revision of the paper "Chinese Food and Foodways in Southeast Asia: An Overview" presented at The 10th Symposium on Chinese Dietary Culture: Chinese Food in Southeast Asia. The transcription of Chinese words is in Hokkien (H) or Mandarin (M), as the case may be. Local names including food names are transcribed according to the local usage, while standard Minnan (Hokkien) words are transcribed according to the system used in the Minnan dictionary *Putonghua Minnan Fangyan Cidian* (Fuzhou: Fujian Renmin Chubanshe, 1982). I thank Prof. Sidney Mintz for giving me his valuable comments on this chapter.
2. Chinese form around 26 per cent of the 28 million population of Malaysia, while they make up around 75 per cent of a total of the 5 million people in Singapore.
3. I have in Tan (2001) written about food and ethnicity with reference to the Chinese in Malaysia. I will do my best to avoid similar examples.
4. See Dunlop (2008: 112–3) for a classification of the complex flavours of Sichuan.
5. For a description on foods developed in China, see Chang (1977).
6. See Wong 2003 (pp. 213–22) for some recipes of Chinese confinement food in Penang.
7. As new foods are created locally, the Chinese speech groups are also associated with a number of traditional and local Chinese foods. Thus Yeap (1990: 80) writes, "The Hokkiens stick to Prawn Noodle Soup, Poh Piah, Laksa, Fried Yellow Noodles and Rojak; the Teochews stick to Dry Fried Noodles, Oyster Omelette, Rice Noodle Soup, Fish Congee; the Cantonese stick to Fried Rice Noodles with gravy, Fried Rice Vermicelli and Meat Congee; the Hainanese stick to Chicken Rice and Boiled Rice with an assortment of dishes and beverages." While generally these foods are so identified with certain speech groups, they are sold by sellers of different speech groups rather than by a particular speech group.
8. For recipes, see Lee (1974: 51), Leong (2004: 20–1), Cecilia Tan (1983: 31) and Wong (2003: 58).
9. The parents of this woman in her fifties migrated to Phnom Penh from Vietnam. I visited her in her house in August 2009.
10. I thank Dr Myra Sidharta for this information.
11. I am grateful to Dr M.L. Walwipha Burusratanaphand for this information.
12. For some examples of popular Chinese festive foods in Penang, see Yeap (1990: 53–78).
13. See Guo (2000) for a description on the making of *ku* in Taiwan.
14. *Zhenzhu Naicha* literally means "pearl milk tea" and is sometimes referred to as "bubble tea" in English. This is milk tea mixed with "pearls" called *fenyuan* (粉圆) which is made of sweet potato flour.

Southeast Asian Chinese Food 43

15. The Cantonese pronunciation shows the Cantonese origin of this dish.
16. As in China, many famous Chinese dishes are place associated, thus Ipoh Hofan, Basheng Rugoucha (Klang Bah Kut Teh 巴生肉骨茶), and so on.
17. For a description of the Chinese Peranakan in Southeast Asia, see Tan (2010).
18. *Rendang* is meat (beef or chicken) cooked with various spices (shallots, garlic, chilli, galingale, turmeric, lemon grass, etc.) and simmered in coconut milk. Malays of different regions have their respective styles of *rendang* dishes, differing somewhat in the use of ingredients and the style of cooking. For a description of the various kinds of *rendang* dishes in Malaysia, see Yew (1982).
19. One should not assume that the Hokkien term *ge* is derived from the Malay term *kuih*, since this Minnan term is used by the Minnan people in Fujian and Taiwan.
20. This is cookie baked from sago or tapioca flour mixed with egg yolks and egg whites, coconut milk and other ingredients. For a recipe, see Ng (1979: 145). *Kuih bangkit* has been so accepted by the Chinese in Indonesia and Malaysia that I find the Chinese Indonesian re-migrants in Quanzhou, Fujian still make this *kuih* for their Chinese New Year. In my July 2009 visit to Xinlong Overseas Chinese Farm (兴隆华侨农场) in Hainan, *kuih bangkit* and other Indonesian *kuih* were sold there.
21. For a recipe of this popular snack in Penang, see Leong (2004: 22) and Wong (2003: 46).
22. In his interesting paper on *xiaoye* in Malaysia, Yao (2000) relates *xiaoye* to sex trade.
23. According to the Indonesian Chinese researcher Myra Sidharta (personal conversation), there is Restaurant Penang in North Jakarta and it has two branches in West and East Jakarta, as well as a branch in Semarang. There is also Penang Bistro in South Jakarta and Penang Corner in Plaza Indonesia, also in Jakarta.
24. I suspect it was the Teochius who introduced this sweet desert soup to Southeast Asia, as it is also available in some Chaozhou (i.e., Teochiu) restaurants in Hong Kong.
25. Unlike some Baba food outlets which closed after a few years, Little Penang House Malaysia restaurant at Sung Kit Street in Hunghom has been in operation for many years. Other than the *laksa asam*, it also sells other popular Malaysian street foods including Hokkien Mee or Prawn Noodle. There are a number of small restaurants in Hong Kong where one can eat popular Chinese Malayan food such as Laksa, Fried Kway Teow and Hainanese Chicken Rice. Another small Malaysian restaurant that I have known since my arrival in Hong Kong in 1996 is Good Satay at the Houston Centre at Mody Road in Tsimshatsui East, where one can eat Hainanese Chicken Rice

and other popular Malaysian foods including Satay. Interestingly a quite good and inexpensive Chicken Rice that I have eaten in Hong Kong was in a small restaurant called Wenhua Jifan (Wenhua Chicken Rice) at Austin Road. At the time of writing this restaurant has just moved into a bigger shop at Hillwood Road. Other well-known Malaysian and Singaporean restaurants include Sabah Malaysian Cuisine, Malaymama, Katong Laksa·Prawn Mee, and others.

26. Wrapped in banana leaf, Otak-Otak contains fish fillet and eggs and many kinds of ingredients including coconut milk, finely sliced kaffir lime leaves, *kadok* leaves, galangal, lemon grass, turmeric, *belacan* (shrimp paste), etc. The *kadok* leaves give the dish its unique taste and smell. These are leaves of the vine called *Piper sarmentosum* Roxb. While the vine is common in Southeast Asia, I find this plant grows very well in a park in Guangzhou in China.

27. This dish is known as Cha Cha in Hong Kong, and the ingredients differ somewhat, with more use of beans than sweet potato and taro.

28. Interviewed Mr. Jiang on 29 June 2008 and the manager of Indonesia Restaurant, Mr. Zheng on 29 June 2009.

29. The chicken rice, referring to the rice, was excellent. Called Bing's Malaysian Restaurant, this restaurant serves popular Malay, Malaysian Chinese and Malaysian Indian dishes such as *nasi lemak*, Curry Laksa, Hokkien Mee, Roti Chanai, various kinds of Thosai, etc.

30. In fact the article by Chua and Rajah is published in the book edited by me and my senior colleague (Wu and Tan 2001). As editor, I refrained from imposing my theoretical orientation on contributors even though I was very familiar with the topic written.

References

Anderson, E.N. 2007. "Malaysian Foodways: Confluence and Separation." *Ecology of Food and Nutrition* 46 (3): 205–19.

Chang, K.C., ed. 1977. *Food in Chinese Culture: Anthropological and Historical Perspectives*. New Haven: Yale University Press.

Chua Beng Huat and Ananda Rajah. 2001. "Hybridity, Ethnicity and Food in Singapore." In *Changing Chinese Foodways in Asia*, ed. David Y.H. Wu and Tan Chee-Beng. Hong Kong: The Chinese University Press, pp. 161–97.

Clifford, James. 1997. *Routes: Travel and Translation in the Late Twentieth Century*. Cambridge, Mass.: Harvard University Press.

Dunlop, Fuchsia. 2008. *Shark's Fin and Sichuan Pepper: A Sweet-Sour Memoir of Eating in China*. New York and London: W.W. Norton & Company.

Duruz, Jean. 2007. "From Malacca to Adelaide…: Fragments towards a Biography of Cooking, Yearning and Laksa." In *Food and Foodways in Asia: Resource,*

Tradition and Cooking, ed. Sidney C.H. Cheung and Tan Chee-Beng. London: Routledge, pp. 183–200.

Guo Jingyuan 郭景元. 2000. "Gao bing shijie li de 'gui yu guo' 糕饼世界的'龟与粿' (*Gui* and *guo* in the world of cakes and pastries)." *Zhongguo Yinshi Wenhua* 中国饮食文化 (*Quarterly of the Foundation of Chinese Dietary Culture*) 6 (2): 26–31.

Huang Wanling 黄婉玲. 2004. *Qiantan Guzao Wei* 浅谈古早味 (Introduction to Traditional Tastes). Tainan: Tainan Municipal Government.

Ichikawa, Tetsu. 2004. "Malaysian Chinese Migration to Papua New Guinea and Transnational Networks." *Journal of Malaysian Chinese Studies* 7: 99–113.

Inda, Jonathan Xavier and Renato Rosaldo. 2002. "Introduction: A World in Motion." In *The Anthropology of Globalization: A Reader*, ed. J.X. Inda and R. Rosaldo. Oxford: Blackwell Publishers, pp. 1–34.

Lee Chin Koon, Mrs. 1974. *Mrs. Lee's Cookbook: Nyonya Recipes and Other Favorite Recipes*, ed. Pamela Lee Suan Yew. Singapore: Mrs. Lee's Cookbook.

Leong Yee Soo, Mrs. 2004. *Nyonya Specialties: The Best of Singapore Recipes*. Singapore: Marshall Cavendish.

Liu Haiming. 2010. "Kung Pao Kosher: Jewish Americans and Chinese Restaurants in New York." *Journal of Chinese Overseas* 6 (1): 80–101.

Mintz, Sidney W. 2007. "Diffusion, Diaspora and Fusion: Evolving Chinese Foodways." In *The 10th Symposium on Chinese Dietary Culture: Proceedings*. Taipei: Foundation of Chinese Dietary Culture, pp. 1–14.

Ng, Dorothy. 1979. *Complete Asian Meals*. Singapore: Times Books International.

Ong Aihwa and Donald Nonini, eds. 1997. *Ungrounded Empires: The Cultural Politics of Modern Chinese Transnationalism*. London: Routledge.

Tan, Cecilia. 1983. *Penang Nyonya Cooking: Foods of My Childhood*. Singapore: Times Books International.

Tan Chee-Beng. 2001. "Food and Ethnicity with Reference to the Chinese in Malaysia." In *Changing Chinese Foodways in Asia*, ed. David Y.H. Wu and Tan Chee-Beng. Hong Kong: Chinese University Press, pp. 125–60.

———. 2003. "Family Meals in Rural Fujian: Aspects of Yongchun Village Life." *Taiwan Journal of Anthropology* 1 (1): 179–95.

———. 2007. "Nyonya Cuisine: Chinese, Non-Chinese and the Making of a Famous Cuisine in Southeast Asia." In *Food and Foodways in Asia: Resource, Tradition and Cooking*, ed. Sidney C.H. Cheung and Tan Chee-Beng. London: Routledge, pp. 171–82.

———. 2010. "Intermarriage and the Chinese Peranakan in Southeast Asia." In *Peranakan Chinese in a Globalizing Southeast Asia*, ed. Leo Suryadinata. Singapore: Chinese Heritage Centre, pp. 27–40.

Wong, Julie, compiled and ed. 2003. *Nyonya Flavours: A Complete Guide to Penang Straits Chinese Cuisine*. Penang: The State Chinese (Penang) Association and Star Publications (M) Berhad.

Wu, David Y.H. 1982. *The Chinese in Papua New Guinea: 1880–1980*. Hong Kong: Hong Kong University Press.

Yao Souchou. 2000. "*Xiao Ye*: Food, Alterity and the Pleasure of Chineseness in Malaysia." *Ne Formations* 40 (Spring): 64–79.

Yeap Joo Kim. 1990. *The Penang Palate*. Penang: Yeap Joo Kim.

Yew, Betty. 1982. *Rasa Malaysia: The Complete Malaysian Cookbook*. Singapore: Times Books International.

CHAPTER

2

Gastronomic Influences on the Pacific from China and Southeast Asia

Nancy J. Pollock

Global flows of food out of Asia have a long time depth as people migrated south and east out of China across the Pacific, and around the world (Irwin 2006; Flannery 1994; Bellwood 1985). But this track has been previously overlooked as globalization of foods and other consumer goods has been attributed to a much later process of "Westernization" and the consumer revolutions emanating from Europe, and later the United States of America (Appadurai 1996; Stiglitz 2006). Evidence for gastronomic links between Asia and the Pacific to archaeological finds and prehistoric reconstructions of crops are beginning to emerge as China scholars offer English readers more and more insights into early social life in China (e.g. see illustrations in Chang 1977). When we add these early artistic representations of domestication and settlement patterns to linguistic, micro-biological and other scientific findings, reconstructions of the gastronomic past are clarifying those gastronomic links between Asia and populations that resettled across the islands of the Pacific.

Global flows of migrants bearing goods and ideas are the dominant theme of Appadurai's (1996) discussion of links between the past and modernity across the globe. He suggests we need to focus on the disjunctures as well as conjunctures that have occurred over space and time, where and when global flows of goods have undergone "mutual cannibalization" of sameness and difference (p. 43). Arguments of "production fetishism," reinforced by neoclassical economics, have overwhelmed our understanding of the role of the consumer as chooser. He cites food as one of these practices of consumption that acquire uniformity through habituation. "It is only in ostentation that we take notice of consumption," he argues, yet the underlying bodily forces of food consumption set a temporal rhythm in organizing large-scale consumption patterns that may be repetitive or improvised (1996: 67–8). The resulting distortion of our approaches to production as a leading argument in cultural reconstruction needs to be redirected towards a view of consumption patterns that are integral to gastronomic choices.

Appadurai's approach to global cultural flows is framed in terms of several fluid and irregular landscapes that are the building blocks of "imagined worlds." These are constituted by the historically situated imaginations of persons and groups spread around the globe that can be captured in "ethnoscapes" as ever-changing cultural views of a world in which human motion plays a major part. We can add foodscapes to the mediascapes, technoscapes, financescapes and ideoscapes he addresses (1996: 33). Foodscapes are thus imagined depictions of changes and con-tinuities in gastronomies over time, where not just the material components of foodstuffs are selected for or against, but broader elements of food systems such as cultural ideology, processing, preparation and allocation are integral features. Gastronomy as offered by Brillat-Savarin (1825/1970) includes a range of tastes and ideologies associated with food preparation and consumption from a European perspective. Globalization of gas-tronomies seen through foodscapes is thus a process of linking imagined reconstructions of the past with retrospections from the modern era.

Gastronomic links between the Pacific and China will be discussed by examining four foodscapes that uphold key shared cultural principles. Firstly, the basic elements of any main Chinese/Southeast Asian food intake must include a starch component accompanied by small dish(es) of vegetables and spices, sometimes including small portions of fish or meat; this ideology continued in the Pacific but rice was replaced by taro and other root and tree starches, while the accompanying dishes were limited to small portions of fish, coconut or (today) noodles. All these foods had to be cooked, and some were preserved. Taste as well as texture/"mouth feel" are vital to an eating experience. This basic pairing of the starch food with an accompaniment, as the base of Chinese foodways that moved into the Pacific, provides our first foodscape.

The second foodscape comprises the means to assess ways of reconstructing these linkages. Discoveries of the past are channelled through our imaginations which are fuelled in this case by literary and material evidence, whether from Chinese early texts, or prehistorians' reconstructions from archaeological remains. An useful overview of recent Chinese experiences in the Pacific (Willmott 2007) appears in the first publication of the newly established Centre for the Study of the Southern Chinese Diaspora, ANU, Canberra, Australia. A volume of writings by historians, edited by Reid (2008), includes overviews of recent connections, i.e., from the 1840s to the 1950s, but there are scant references to gastronomic influences on food; the establishment of Chinese restaurants, for example, clearly awaits further in-depth research.

Understanding the centrality of foodways in Chinese culture is growing as scholars such as Wu and Tan (2001) and the Foundation of Chinese Dietary Culture publications bring together the wider aspects of gastronomy in the Chinese diaspora. Looking back at past gastronomies is enhanced by the availability of texts for non-Chinese readers, thus increasing awareness of key cultural differences from European gastronomic traditions.

The third foodscape addresses the key principle of sharing food. Early settlers in the Pacific had to generate new food resources that differed from original Asian stocks, as rice proved unsuitable to Pacific island environments. Imports by travellers from the west provided an ever-widening base of biodiversity in foodstuffs that were shared for security of supply (Pollock *in press*). Similarly, cooking techniques necessitated adjustments. Cultural feeding practices both within households and between communities also diversified in island settings. The banquets and feasts which are expressions of the base principle of sharing are a key feature of both Chinese and Pacific gastronomy. Processes of reconfiguration of Chinese dietary principles were necessary across the Pacific.

The fourth foodscape assesses the continuities and disjunctures of those gastronomic principles in modern times. A strong Chinese gastronomic presence in the Pacific has developed with the proliferation of market gardens, Chinese restaurants and takeaways all used by both the Chinese and Pacific communities. The continuities and transformations have occurred over a period of at least 3–4,000 years, and cover almost two-thirds of the world's surface. They have resulted in a rich biodiversity that

50   *Nancy J. Pollock*

affords food security for island populations from local resources (Pollock *in press*). These principles precede modern day food globalization by several thousand years.

Foodscape 1: Gastronomic Resources

The centrality of food in Chinese culture is expressed in several key principles. As Confucius said "knowing how to eat properly has always been a metaphor for knowing how to live" (cited in Dunlop 2008: 208). The starch food(s) together with accompanying dishes (*fan/cai*) is the base on which other gastronomic principles are built. The accompanying dish of vegetables and pieces of meat or fish, with spices provides the tastes, textures and aromas that appeal to diners (Chang 1977; Dunlop 2008; Wu and Tan 2001). Ways of preparing, cooking and presenting foods add flexibility and adaptability throughout regions of China, as well as to Chinese food overseas. Sharing food for health and well-being included ancestors in the community of diners. Records indicate that any Chinese gentleman showed his qualifications in terms of his knowledge and skill pertaining to food and drink (Chang 1977: 6–11).

The vitality of food in Chinese dietary history is attributed by several authors to Yi Yin's theory of cuisine and gastronomy. Developed from the sixteenth century BC it "became a major point of reference for posterity, setting out culinary principles that have remained the implicit standard adopted by subsequent authors and chefs" (Sabban 2000: 1164; see also Chang 1977: 11; Dunlop 2008: 102, 106). These principles have lasted down to current times. Dunlop discovered that "experiences of eating and learning to become a chef in China imprinted on her experience and imagination the key principles of cooking to produce delectable foods" (2008: 208).

"Eating properly" is characterized by a complex of interrelated variables essential to a balanced meal. The essential features are *fan*, grains and other starch foods, complemented by *cai*, vegetable and meat dishes. These foods are drawn from an assemblage of plants and animals that grew prosperously in the Chinese lands for a long time. Cooking transforms these key elements to provide the tastes, smells and textures that distinguish variations in Chinese gastronomy (Chang 1977: 7–8; see also Wu and Tan 2001: preface). The result is "The artistry of the finest Chinese cooking with its subtle command of colour, aroma, taste and mouth feel." Dunlop enthuses about the skill of combining these elements

Gastronomic Influences on the Pacific 51

in Chinese gastronomic culture that opens up whole new fields, particularly the understanding of texture (Dunlop 2008: 145).

Whereas the starch element comprises the bulk of any meal, it is the subtleties of the accompanying dish(es) that provide the distinctive tastes that linger. The *fan/cai* complementarity provides the cook with opportunities to tempt his diners with spices, textures and smells. The starchy foods, millet or wheat in northern China or rice in the south, provide the platform on which an array of colours, textures and aromas is displayed. The diversity of plant and animal resources used in small amounts allows for regional variations and further substitutions as Chinese dietary cosmology and practice has spread out from Asia (Wu and Tan 2001).

Early settlers in the Pacific carried these base principles with them. Rice did not penetrate beyond Guam in the northern Pacific probably because of ecological and edaphic differences. Rice was presented for sale to Magellan's expedition in 1521 when they arrived in Guam from the east (Pollock 1983), but we have no records of it being grown successfully elsewhere until the modern era. Shortage of available fresh water on atolls and low lying islands of Micronesia may have been a major deterrent to growing rice in the islands.

Instead, taro and other root and tree starches became the natural resources that provided the basic starch component in the Pacific. All of these required human intervention for their reproduction. Vegeculture, that predominates in East Asia and the Pacific, allowed for ongoing selection of chosen attributes of crops by replanting parts of the original corm or shoots (Shuji and Matthews 2003).

Domestication of taro as it was carried out of India and China to tropical settings has included increasing the size of the corms, reduction in the oxalate crystals under the skin making it sweeter (hence *Taro esculenta*) and selection of species suitable for irrigation in contrast to dry-land or upland taro; these developments closely parallel rice domestication (Pollock 2000; 2003). We know that taro was cultivated in early times in China, but we have less evidence for its history than for rice. It has been suggested that it was not regarded as highly as the *fan* component.

In the Pacific the essential features of the gastronomic principle, namely the starch component as the base for a tasty accompaniment, has endured to the present though with transposures over time and space. In Fiji, for example, taro is known as "real" food (*kakana dina*) but only if it is eaten with a little accompaniment (*I coi*). Together these key foods are essential for a Fijian or other Pacific person to say they have eaten, and feel satisfied and a sense of well-being.

Other starch foods domesticated in Asia included Dioscorea yams, Alocasia taro, breadfruit, bananas, arrowroot and pandanus. These must have been carried aboard settlers' canoes as they moved through Southeast Asia into the Pacific (Irwin 2006; Pollock 2003). All these starchy foods had to be cooked, thus necessitating various uses of fire and utensils, as discussed below.

Accompanying foods in the Pacific were more limited than in China. Taro leaves, fish and coconut provided the main ingredients. Archaeological evidence from bones in middens indicates that fish and birds provided readily available food for coastal dwelling populations. Recent ethnographic evidence underlines that those assembled to eat did not feel satisfied unless they had had their taro, or breadfruit accompanied by a small taste of fish, or coconut, or even just salt water (Pollock fieldnotes 1986). Major

Lap-lap in Vanuatu made from taro or other roots, baked in leaves with coconut cream, is used as an accompaniment to rice. This dish parallels the many tasty Chinese dishes used to accompany rice. (Photograph by Nancy Pollock)

Gastronomic Influences on the Pacific 53

developments in recent Pacific gastronomy have come from an increased array of foods to accompany taro or rice, such as ramen noodles, or canned fish or corned beef.

Cooking has remained an aesthetic principle of Chinese gastronomy as transferred into the Pacific. Both rice and the root starches had to be cooked to make them edible. The elaboration of cooking and kitchens over the last 2–3,000 years has been well recorded in China, particularly for the Han period 100 BC–600 AD (Chang 1977; Dunlop 2008). Such elaboration has been on a lesser scale in the Pacific. Not only is the pictorial and descriptive evidence missing for Pacific communities, but the environment was not conducive to vast kitchens and the diverse array of foodstuffs which imperial rulers demanded. Simple ways of cooking rice for ordinary households probably relied on bamboo containers. Pottery utensils and bronze containers would not have been accessible to peasant farmers in China. Just how they cooked their rice requires further explanation.

The earliest cooking fires in the Pacific are not well documented, but may well have been similar to those in rural Southeast Asia (Alice Ho 1995) and across the Pacific today (Pollock 1992). A fire built in a hollow in the sand, or earth enabled the cook to place the taro corms or breadfruit to roast directly in the embers. Such fireplaces leave less evidence than the fire pits, or *umu* in which larger quantities of roots and tree foods could be cooked (Leach 2007). Rice would have been difficult to cook in the absence of a vessel in which it could be steamed.

Lapita pottery has become a key feature in the reconstruction of the past of communities across the Pacific (Kirch 2000; Flannery 1994: 164–75; Irwin 2006; Spriggs 1997; Marshall 2008). Prehistorians have constructed a Lapita culture around a particular style of pottery finds originating in a New Caledonia site, in association with the spread of the Austronesian language family across Near and Remote Oceania over the last 3,000 years. That Lapita culture is said to represent a new phase in "agriculture" with the spread of crops, such as taro, yams, breadfruit, as well as pigs, dogs and chickens with travellers moving east towards the islands of Remote Oceania (Kirch 2000). Canoes and maritime technology were essential to this innovative phase (Irwin 2006). Whether the Lapita pottery is closely modelled on pottery in Taiwan, where the Aboriginal population is reputed to have spoken early forms of the Austronesian language is the subject of debate. The alternative argument (according to White cited in Flannery 1994) is that Lapita culture developed within

Melanesia. How the various types of Lapita pottery were used, whether for burials, cooking, water carrying is still subject to inquiry (see Marshall 2008).

Preservation of foods was also a technique developed in China (Chang 1977; Dunlop 2008) that may account for similar developments in Pacific communities. Whereas Chinese developed a range of practices, fermentation was the most widely known practice in the Pacific. Fermented taro or breadfruit provides an alternative, acidic taste to the bland fresh products. It is also a means of preserving excess seasonal foods such as breadfruit so that careful burial in pits can provide food for lean times (Pollock 1984; Yen 1975). "Poi" made from fermented taro in Hawaii, but also preserved elsewhere, provided a gastronomic variant that added a different taste, colour and texture to the cooked corm. Drying and salting any excess fish in a catch also added to the culinary pool. The art of preserving these foods by fermentation may well have been transferred across the Pacific from Chinese origins.

Local food resources in the islands of the Pacific thus provided a base for small tasty accompaniments, mainly fish. The diversity of starch foods in the Pacific, namely root and tree crops, is in marked distinction to the ubiquity of rice in China and Southeast Asia, while continuing to provide a base of local gastronomy.

Foodscape 2: Literary Evidence

Each foodscape is compiled from evidence drawn from a number of different sources, whether from the past, or present. All are reconstructions from what Appadurai terms "the imaginary" (p. 31). For China we have a rich array of sources that includes translations of old texts, reproductions of early drawings, as well as archaeological and prehistorians' reconstructions. Translations and documents in English, such as Chang (1977) or Dunlop (2008), provide a beginning. For the Pacific we have no early written sources before European accounts from the sixteenth century, as early settlers have left only oral traditions such as Taonui's compilation for Polynesia (2006: 28–30). We must rely on prehistorians' reconstructions as well as extrapolations from the sixteenth- and seventeenth-century European perspectives, such as Cook and missionary Williams, together with ethnographic records for the last 100 years.

The evidence from China suggests that gastronomic practices have been developed over a long period of time (e.g., Sabban 2000; Chang

Gastronomic Influences on the Pacific

1977; Dunlop 2008; Wu and Tan 2001; Anderson 1988). Chinese literary sources take us back 6,000 years, while archaeological sources suggest a longer history of the domestication of food crops in the Asian region (Bellwood 2002). Depictions in prose and art of culinary activities establish a time depth of some 3,000 years (e.g. see Chang 1977). Yi Yin, Prime Minister in the Shang dynasty (3,600 years ago), is credited with inventing the theory of cuisine and gastronomy that has lasted down the ages. He not only classified foodstuffs according to a number of criteria, but stressed the mastery of five flavours and of the elements of fire, water and wood (Sabban 2000: 1165; Dunlop 2008: 55, 102). Bamboo slips from Madam Li's tomb at Mawangdui reveal not only lists of foods used in the Han era, 175–145 BC, but a variety of dishes and the parts of animals used as meat (Ying-Shih Yu 1977: 55–8 and illustrated fig. 19, p. 186). Chefs in Hunan province still revere Yi Ya as the ancestor of their profession from 2,000 years ago. Yuan Mei is reputedly the most famous of these chefs for his prose and poetry that depicts the way flavours should be blended. Writing in the eighteenth century he has immortalized how foods should be selected, and brought together in his cookery book entitled *The Food Lists of the Garden of Contentment* (Dunlop 2008: 55). These literati in Chinese culinary history brought renown to Chinese gastronomic practices, but it was the multitude of chefs who could not read these recipes who perfected their culinary skills and passed them down the generations by word of mouth (Dunlop 2008: 54).

According to Chinese legend Shennong, the Divine Farmer, one of three august sovereigns, taught men to cultivate and thus cooking became the foundation of civilization. Cooking, cultivation and consumption of cereals became associated with the Han people (Sabban 2000: 1165). The diversification over time of populations has led to a range of gastronomic styles which Sabban summarizes as Northern Chinese characterized by wheat products, cakes and noodles, Southern Chinese characterized by rice and fish, Sichuan by intricate use of spices and Cantonese by dim sum, clear soups and fish. For the current era Dunlop provides ethnographic details of the developments of these regional cuisines, beginning with Sichuan, as produced both by grand chefs, and village chefs. From the lean times of the Cultural Revolution each of the provinces is rediscovering its gastronomically distinctive dishes (2008).

Archaeological material from Asia provides increasing evidence for the early domestication and cultivation of rice south of the Yangtze, with millet the crop more suited to conditions north of the river (Lu 2005).

Bellwood (2005) has drawn the archaeological and historical linguistic material together into a "farming/language dispersal hypothesis" that suggests that domesticated rice enabled population expansions southward in China to Taiwan and the emerging islands after the sea level rise that separated the Sunda from Sahul land masses and the islands of Southeast Asia some 5,000–6,000 years ago. Linguistic reconstructions of early (Proto-Malayo-Polynesian) terms indicate that various aspects of the gastronomic uses of rice emerged perhaps around 6,000 years ago (Blench 2005: 41–2). He argues that Austronesian speakers had some form of rice when they began to colonize Taiwan, probably growing upland rice, together with taro and millet as the dominant crops (Blench 2005: 45).

Taiwan plays a central role in the reconstruction of these early global flows of people and their foodways. Since present day Taiwan aborigines living in the southeast corner of Taiwan, speak languages related to the Austronesian family of languages, reasoning back in time has led to theories placing Taiwan as the "homeland" of Pacific or Polynesian peoples. For example, Irwin (2006) notes that Taiwan was settled by hunters and gatherers 15,000 years ago, probably from southern China. Archaeological sites from 4,000 years ago have revealed pottery, stone tools and the beginnings of agriculture, e.g. TPK (Sagart 2005). Irwin suggests that sea-farers spread into the northern Philippine islands 4,000 years ago and also through island Southeast Asia, where sites contain evidence of domesticated plants and animals, pottery, shell tools, and ornaments (Irwin 2006: 64).

These various reconstructions from archaeological remains have been associated with time scales for domestication and the production of food crops. However there are no indications as to how those crops were used gastronomically until we read the early Chinese documents.

Two great colonizations of the Pacific from Asia have been suggested, based on assessments of human remains (Pietrusewsky 2005). He suggests the first colonization occurred before the last Ice Age (10,000 to 6,000 years ago) perhaps 40,000 years ago, when a single land mass known as Sunda included China and the rest of Asia separated from a southern single land mass known as Sahul, that is now Australia, New Guinea and the Bismarck and Solomon Islands. This first period of settlement necessitated people and plants and animals crossing the Wallace trench, perhaps by raft, during the last Pleistocene (47,000 bp) (Pietrusewsky 2005: 201). Whether these were intentional or accidental crossings are the subject of consider-

Gastronomic Influences on the Pacific 57

able debate amongst those contributing to these prehistoric reconstructions (Irwin 2006: 61). When gastronomic questions are included, it is clear that to survive such journeys these voyagers would have had to carry foods and knowledge of cooking them and key gastronomic principles out to the islands that lay to the east.

The second great colonization of the Pacific, as reconstructed by Pietrusewsky, occurred between 6,000 and 3,000 bp with another movement out of Asia, both west to Madagascar, and as far east, eventually, as Easter Island (2005: 202). The spread of peoples in this latter period necessitated development of maritime skills, both to construct suitable sailing craft, and the navigation skills to cross short distances between islands, and later across longer stretches of water. But the lack of any archaeological evidence of canoes is a concern in these reconstructions (Irwin 2006: 73).

Further evidence for these early global flows of people and their food systems eastwards out of Asia is emerging with advances in various microbiological techniques in the new millennium. Whether the ancestors of the taros (*Colocasia, Alocasia or Cyrtosperma*) were first domesticated from wild plants in India or the Asian mainland or in New Guinea has become the subject of several alternative theories (Allaby 2007; Walter and Lebot 2007). These authors draw on archaeobotanical techniques, including molecular biology to establish the pre-existence of wild forms of key food plants in New Guinea (see also Matthews 2006: 94). It is thus possible that taro, breadfruit, bananas, coconut and sugar cane which have a natural range that spans tropical and sub-tropical latitudes from India to China and New Guinea have been derived from the basic genetic stock found in the various Pacific islands in the twentieth century. These root and tree starches leave very little evidence other than starch granules on digging sticks from 28,000 bp (Spriggs cited by Kirch 1997: 281n25) from which to derive direct evidence of cultivation.

The diminishing number of species of these root and tree starch crops eastward across the Pacific is one indication that fewer voyagers were able to cultivate and diversify the types of taro and other food crops on Tahiti than in New Caledonia for example. Some 300 species have been recorded for what prehistorians call Near Oceania (New Guinea and Bismarcks etc.) while only 100 species have been documented for Remote Oceania, the islands further east (Walter and Lebot 2007). In total Kirch (2000: 109) has listed 28 crop plants transported by this second wave of colonists, 15 attested by botanical remains, and 13 by linguistic and other evidence. The economic picture of the Pacific some 3,000 years ago is thus characterized as a mixed horticulture–maritime economy with root and tree crops, pigs, dogs, chickens, fish, shellfish and birds (Irwin 2006: 75). How these plants and animals featured gastronomically in early times has not been considered in the reconstructions of their domestication.

Animal remains across the Pacific are very limited. Pigs, dogs and chicken bones have been analyzed as domesticated animals that were found in settlements on the islands, but how they were used as food remains speculative. Several authors suggest that the Polynesian rat was eaten since it was also found in association with settlements, but that cannot be confirmed. Rather, current residents in the Cook Islands hotly deny that their ancestors ate rats (Pollock fieldnotes 1996).

Fish is the most readily available source of accompaniment to the starch foods discussed in Foodscape 1. It would have been readily available to generations of peoples moving around between the gradually emerging islands off East Asian shores. The bones collect in middens more readily than evidence of the main starch foods. Thus it is easy to propose fish and shellfish were the dominant foods, rather than the taro and starches.

Pigs, dogs and chickens have all been the subject of modern micro-biological analysis to reveal DNA connections. Analysis of pig bones has distinguished one species possibly domesticated in Taiwan (*Sus scrofa*) from a second derived from the Celebes and islands of the lesser Sundas (*Sus celebensis*). "The complete absence of Pacific Clade haplotypes [of pigs] from modern and ancient specimens from Mainland China, Taiwan, the Philippines, Borneo and Sulawesi suggests that any human dispersal from Taiwan to the New Guinea region via the Philippines, as purported by the 'Out of Taiwan' model did not include the movement of domestic pigs.... The most parsimonious explanation is a west to east dispersal trajectory, as supported by relative frequencies of Pacific Clade pigs identified across this distribution" (Larson *et al.* 2007: 4837; Matisoo-Smith and Robins 2004: 9167).

DNA reconstructions from chicken bones suggest domestication derived from jungle fowl, centred in Vietnam and peninsular Southeast Asia. These chickens may have been carried along with the pigs in the voyaging canoes that journeyed between islands of Southeast Asia and Oceania. Analysis of chicken bones from a site in Chile, South America, suggests close similarities to chicken bones found in Tonga and dated to 1,500 years ago (Storey in Larson *et al.* 2007: 4838). Wide dispersal of these animals is affirming links between the peoples of Southeast Asia

Gastronomic Influences on the Pacific 59

and settlements across the Pacific, but their gastronomic usage remains to be affirmed.

Pietrusewsky's second colonization alongside the work of many archaeologists and prehistorians broadens the analysis of Lapita culture as the foundation of the spread of peoples out from Near Oceania or Melanesia to Remote Oceania, particularly the islands of Polynesia (Kirch 1997). From 3,500 bp a common pottery style became dispersed from New Caledonia to Fiji and Tonga, until it disappears in the archaeological record for Samoa in about 400 AD. Prehistorians base their argument on the pottery as a diagnostic tool for the establishment of this new Lapita culture.

Whether this pottery was used for cooking remains an open question. As Kirch notes the differing functions of the pots have been little studied though pots were (apparently) not used directly over cooking fires, so many have been used as serving vessels, or storage (1997: 120). The history of a cuisinary pattern is not well developed, but Kirch suggests that what he terms "the archaeogastronomy of Lapita cuisine" was based on a staple carbohydrate core of the diet, using taro, yams, bananas, breadfruit plus nuts and fruit, together with protein from the sea and some meat (Kirch 1997: 212–3).

Evidence for cooking in shallow pit ovens and fermentation and pit ensilage is derived from archaeological excavations as well as linguistic reconstructions, such as the term **qumum*[1] as the Proto-Austronesian word for the earth oven (*umu*).Whether pottery was used to boil taro, as distinct from roasting the corms and breadfruit etc. in the coals or in an earth oven is a significant gastronomic point yet to be resolved (Pollock n.d.). Leach (2007) in her reconsideration of Lapita cookery suggests that the earth oven was more useful for traditional cooking of starches than pottery.

So the gastronomic background of Lapita peoples requires further exploration. Kirch claims taro "was a major staple food" (1997: 37) though evidence of how it was prepared and the occasions on which it was eaten are not available. The place of gastronomy in early cosmology and how foods were processed for cooking, who cooked and how widely the food was distributed are questions yet to be answered. It would be useful to know the criteria by which farmers selected or rejected specimens from the crops grown in order to trace new gastronomic influences. It is likely that continuing waves of settlers sailing east brought innovative ideas about gastronomy, along with the crop material on their canoes.

The evidence for developments in Pacific gastronomy is thus subject to prehistorians' reconstructions rather than literary evidence. It is not as extensive as that for developments in Chinese gastronomy. The principles and ideologies expressed in recipes and modes of food presentation by Chinese scholars are not matched in the Pacific, where oral history was the main means of transmission of ideas across the generations.

Ethnographic descriptions of food usage and principles, until recently have largely addressed food as an economic good, focusing on production rather than consumption. Retrospection from today's values inevitably dominates any of these reconstructions. Considering the starch foods as the dominant component of any meal, eaten with a little fish or coconut is the reverse of European values, which place meat as the main component of the diet (e.g. Smil 2002). Reasoning from today's European values is thus dangerous for the reconstruction of gastronomies elsewhere in the world from previous times.

My own interest in the Pacific/China gastronomic links was stimulated by issues that confronted me during periods of ethnographic fieldwork across the central and eastern Pacific (Pollock 1992). As I gained understanding of their gastronomic ideology it became apparent that Pacific communities placed different values on the components of their daily eating experiences to those I was used to. The importance of the starchy food, whether rice or breadfruit eaten with a piece of coconut or fish, stimulated my investigations into wider Pacific experiences, where I found this key food classification principle expressed (Pollock 1986).

The literature on the Chinese diaspora in the Pacific is growing, but focuses on the last 150 years, rather than the earlier influences discussed here. The new Chinese arrivals (Willmott 2007) sought to re-establish as nearly as possible their lifestyle from their former homelands. They not only established market gardens to produce the vegetables necessary for their accompanying dishes, but also set up restaurants and later take-aways for others to purchase their food styles, as discussed below.

Foodscape 3: Sharing and Generosity with Food

Any foodscape must include the practices whereby food was shared whether within or between households, or with the larger community. Daily food use in the household, as well as gifts to kin and neighbours and receiving a share from feasts, banquets that cater for large social gatherings, or special events — all these modes of sharing are culturally proscribed.

Gastronomic Influences on the Pacific 61

While food is a key element of festive sociality, it is accompanied by other forms of celebration, such as dancing, singing and laughter. Sharing food spreads general good will, as well as indicating the well-being of the host community.

The principle of sharing food is apparent in the literature on Chinese gastronomy (see Chang 1977 for the various dynasties), as well as in any Pacific experience (Pollock 1992 and ethnographies). Such elaborate presentations of vast amounts of food in the 1880s in Fiji (see illustration in Pollock 1992: 116) may be seen as shockingly wasteful by European values where parsimony dominates. Captain Cook and missionaries after him were overwhelmed by the amount of food and its distinctive features from what they were used to (e.g. Banks 1769). Missionaries, such as Ellis, considered the Pacific communities to be profligate, as they expected that much of this food would be wasted. They were not familiar with the cultural protocols of sharing food.

Sharing and generosity with food has been considered in the anthropological literature as part of the general principle of exchange, and thus part of the economy. For example the exchanges of food that take place between communities participating in a Trobriands Kula Ring have been reported as exchanges between trading partners (Malinowski 1935). Such an approach denies the cultural place of food as a key element in the gastronomic experience, which may extend from the gathering and cooking of the foods, to the style of presentation on a table, or mats, and the dancing and singing that may be part of the experience. Sharing and generosity with food is more than giving and taking. It is a very deeply seated cultural principle.

Sharing was a dominant feature of Chinese gastronomy. The Chinese literature (referring mainly to the upper classes) has left a detailed record of early feasts, and the principles by which they should be run. As early as the late Han dynasty 2,000 years ago, we have illustrations of elaborate feast scenes and their contents in manuscripts and paintings on the walls of tombs, unearthed by archaeologists in the 1970s. Inscribed bamboo slips found in the tomb of a prominent lady of Hunan who lived about 120–170 BC give details of a number of foodstuffs as well as the seasonings and methods used in Han-period cooking. The contents of this lady's stomach gives us further indications of what she had been eating before her death (Chang 1977: 55–9, and illustration #19, p. 186). Ying Shih Yu's detailed record of the findings from these archaeological discoveries also includes references to literary pieces (p. 67) that record foods not known today and ways of special cooking to such feasts (Chang 1977: 53–81, see also illustrations #20–22, pp. 187–9). We are not told just how extensive the guest list was for such events, but must surmise that large numbers of families gave and also received. Such elaborate feasts must have taken their toll on the food supply of the peasant households that contributed to them, at the same time as those peasants also shared in the joy of the occasions. As the poem translated as "The Summons of the Soul" from the Chou dynasty shows, many dishes very elaborately prepared "ranked among the best-treasured enjoyments of life." These were offered to lure back lost souls (Chang 1977: 32).

Similarly details of kitchens of several types for the Emperor's household are depicted on the walls of tombs. Dunlop's contemporary report of the many kitchens she visited indicates the wide range from elaborate kitchens to tiny spaces, enough for one wok and street vendors. Dunlop saw for herself in 2001 how the last Emperors regaled their visitors with food when she gained access to forbidden parts of Beijing's Forbidden City, and the storerooms that have never been emptied since the fall of the last Emperor in 1908 (2008: 203–4). This rich gastronomic array, left to decay during the Cultural Revolution, reminds today's chefs of the glories of the past as they slowly recreate the elaborate banquet culture of China's heritage. Feasting reached elaborate heights in China, both in quality and quantity of shared foods.

In the Pacific evidence of sharing and feasting can only be surmised from archaeological remains. Only when we read the reports by early European visitors from the sixteenth century onward such as Magellan, Captain Cook, etc., can we begin to form a picture of elaborate food sharing with guests. Their accounts are amplified by those of missionaries who took up residence and had very different ideas as to the amount and style of food offered at feasts. These sources depict the large collections of taro roots, kava stems, yams and mulberry that they saw piled on and around heaps of roasted pigs. Photos, such as that of "a wall of food" in Fiji in 1876 (Pollock 1992: 116) enhance word pictures such as a visitor's description of a Fijian *magiti* as an occasion of "prodigal abundance" (Derrick 1946 cited in Pollock 1992: 116). But we lack any information on how the local people participated in the consumption of such bounty. Archaeological middens near elevated sites have been interpreted as indications of high ranking individuals attracting tribute for such large feasts. These outsiders described the bounty in those feasts from their own values, by which they seemed excessive. They did not

Gastronomic Influences on the Pacific 63

perceive the feast within the wider social context of irregular eating and community sharing.

However our "imaginary" can suggest some depictions of feasting in the Pacific past. Maritime guests from across the waters would have been greeted by those already settled with whatever foods were available, while the new arrivals also contributed any remaining planting material that they had carried with them. Their arrival was a celebration in itself. For those who had left their extended family and political networks whether in Southeast Asia and China, or nearby islands, were likely to carry with them the principles behind tribute and sharing for feasts that were part of their heritage. In the Pacific the food resources were less varied so "a feast" was made of what was available. On Namu in 1968 the community had run out of food; there was no local breadfruit or rice (purchased) with which to celebrate Christmas, so our "feast" consisted of ship's biscuits and Hawaiian punch (my contribution) (Pollock fieldnotes 1967). But there was also dancing and singing and a Church service to mark the occasion. It was a noteworthy celebration for me.

The social organization of contributions to Pacific feasts was so important that it became a specified role in some Polynesian hierarchies. Just as the role of distributor of foods was a politically important one in China, it became so in parts of the Pacific such as Tonga. The distributor was in charge not only of the allocation of contributions by family households, but also of redistribution after guests had left. He designated who should receive the baskets of leftover coconuts, or pieces of cooked pig. A visitor to a feast in a Pacific village today is likely to take home a basket containing the taros, and coconuts and a remaining cut of pork — to be given to the family hosting that visitor. How recent is this formalized role? In some Pacific communities women's committees have taken over this role (Pollock fieldnotes 1983).

The ancestors were important participants in feasts. Practices of sharing foods with the ancestors are widely documented for China, whether at mourning feasts, family events, or as propitiation for favourable crop growth (Chang 1977: 18). In the Pacific funeral feasts are among the largest family events that include the living community, the deceased as well as the ancestors, with the development of elaborate graves at which food and flower offerings are still in practice, as in Tonga and Guam for example (Pollock fieldnotes 1986). First fruits ceremonies honour the ancestors and the gods, as Captain Cook and others noted for Tonga, and Cook also found at cost to his life in Hawai'i. Malinowski's two volumes (1935) document the attention paid to ancestors with food in the Trobriands, while Firth (1967) has left a detailed account of how Tikopians incorporated their ancestors and other gods in their rituals by sharing food.

Pacific feasts provide elaborate displays of food that catch the eye, stimulate the taste buds and draw commentaries from participants as well as visitors and onlookers. Today tourists are regaled with such a feast during their stay at a resort hotel. While Chinese banquets are more elaborate in the number of courses served and attention to detail in the many foods presented (Dunlop 2008), Pacific feasts display the best of their delicacies on a series of tables, buffet style. The best food may be a select variety of yam (Dioscorea species) in a Pacific community (Pollock 1992 Appendix a), or a taro leaf wrapped pudding. Turtle is a highly prized feast food in the Pacific. Fish has brought delicate flavours to feasts and banquets as evidenced in Han dynasty tile reliefs from 206 BCE to 220 CE (Wang 2008: 78) and middens in many Pacific archaeological sites (Kirch 2000). Fish feature prominently in Michel Tuffery's contemporary "gastronomic art," alongside his "Povi" life-size cow structures made of corned beef tins (Pollock 2008). These elaborations of the gastronomic elements carry the food beyond the material into strong symbolic realms, resonant for those sharing the experience.

In modern times lavish Pacific feasts take place either in village settings or urban settings. They draw on kinship and political ties to chiefs, nobles and leaders. Communities contribute the best they can offer, whether in the form of cooked dishes, or pigs, chicken or crabs. But in modern times their resources are severely challenged. As in China (Dunlop 2008: Ch. 8) prominent people in urban Pacific communities are moving their entertainment with food into catered establishments where "western," local and Chinese, Korean, or Indian foods may be served. Ironically the largest venue for a political feast in Majuro, Marshall Islands in the 1970s was a Chinese restaurant; they served steaks and fried chicken dishes alongside variants of Cantonese dishes.

Feasts in the Pacific, as well as in China (e.g. Han in Chang 1977: 62–70) represent a manifestation of wide social commitments and responsibility to both people and events. Whether social hierarchies developed around the giving of food is indeterminate, though widely considered. In Marxists' views they may be analyzed as exploitation of the masses by the elites, and thus pressure to give, or as a form of "consumer production" (Foster 2008).

Gastronomic Influences on the Pacific 65

An alternative explanation of the development of a strong ethic of generosity becomes apparent when viewed from the perspective of social responsibilities rather than material factors. The cultural joy of contributing in kind and spirit to a communal event is accepted and welcomed as a diversion from ordinary day to day life, even though it may seriously deplete local resources; my questions to Namu people about why they were giving a boat-load of pandanus fruits, breadfruit paste and coconuts, the last of their local resources, to their Iroij (chief) living amidst plenty on Ebeye were greeted with puzzled expressions; why was I questioning such a joy (Pollock fieldnotes 1968). Through feasts a community expresses its material well-being as well as their loyalty to the chiefs who represent them to the wider social world. The people contribute and the chiefs redistribute, so that any concept of waste is derived from external interpretations that devalue the social importance of food sharing.

Generosity with food in Pacific societies, both for spiritual as well as material reasons, thus replicates similar principles that have dominated Chinese gastronomy. The influence of new arrivals from across the ocean to the west left a strong imprint on future generations of Pacific peoples. The evidence for China is as strong as it is multi-faceted, whereas it can only be surmised for the Pacific. Present day ethnographic experiences provide indications that sharing food continues to be essential to Pacific culture.

Foodscape 4: Modern Day Chinese Influences on Pacific Gastronomy

Sharing food has developed in Pacific communities continuing the Chinese influence in two ways. Not only have Chinese set up market gardens to supply key ingredients for their own cuisine, but they contribute these vegetables to the urban markets, as well as through their Chinese restaurant establishments. This more economic form of sharing is based on payment by clients, whether as purchasers in the markets, or as guests to a proprietor, rather than goodwill between extended kin. The employees in small Chinese restaurants are often kin who mediate the social distance between guests and hosts. Chinese restaurants as they have become established in the Pacific are notably different from Pacific feasts, though hotel luaus and replications of Pacific feasts for tourists are an attempted approximation. Chinese restaurants in the Pacific offer a distinctive gastronomic experience, and thus contribute to an alternative foodscape. They are not yet well documented in the ethnographic literature, but visitors may recognize the

66   *Nancy J. Pollock*

general patterns reported by David Wu in this volume, and the writer's personal experiences.

Chinese arrived in the Pacific in the mid-nineteenth and early twentieth centuries as indentured labourers in mines in New Caledonia and Nauru, and in sugar cane and oil palm plantations in Fiji and Papua New Guinea (see Willmott 2007). These new residents not only developed small gardens in which to plant their favourite vegetable accompaniments, but also traded in delicacies shipped to China from the Pacific, such as shark's fins, and sea cucumbers which were in high demand. Trade thus linked the homelands of the early restauranteurs to their Pacific base.

The need for fresh vegetables for their accompanying dishes gradually increased a commitment to the development of extensive market gardens providing cabbages, tomatoes and other fresh produce in Tahiti, Fiji and New Zealand, for example. Family labour is a hallmark of these gardens, as it is of the various types of restaurants which draw on this food supply. Chinese market gardens have flourished as they provide a range of foodstuffs that differ from the traditional Pacific food crops. With an increase in tourism and western style restaurants' demands for fresh vegetables, these market gardens continue to play an important role in Pacific gastronomy.

Chinese restaurants are characterized by the regional styles of *cai,* dishes that accompany the rice. Major urban centres each have their own dishes appropriately identified: *jingcai* (Peking dishes), Shanghai, Cantonese/Hong Kong and Taipei. Each style has become used as a classification of restaurants themselves rather than regional styles (Chang 1977: 15). These styles have been carried by Chinese moving out of Asia, with Cantonese being the most common style in the Pacific.

In China, these restaurants developed in the eighth century to serve weary travellers tea and wine and food at Buddhist or Taoist monasteries, as documented for the Tang period. Inns, taverns, hostels and restaurants offered abundant cheap food (Chang 1977: 137) that allowed a range of choice depending on social class. In Sung times large rectangular tables became common, along with chopsticks, spoons and wine cups — with silver cups being offered in the highest class of restaurants (Chang 1977: 153). Regional cooking styles became available beyond the native region; "thrown in contact with all the other kinds of cooking ... [they] adopted the ingredients from one region, the nuance of seasoning from another, until cooking was indeed 'mixed up'" (Freeman in Chang 1977: 175). By the time of the Qing dynasty restaurants were available for every level of

Gastronomic Influences on the Pacific 67

expense and taste, from opulent settings on floating boats to small town inns and restaurants which were "centers for social contact and gossip" as reported by writers of those times (Spence 1977: 289). A common characteristic of Chinese restaurants was that many customers ate in private rooms, separated by walls or screens, so that one establishment catered to different purses; those dining at "*badawan* feasts" (eight course dinners) shared the physical setting with those eating a simple "fire pot" (Hsu and Hsu 1977: 307). Modern day travellers or businessmen choose a suitable level of formality, some establishing daily office hours at a specific time at a specific shop (Anderson 1977: 371). The range of cooking styles took Dunlop on her journey across six provinces of China to document a range of offerings (Dunlop 2008). McDonald's restaurants have developed a following that appeals mainly to younger Chinese in Hong Kong and Beijing who see them as a place to congregate and try some different foods while scarcely recognizing that the franchises have been imported from the US (Watson 1997).

It was inevitable that Chinese restaurants should become established in Pacific urban centres as part of the global spread (see Liu 2009; Wu 2007). A meal in a Chinese restaurant caters to different types of Pacific feasting and sharing. The banqueting needs of government and business officials to entertain visitors can be met by Chinese style dining facilities and food offerings. Family members in Pacific communities, organizing large gatherings for birthdays, farewells, and other rites of passage, likewise may choose to gather in a Chinese restaurant (Pollock fieldnotes; Majuro 1996). Such feasting includes several courses of different accompanying foods, such as beef in black bean sauce, but always served with rice as the basic food. On a smaller scale, office workers and those with cash may choose a Chinese meal for lunch, consisting of one or two dishes accompanying the rice, perhaps to be shared with others. In Honolulu, the single serve "plate lunch" served in a styrofoam container has become a favourite, to be taken away and eaten elsewhere either alone or with others.

Various forms of eating Chinese food have developed in the Pacific over the 150 years since Chinese contract workers have made their contributions to gastronomic culture. Roberts' account of the development of Chinese restaurants and Chinatowns in the US from the early period of Chinese migration to the US in the late nineteenth and early twentieth centuries (Roberts 2007) may have parallels in the Pacific. He notes that European writers distinguished between early nineteenth century (derogatory) reactions to Chinese food and those at the turn of the century, as these changed in Communist China. Curries, hashes, and fricassees became dominant dishes, with large restaurants in San Francisco catering for the "less sophisticated" with all-you-can eat meals. Spaces in these large restaurants could be rendered private with the use of screens. Smaller establishments increased in number and diversified from seating for guests to take-aways, and thus a cheaper style meal. The result is that today there is a wide range of Chinese dining available, from the elaborate large rooms offering banquet style menus of many dishes, to the small leased space with one or two wok on which to cook the accompanying dish(es) of choice to be taken and eaten elsewhere.

Chopsuey is one dish that has become widely established across the Pacific. It may be unrecognizable to a new Chinese arrival, because it has been adapted into many forms, whether for household servings, or celebratory events such as feasts. It is a common form of Chinese take-away in urban centres, as well as a popular dish to be shared with a few friends. Samoan *sapasui* may be made with beef marinated in soy sauce, or corned beef, together with ginger, garlic and onions, served with vermicelli (see <www.samoa.co.uk/food&drink/html>), or with tinned vegetables.

Chinese food in the Pacific is seen as cheap, filling, tasty and cosmopolitan so that similar named dishes can be found in a Chinese restaurant in Papeete, Suva or Honiara. The owners are often the chefs and provide the necessary labour for waiting on tables, washing dishes as well as the administration. They offer an amazing range of *cai* dishes produced with very limited cooking facilities. During the holding of Pacific Forum meetings on Nauru in 1993, 53 new Chinese establishments were set up in this small island nation, many of the operators being new arrivals from China, just for the occasion of making money by serving food for this two week event (Pollock fieldnotes 1994). Fresh vegetables are hard to come by on Nauru, other than from a UNDP garden run by a Chinese — who welcomed this new outlet for produce that Nauruans themselves rarely bought.

Key features that distinguish Chinese food for diners are the range of establishments, and of food offerings, as well as the gastronomic accoutrements that differ from European style restaurants. Chinese operators work in premises that vary from large establishments to small leased premises, often little more than a shop front. Their distinctiveness is denoted with a sign in Chinese and English that reflects Chinese thought. Inside, tables, often round seat 8, 10 or 12 guests, complete with lazy

Gastronomic Influences on the Pacific 69

susan in the middle, indicating that all dishes will be shared between the diners. Both chopsticks and western style spoon and fork may be provided. The menu is as likely to list offerings in Chinese or English script, with numbers that make for easy ordering. Rice is the unscripted stage for presentation of a variety of tastes and textures. Meats such as pork, beef and chicken comprise only a small portion of these dishes, chopped in bite size pieces amid the vegetables. Fish may be offered whole, or in a vegetable dish. Ingredients are usually sourced from local market gardens as vegetables should be served fresh. Other ingredients such as spices may be imported from China. Soy sauce has become an accepted accompanying dipping dish. In New Zealand in the early days of development of Chinese restaurants, these establishments offered a large stack of sliced bread already buttered but this practice has been discontinued.

Chinese restaurants in the Pacific thus follow on from a long tradition in the homeland, albeit with necessary changes due to distance from the source of spices and the available range of vegetables. They enhance Pacific gastronomy with a variety of dishes only a few of which may be cooked at home. Chopsuey, Pacific style, consisting of noodles, mince and a few carrots and peas is a dish frequently cooked by Pacific women for special events, and feasts whether in Samoa, or in New Zealand. The *fan/cai* principles become amalgamated in one dish.

Conclusions

The four foodscapes discussed above provide perspectives on Chinese influences on Pacific gastronomy over time. The resources that have been developed as consumables illustrate a disjuncture with grains to root and tree crops, with taro, yams, breadfruit etc. replacing rice as the base foods. Yet they represent a similar balance between starch and accompaniments. The long span of literary descriptions of Chinese cuisine contrasts with oral traditions in the Pacific and prehistorians' reconstructions. Sharing is the key ideology that provides continuity to link Chinese with Pacific socially based gastronomies. Moving up to present times, the (preliminary) foodscape of Chinese contributions through market gardens, restaurants, and takeaways provides a contrasting perspective to the gastronomic globalization out of the "West," that is, Europe and America.

When viewed from a perspective of globalization, these early gastronomic influences that emanated from China have become accepted in many nations around the world, even beyond the places where the Chinese diaspora is strong. When we view these "as a network of connections that define an enlarged world [as] held together by commodities" (Foster 2008: xii), we have pushed the time frame for these "commodity connections" as Foster labels them, back some 3,000 to 4,000 years. So the gastronomic connections are not "recent" as he argues for Papua New Guinea or elsewhere across Oceania. They have become so deeply embedded that they have not been recognized by those reconstructing an Oceanic past from a Euro/American perspective on gastronomic values.

Chinese gastronomic globalization across Oceania is thus marked by continuities on two levels as well as disjunctures on two levels. The consumer style for use of resources (starch/accompaniment) has provided continuity of principles across time and space. Adaptations of those base principles has allowed for inclusion of substitute resources such as taro, and much later sweet potato, thereby establishing a strong biological foundation for food security in the islands. The disjuncture between rice and taro, and hence cooking styles and preservation techniques is thus interwoven with this continuity of resources.

The principle of sharing, whether within households, or communities, or at feasts is a means of strengthening social networks across land and water, but on a different scale in the Pacific from that in China. Furthermore this sharing goes beyond an economic analysis involving material exchanges. Rather it represents a deep-seated reciprocity based on fundamental tenets of generosity and social obligations. Even without direct Chinese presence in the Pacific for some 2,000 years, the key gastronomic principles persisted with adaptations, to be renewed by Chinese settlements across Oceania in the last 150 years.

Another major disjuncture is apparent between two concepts of globalization. This early establishment of Chinese gastronomic influences must be distinguished from the more recent, much publicized, form of "western" globalization. Multi-national transfers of commercialized foods, such as McDonald's or Coca Cola, out of industrialized nations to remote parts of the world such as islands of Oceania, is very different from the earlier globalization out of China, discussed here. Not only does this later expansion consist of processed foods largely derived from imported resources, but the new foods form part of modern systems of trade and commercial activity. They are part of a cash based world system, rather than derived from a subsistence base. New western foodstuffs are globalized through trade networks rather than social networks. And western globalized

Gastronomic Influences on the Pacific

"commodity connections" direct their appeal to individual consumers, rather than as shared experiences.

Foodscapes thus provide a means to construct perspectives on significant changes to the gastronomic support of communities over space and time. They direct us to rethink the global flows of goods vital to well-being, namely foodstuffs, while placing those material resources in a wider ideology that stresses social networking. Oceanic communities have a long heritage of connections with peoples to the west, with food and gastronomic principles providing vital traceable linkages to an Asian heritage.

Note

1. The * refers to a linguistic reconstruction of a term that may not have been spoken.

References

Allaby, Robin. 2007. "Origins of Plant Exploitation in Near Oceania: A Review." In *Population Genetics, Linguistics and Culture: History in the South West Pacific*, ed. J. Friedlaender. Oxford: Oxford University Press, pp. 181–98.

Anderson, E.G. 1988. *The Food of China*. New Haven: Yale University Press.

Appadurai, Arjun. 1996. *Modernity at Large: Cultural Dimensions of Globalization*. Minneapolis: University of Minnesota Press.

Banks, Joseph. 1769. *Journal of Sir Joseph Banks*, ed. Sir Joseph Hooker. London: Macmillan, 1896, Reprint.

Bellwood, Peter. 1985. *Prehistory of the Indo-Malaysian Archipelago*. Sydney: Australia Academic Press.

———. 2002. "5000 Years of Austronesian History and Culture: East Coast Taiwan to Easter Island." In *Proceedings of Taro Symposium*, USP, pp. 2–18.

———. 2005. "The Farming/Language Dispersal Hypothesis in the East Asian Context." In *The Peopling of East Asia*, ed. L. Sagart *et al.* Abingdon, Oxon: RoutledgeCurzon Press, pp. 1–26.

Blench, R. 2005. "Geography of Rice." In *The Peopling of East Asia*, ed. L. Sagart *et al.* Abingdon, Oxon: RoutledgeCurzon Press, pp. 36–48.

Brillat-Savarin, Jean-Anthelme. 1970. *The Philosopher in the Kitchen*. Penguin: Middlesex [reprinted from Le Physiologie du Gout, 1825].

Chang K.C., ed. 1977. *Food in Chinese Culture: Anthropological and Historical Perspectives*. New Haven: Yale University Press.

Chang Te Tzu. 2000. "Rice." In *The Cambridge World History of Food*, ed. K. Kiple and K. Ornelas, II.A.7. London: Cambridge University Press, pp. 132–48.

Dunlop, Fuchsia. 2008. *Shark's Fin and Sichuan Pepper: A Sweet Sour Memoir of Eating in China*. London: Ebury Press for Random House Group.

Firth, Raymond. 1967. *The Work of the Gods in Tikopia*. Melbourne: Melbourne University Press.

Flannery, Tim. 1994. *The Future Eaters*. Chatswood, NSW: Reed Books.

Foster, Robert. 2008. *Coca-Globalization — following soft drinks from New York to New Guinea*. New York: Palgrave Macmillan.

Freeman, M. 1977. "Sung." In *Food in Chinese Culture*, ed. K.C. Chang. New Haven: Yale University Press, pp. 141–92.

Handy, E.S.C. and E.G. Handy. 1972. *Native Planters in Old Hawaii*. Honolulu: Bishop Museum Bulletin #233.

Hsu, Vera and Hsu, Francis. 1977. "Modern China: North." In *Food in Chinese Culture*, ed. K.C. Chang. New Haven: Yale University Press, pp. 295–316.

Irwin, Geoffrey. 2006. "Voyaging and Settlement." In *Vaka Moana*, ed. K.R. Howe. Auckland War Memorial Museum and David Bateman, pp. 54–99.

Kirch, Patrick. 1997. *The Lapita Peoples — Ancestors of the Oceanic World*. Oxford: Blackwell.

———. 2000. *On the Road of the Winds*. Berkeley: University of California Press.

Larson, Greg *et al.* 2007. "Phylogeny and Ancient DNA of Sus Provides Insights into Neolithic Expansion in Island South East Asia and Oceania." In *Proceedings of the National Academy of Sciences* 104 (12): 4834–9.

Leach, Helen. 2007. "Cooking with Pots Again." In *Vastly Ingenious, the Archaeology of Pacific Material Culture*, ed. A. Anderson, K. Green and F. Leach. Dunedin: Otago University Press, pp. 53–68.

Liu Haiming. 2009. "Chop Suey as Imagined Authentic Chinese Food: The Culinary Identity of Chinese Restaurants in the United States." *Journal of Transnational American Studies* 1 (1): 1–24.

Lu, Tracey. 2005. "The origin and dispersal of agriculture and human diaspora in East Asia." In *The Peopling of East Asia*, ed. L. Sagart *et al.* Abingdon, Oxon: RoutledgeCurzon Press, pp. 51–69.

Malinowski, Bronislaw. 1935. *Coral Gardens and their Magic* (2 vols.). London: Allen and Unwin.

Marshall, Yvonne. 2008. "The Social Lives of Lived and Inscribed Objects — A Lapita Perspective." *Journal of Polynesian Society* 117 (1): 59–74.

Matisoo-Smith, E. and J. Robins. 2004. "Origins and Dispersals of Pacific Peoples: Evidence from mtDNA Phylogenies of the Pacific Rat." In *Proceedings of the National Academy of Sciences* 101: 9167–72.

Matthews, Peter. 2006. "Plant Trails in Oceania." In *Vaka Moana*, ed. K.R. Howe. Auckland War Memorial Museum and David Bateman, pp. 94–7.

Pietrusewsky, M. 2005. "The Physical Anthropology of the Pacific, East Asia and South East Asia." In *The Peopling of East Asia*, ed. L. Sagart *et al.* Abingdon, Oxon: RoutledgeCurzon Press, pp. 201–35.

Gastronomic Influences on the Pacific 73

Pollock, Nancy J. 1983. "Rice in Guam." *Journal of Polynesian Society* 92 (4): 509–20.

———. 1984. "Breadfruit fermentation practices in Oceania." *Journal Societe des Oceanistes* 79: 151–64.

———. 1986. "Food classification in Fiji, Hawaii and Tahiti." *Ethnology* 25 (2): 107–18.

———. 1992. *These Roots Remain — Food Habits in Islands of the Central Pacific.* Hawaii: The Institute for Polynesian Studies and University of Hawaii Press.

———. 2000. "Taro." In *The Cambridge World History of Food*, ed. K. Kiple and K. Ornelas, II.B.6. London: Cambridge University Press, pp. 218–30.

———. 2002. "Vegeculture as Food Security for Pacific Communities." In *Vegeculture in Eastern Asia and Oceania*, ed. Shuji Yoshida and Peter Matthews. Osaka: JCAS, National Museum of Ethnology, pp. 277–92.

———. 2008. "Chinese Dietary Influences in the Pacific." In *The 10th Symposium of Chinese Dietary Culture*, Taiwan, pp. 265–93.

———. In press. "Diversifying Pacific Foodscapes over time and tastes." In *Proceedings of European Society for Oceanistes*, Verona.

Reid, Anthony, ed. 2008. "The Chinese Diaspora in the Pacific." In *The Pacific World*, vol. 16, Ashgate Variorum, Aldershot, Hants.

Roberts, J.A.G. 2003. *China to Chinatown: Chinese Food in the West.* London: Peakton books.

Sabban, Francoise. 2000. "China." In *The Cambridge World History of Food*, ed. K. Kiple and K. Ornelas, Vol. 2. V.B.3: 1165–74. Cambridge: Cambridge University Press.

Sagart, L. *et al.*, eds. 2005. *The Peopling of East Asia.* Abingdon, Oxon: RoutledgeCurzon Press.

Smil, Vaclav. 2002. *Feeding the World: A Challenge for the Twenty-first Century.* MA: MIT Press.

Spence, Jonathan. 1977. "Ch'ing." In *Food in Chinese Culture*, ed. K.C. Chang. New Haven: Yale University Press, pp. 259–94.

Spriggs, Matthew. 2002. "Taro Cropping Systems in the Southeast Asian Pacific Region; An Archaeological Update." In *Vegeculture in Eastern Asia and Oceania*, ed. Yoshida Shuji and Peter Matthews. Osaka, Japan: JCAS Symposium Series #16, pp. 77–94.

Stiglitz, Joseph. 2006. *Making Globalisation Work.* N.Y.: W.W. Norton & Co.

Tan Chee-Beng. 2001. "Food and Ethnicity with reference to the Chinese in Malaysia." In *Changing Chinese Foodways in Asia*, ed. David Y.H. Wu and Tan Chee-Beng. Hong Kong: The Chinese University Press, pp. 125–60.

Wang Ren-xiang. 2008. "A Study on the Fish Designs in Han dynasty Stone and Tile Reliefs." *Journal of Chinese Dietary Culture* 4 (2): 78–114.

Walter, Annie and Vincent Lebot. 2007. *Gardens of Oceania.* Canberra: ACIAR, Australian Centre for International Agricultural Research.

Watson, James. 1997. *Golden Arches East — Macdonalds in East Asia*. California: Stanford University Press.

Willmott, Bill. 2007. "Varieties of Chinese Experience in the Pacific." *CSCSD Occasional Paper* #1, ejournal, <rspas.anu.edu.au/cscsd/publications.php>.

Wu, David Y.H. 2002. "Improvising Chinese Cuisine Overseas." In *The Globalization of Chinese Cuisine*, ed. David Y.H. Wu and Sidney Cheung. RoutledgeCurzon Press, pp. 56–66.

Wu, David and Tan Chee-Beng, eds. 2001. *Changing Chinese Foodways in Asia*. Hong Kong: The Chinese University Press.

Yen, Douglas. 1975. "Indigenous food processing in Oceania." In *Gastronomy*, ed. M. Arnott, *World Anthropology Series*. The Hague: Mouton, pp. 147–68.

Yen Ho, Alice. 1995. *At the South East Asian Table*. Kuala Lumpur: Oxford University Press.

Yoshida, Shuji and Peter Matthews. 2002. *Vegeculture in Eastern Asia and Oceania*. Osaka: JCAS, National Museum of Ethnology.

Yu Ying-shih. 1977. "Han." In *Food in Chinese Culture*, ed. K.C. Chang. New Haven: Yale University Press, pp. 53–84.

CHAPTER

3

Global Encounter of Diasporic Chinese Restaurant Food

David Y.H. Wu

Introduction: Theoretical Considerations

I write this chapter to make sense of what constitute Chinese cuisines and how they represent Chinese cultures or Chineseness overseas. Since my childhood, I have tasted Chinese food in restaurants and food stalls in large and small cities, in private and public banquets, and in remote village markets all over the world.[1] This paper discusses the complexity of Chinese cuisines in the context of a historic process of global expansion, drawing on my life-long experience as well as scheduled fieldworks conducted during the past two decades. My experience of eating Chinese food inside and outside of China, combined with my eating in ordinary and upscale "Western" restaurants, allows me to present personal judgment of global variations and tastes of diasporic Chinese cuisines.

In terms of theoretical thinking, I shall frame my analysis of current global variations of Chinese culinary culture and restaurant food in terms of three theoretical considerations:

(1) There are many Chinese cuisines, and they symbolize many intra-Chinese culinary divisions and ethnic identities;

75

76 *David Y.H. Wu*

(2) Contemporary Chinese cuisines can be placed within a larger global process of transnational flows of people, ethnicity, capital and imagination as proposed by post-modern scholars such as Appadurai (1990, 1996, 2001), and Beriss and Sutton (2007);

(3) Chinese cuisines on the world arena continue to face challenges of negative social stigma, discrimination and colonial imagination in a world of "Western domination."

An important argument is that the spread of the diasporic Chinese cuisines around the globe during the twentieth century parallels two major historic developments: Euro-American colonialism and increased consumption of commercially prepared food in restaurants, or "eating out." The former development brought a peasant class of southern Chinese to work around the world, and the latter provided opportunities for the Chinese who settled on foreign lands to engage in food trade and restaurant business. It is in this sense, that is, the Chinese restaurant being a familiar global phenomenon in contemporary dining-out culture that my personal encounters with Chinese restaurants in many parts of the world informs on anthropological and theoretical inquiries about Chinese food overseas.[2]

I myself become a diasporic person and have lived outside of China for more than 40 years, yet I paid regular, almost annual, visits to my Chinese "homeland." I also annually took several trans-continental trips and have frequented Chinese restaurants operated by Chinese migrants in different parts of the world. Whether doing fieldwork or not, I habitually collected the menus of the restaurants I visited, including banquet menus prepared for special social occasions. I shall in the first part of this chapter describe my encounters with Chinese restaurants in Australia, Europe, Japan, North America and Papua New Guinea. My initial encounters with the diasporic Chinese food overseas, mainly in the United States, gave me unprepared cultural shocks, for which I present stories in the following three sections. I also provide common sense explanations for the reasons why the diasporic Chinese cuisine appeared to be so foreign and unacceptable to a new comer from the "homeland." In the final sections, I shall engage in theoretical discussions that offer new meanings to diasporic Chinese cuisines and cultural representations of Chinese food in contemporary global culture.

My Papua New Guinea Encounter

In the early 1970s I lived for two years in the present day South Pacific nation of Papua New Guinea (hereafter PNG). With the assistance of my

Diasporic Chinese Restaurant Food   77

late wife Wei-lan, I conducted anthropological fieldwork in the Chinese communities. I believe an ethno-historical account about the Chinese foodways in PNG helps us to understand how in the beginning an overseas Chinese cuisine could have been developed in any parts of Southeast Asia or Pacific island nations. The Chinese community in Papua New Guinea has a short history of 120 years (Wu 1982). At the beginning of the twentieth century, the German governor began to develop the small port city of Rabaul, New Britain, as the headquarters of the German colony of New Guinea. The governor envisioned a prosperous second Singapore in the future, but the First World War interrupted this development. With a population of less than two thousand Chinese residents, Rabaul can be considered a typical example of early settlements among overseas Chinese in the European colonial South Seas that resembles any emerging small Chinese towns one or two hundred years earlier in many parts of Southeast Asia.

There are two common elements in the development of diasporic Chinese cuisine and restaurants in a typical frontier migrant society. First, in order to maintain Chinese foodways the migrants must introduce new kinds of agricultural produce. Second, Chinese restaurants evolved on the basis of Chinese socio-political associations. At the turn of the twentieth century, all Chinese arrivals in the largest urban centre — Rabaul, New Britain — were single males. They formed clan and hometown associations for mutual aid. They constructed association halls in Rabaul to provide room and board for members and newcomers. Food cooked and served at the *huiguan* (Chinese associations) marks the beginning of a PNG Chinese restaurant cuisine.

Chinese migrants brought cooking ingredients to New Guinea for preparing "Chinese meals." Botanical records show new varieties of vegetables introduced by the Chinese at the end of the nineteenth century to these tropical islands, such as Chinese cabbage, squash, radish, taro, ginger and Chinese parsley (Wu 1977). The Chinese later (since the 1930s) also imported directly from south China or via Sydney (arranged by Chinese merchant brokers) dehydrated cooking ingredients, such as dried mushrooms, dried tree fungus, dried shrimp, dried oysters, dried bean curd and cured meats including Chinese sausages (*lap chong*). Chinese cooking methods were maintained, although it was also necessary to incorporate ways borrowed from European and native cultures in the foreign countries. This is comparable to the familiar situation in Southeast Asia in the development of *Nonya* (indigenized and creolized) cooking (Tan 2007).

A former PNG resident (who now lives in Australia, as the majority of PNG Chinese do) recalls his favourite dishes served at Chinese gatherings when he was a teenager in Rabaul during the 1960s. The dishes included roast chicken, deep fried battered chicken wings (seasoned with Chinese five spices), mild curry dishes, chopsuey (meaning chopped vegetables stir fried with finely chopped meats), roast pork (with crispy skin), *char siew* (sweet barbecued pork), braised whole black mushrooms, fried rice, fried noodles, etc. These dishes are similar to what I encountered at Chinese parties in Rabaul during the early 1970s. Also similar dishes were served in the Chinese restaurants in Rabaul and Port Moresby. During my three-year sojourn in Rabaul I observed that two Chinese trade stores sold homemade roast whole chickens to fellow Chinese customers. Chinese were able to purchase live chickens and Cantonese vegetables such as *choy-sam* (green leafed cabbage) in the "native market" where the indigenous Tolai people placed their garden produces for sale. The PNG Chinese diet certainly included all the local tropical fruits. There were also plenty of fresh fish and seafood from the surrounding seas. The giant fruit bat, locally named "*fei shi*" (flying fox, in Cantonese), and wild pigeons (*bagga*, Cantonese, literally means white pigeon, but actually dark coloured) were local delicacies. Chinese cooked these with traditional herbal medicine to increase the potency of special medicinal effects. A Chinese butcher killed a pig once a week to satisfy those who desired fresh pork, whereas for daily consumption only frozen pork imported from Australia was available. On the assigned day every week when the butcher arrived with fresh pork, his shop would be overwhelmed with Chinese ladies, fighting for the desirable parts of the pig. One old Chinese man made baked castor-tarts daily at his home kitchen for Chinese customers who pre-ordered them. They are the same "egg tarts" considered a standard desert item today served in almost all Cantonese (style) tea houses (*yam-cha* or dim sum restaurants) around the world. The oven-baked tart apparently has a Western origin; as do lemon chicken and many other dishes in Cantonese cuisine. During the 1970s the "Chinese" dishes found at meal time on the tables of PNG Chinese also included local inventions such as (canned) corned beef stir-fried with onions (*young zong*, literally meaning foreign scallion), which was a popular post-war (WWII) pan-Pacific dish.

One important aspect of change in PNG Chinese foodways concerns the manner in which meals are served, whether at home or in a Chinese restaurant. PNG Chinese put rice and "*sung*" (or *cai*, main dishes, in Mandarin) on a plate and eat the food with a fork and a spoon (in place

Diasporic Chinese Restaurant Food 79

of a knife). It is the same way of serving meal in *Peranakan* homes in Southeast Asia. This habit may have a Southeast Asian origin, as the earliest Chinese settlers in Rabaul were recruited from Singapore. When I questioned this apparent "foreign" habit, some PNG Chinese commented that they are "more Chinese" than the Australian Chinese or American Chinese because they are fluent in the spoken Chinese (Cantonese) language, although they do not use rice bowls and chopsticks to eat their meals as their cousins in Australia or North America do.

Importation of brides from Hong Kong beginning in the late 1960s expanded the variety and style of dishes served in PNG Chinese homes. The PNG Chinese community had become more affluent by the 1970s and many individuals were able to travel to Hong Kong and Taiwan for vacation every year or more often. Although the trips opened their eyes to Chinese high cuisine, they did not alter their foodways in any substantial way.

The population of Chinese in Rabual was small at only one to three thousand during the twentieth century. The small size of the community still allowed it to maintain one or two public eating-places. From the 1950s to the 1980s there were two Chinese restaurants in Rabual. One is actually the Kuomintang Club (PNG official Nationalist headquarters of the Republic of China established in the 1930s). Its main hall occasionally served as a venue for large Chinese banquets or dance parties. In addition to daily operation of a restaurant, its main function was to host national (ROC Double Ten Day) holiday celebrations and Chinese festivities (such as New Year's Day) that were attended by the entire Chinese community. After Australia officially recognized China in 1972, the club name was changed to Taiping (eternal peace) Club. The club/restaurant had a limited menu. I saw mixed blood Chinese workers in the kitchen and they also waited at the tables. At one time in the 1980s the club tried to hire a Chinese cook from a visiting cargo ship. He worked there for only one year.

The other restaurant, the Chung Café, located on the same main street of "Chinatown," was operated by a family so named. It was much smaller in size compared to the KMT Club, having only about six small tables that could seat at one time some two dozen customers. It changed ownership and name many times (e.g., it once was the Bamboo Café), but it was always under the ownership of a Chinese family. It was in operation during the 1980s and was frequented by expatriates (or Europeans — an official "racial category" in PNG referring to Caucasians). This restaurant closed down for good when the majority of the Chinese and Europeans left the country in the late1980s. To me the food was edible but not particularly palatable — a sort of improvised Cantonese style of country cuisine. It was the only place in town for eating out and "eating Chinese."

In Port Moresby, three public eateries served Chinese food during the 1970s. The larger one was an upscale restaurant called the Mandarin Club, which was operated by several Chinese partners. It opened for business only at night, a place for eating out on special occasions or for social engagements, where diners could also enjoy entertainers playing a piano. Several times my wife and I went there with expatriate (white) friends and saw customers were predominantly Europeans. Another small restaurant was also operated by a Chinese family and served Cantonese home (country) style cooking. Both restaurants have changed hands many times. Typically, when one family owner runs into financial difficulty another Chinese family would take over. This pattern is almost universal among Chinese restaurant businesses around the world.

The third place that served Chinese food was the Port Moresby Chinese Association house. To these days the Port Moresby Chinese community has maintained a Chinese Club, which was also called Taiping. Other than for community wide functions, women would occasionally bring dishes cooked at home to the club hall to serve at social gatherings. Even new immigrants or temporary workers from PRC increased to thousands, mainly on the Highlands and Bougainville, they had little contact with the PNG Chinese. A friend told me recently that there was once a cooking class for women to learn how to cook "northern Chinese" dishes, which are not in the foodways of PNG Chinese. I also learned that in the past decade many Taiwanese came to PNG and the Solomon Islands to conduct business. Some of them must have introduced to PNG ladies the so-called northern Chinese cuisine of Taiwan.

In sum, the PNG Chinese did not eat out frequently, especially in Chinese restaurants; because the community was small and restaurant food was no better than food prepared at home for special occasions. I observed in the 1970s that when individual young Chinese eat out on special occasions, they would dine at Western restaurants operated by Europeans. Chinese restaurants in PNG mainly catered to the expatriate (white) community, as these customers did not cook Chinese dishes at home and Chinese meals provided an alternative to the more expensive meals in the hotel restaurant (such as Travel Lodge in Rabaul), or social club for the Europeans. Of course, most expatriate customers were

Diasporic Chinese Restaurant Food

accustomed to frequenting Chinese restaurants in other countries where they had lived.

Mundane Chinese Restaurants in the United States

The global diffusion of food and foodways renders the American culinary scene too complex and too variant to identify an "American cuisine." Sidney Mintz (1996: 107–9) maintains that the United States is a country without a "national cuisine." Until the late twentieth century, ordinary Americans may think otherwise when they disregard the influence of minority ethnic cuisines. Geographer Pillsbury's book (1998) on "The American Diet," has a title of "No Foreign Food," since the book presents a pan-American diet, albeit complex with regional characteristics and historical variations. This book of American diet has only one entry in identifying a food item that can be associated with Chinese cuisine — *chow mien*. In mentioning the term, the author's remarks that "for the mass American population," prepared foods available to any household today includes such "exotic" item as "La Choy Chow Mien," which is an American invention. According to this book, both Chinese and Italian food items are considered "foreign" for "ordinary Americans." This is in apparent contrast to the common practice of millions of Americans frequently consume "Chinese food" when they eat out or buy take-out food. Although the American diet may include a variety of ethnic cuisines, a common image of an "American cuisine" would support Pillsbury's view, which reflects a "(white) middle class American" background. In other words, the Chinese food though omnipresent is still marginal to the American diet both in terms of the range of food consumed and in terms of the perception of what constitutes the American cuisine or food culture. For the majority of Americans, including many ethnic Chinese themselves, eating out in a Chinese restaurant, or eating take-out Chinese food at home, is associated with eating out cheaply, i.e., "cheap eats." Most Americans are quite familiar with the imagery of eating Chinese food from paper containers and with fortune cookies.

Regarding the current situation of Chinese food served by the diasporic Chinese restaurants in the US, I agree with Mintz in his remark:

> (It) has become dilapidated during the last two decades, as regional variants in Chinese cooking were first discovered by Americans, then largely dissolved by the relentless degradation of distinction in bad restaurants (Mintz 1996: 94).

It is this image of incredibly bad food that came to my mind when reminiscing about my first encounters with the diasporic Chinese cuisine in Honolulu and in small towns in Utah and Arizona in the late 1960s. Anthropologists of food realize how important "memory" serves to enhance our understanding of food culture and identity (Holtzman 2006). I now realize that my memory of bad American Chinese food had to do with the fact that I arrived in the United States with fresh memories of good restaurant food in Taipei of the 1950s to the 1960s. More significantly, I then had the expectation that Chinese restaurant food ought to taste good regardless of location, even overseas. When I took my wife for the first time to an established large chopsuey restaurant in Honolulu in 1967, she sobbed in disappointment at the terrible looking, inedible, and unfamiliar "Chinese" food. This also reflects how food can bring out fond memories of good food at home (Taiwan) as compared to unexpected bad food in a foreign land. In 1969 at a Chinese restaurant in a small town of Utah,

David Wu eating *Ganchao Niuruo Hefen* (Fried Beef Flat Rice Noodle) and *Cuipiji* (Crispy Chicken) in a Chinese restaurant in Honolulu, Hawaii. (Photograph by David Ma, 2010)

when my order of a "chow mien" dish arrived, I could not believe my eyes. The dish looked and tasted like today's uncooked instant "cup noodle."

The cultural shock caused by unappetizing American Chinese restaurant food reveals something that we were not aware of during the 1960s. We were not used to American Chinese restaurant food; because during the 1950s and earlier 1960s we had experienced in Taipei good food prepared by the best (refugee) cooks from all parts of China. I shall in a later section elaborate on this historical fact. The mediocre food of American Chinese restaurants in the 1960s and the 1970s — the chopsuey food — is a product of adaptation to foreign tastes and originated from the cuisine of working class southern Chinese peasants of the nineteenth century (Liu 2009). During the 1970s, even with changes and an infusion of new regional Chinese cuisines and the incorporation of Hong Kong style dishes in North American Chinese restaurants, a standardization process continued to corrupt the taste of Chinese restaurant food. Even though in later years I also encountered arguably more authentic and delicious Chinese restaurant food on the United States mainland, especially in large cities such as San Francisco, I am not surprised with Mintz's observation of the bad Chinese restaurant food of the 1990s. An interesting ethnographic study of Chinese restaurants in rural Western Canada reveals that even a good cook from Hong Kong has to re-educate himself of how to cook "(bad) Chinese food" in order to serve foreign customers (Smart 2003). It is quite common today even among Chinese restaurants in large American cities (e.g., Honolulu, San Francisco and Los Angeles) that boast a large ethnic Chinese population, the taste and quality of Chinese restaurant food continue to deteriorate rather than improve (if we apply the standard of restaurant food in Hong Kong, Taipei, or even Singapore). Most of the restaurants today serve dishes that reflect a combination of Chinese ethnic regional cuisines of the 1960s and 1970s. We shall later document a history of a new "Pan-China" cuisine of the 1970s, which later went through the same standardization process that is found at today's "express" Chinese food stalls in shopping malls. Such a trend is what I would like to call the American "*buffetization*" of bad Chinese cuisine (Wu 2008). Today the newspapers often carry advertisements for Chinese restaurants highlighting such a statement: "We serve authentic Peking, Cantonese and Sichuan cuisines."

When Chinese regional cuisines, and the Hong Kong style (seafood) Cantonese cuisine as well, were first introduced to the United States during the 1970s, an experienced Chinese customer could tell which regional

Chinese cuisine the restaurant serves by the way they cooked certain dishes. Take for instance, duck; each of the following duck dishes serves as a marker for one type of Chinese cuisine:

Peking (roast) duck – Peking or other northern Chinese restaurant

siu-up (roast duck) – Cantonese or Hong Kong restaurant

zhangchaya (tea smoked duck) – Sichuan restaurant

xiangsuya (crispy deboned duck) – Shanghai restaurant

taro duck (stuffed and braised) – Hawaiian Cantonese restaurant

If a restaurant had all these different kinds of duck dishes on its menu, a sophisticated Chinese customer may question whether the cook is capable of producing any duck dish with authenticity in taste or style.

Beardsworth (1997), citing Fischer's study (1988), argues that food, as symbols is absolutely essential to our sense of identity — both individual and collective. Eating Chinese is not only an expression of the food habits of some individual Chinese who maintains a strong Chinese identity, it is also a collective "patriotic act" — expressing pride in belonging to a certain "Chinese regional group" or certain ethnicity — northern Chinese, Shanghainese or Cantonese. Indeed many Chinese, whether recent migrants or local born, desire to eat at their favoured "ethnic" (Chinese) restaurants when eating out. This explains why there are numerous Chinese restaurants serving different styles of Chinese regional food in large cities with a large Chinese population.

A Chinese middle-aged couple recently (2007) moved to Hawaii from California and claimed local Chinese restaurants uninviting. When I interviewed them, the wife told me: "There are no *real Chinese* restaurants here in Hawaii; they are all Cantonese." When asked what she meant by real Chinese, she answered: "The kind of food we can eat, like Shanghai or Sichuan dishes." The couple was both born in China, grew up in Taiwan since childhood, and later came to the United States to pursue graduate studies. They have lived in the United States for 45 years. They now fly from Honolulu to Los Angeles several times a year to "enjoy real Chinese food (like the kind of *waisheng cai* to be discussed later)." This couple's preference for "real Chinese" versus "Cantonese" food is not uncommon among my generation of Chinese diaspora of North America. It demonstrates differences in intra-Chinese ethnic identity that contributed to segregation in food habits and restaurant patronage among diasporic Chinese consumers. Later I shall elaborate on the historic development of intra-ethnic Chinese cuisines.

Globalization of American Chinese Fusion Cuisine

Since the end of the twentieth century, a new trend in cuisine occurred in the United States restaurant business, i.e., "fusion," the globalization of cooking techniques and ingredients. Fusion, like globalization, is not really the product of the late twentieth century: it has been happening for thousands of years. However, "fusion food" or "fusion cooking," such as "Pacific Rim Cuisine," has become in recent years a terminology often associated with advertising and promotion among professional chefs and restaurateurs. It is an invention in the restaurant world of a distinct class of cuisine. If modern fusion cuisine assimilates the best of international tastes and cooking techniques into "Western" cuisine, the "buffetization" in contrast brings to the Chinese restaurant the mediocre, or unacceptable, Chinese regional cuisines. A related recent development in Honolulu, for instance, is one in which Chinese dishes are literally served buffet style, similar to buffet breakfasts served in hotels. This is another trend causing degradation in the image and quality of food of the diasporic Chinese restaurant, marking the loss of a distinct culinary identity and guaranteeing poor quality "Chinese" food. In order to compete with other restaurants, some Honolulu Chinese restaurants have advertised proudly that food items on their buffet table include sushi and prime steaks. In contrast to this development that has contributed to the decline of taste and quality of Chinese cuisine in the US, there are also new trends of a different type of "Chinese fusion" cuisine in which diners enjoy refined and delicious Chinese food. It is the Euro-Americanization of "Chinese cuisine" in the United States by non-Chinese for non-Chinese diners. This type of cuisine is an obvious product of late twentieth-century commercialism, public media and globalization, which has not been studied by anthropologists (see Appadurai 1999). It appears we have a new example of "a third world cultural commodity — Chinese restaurant food" that has become localized in this leading capitalist country of the world.

Two restaurants I have encountered serve to illustrate the first type of this new fusion or globalization trend of Chinese restaurants. They are Wolfgang Puck's Chinois in Santa Monica, California, and the chain restaurants of P.F. Chang's China Bistro in many United States cities.

Wolfgang Puck is what in the United States would call a "celebrity chef" — a famous chef, restaurateur, businessman and TV commercial promoter. Twenty years ago he opened his first fusion restaurant in Santa Monica named "Chinois" — or "China" in French. The cuisine is European with a heavy Chinese touch; so is the black costume of the waiting staff, a sort of Chinese martial arts (*"gong fu"*) outfits. The tables are set with chopsticks. The martial arts outfit for the staff and chopsticks apparently intent to evoke a sense of "Chineseness." None of the chiefs busy cooking in the open kitchen was Chinese. If we judge one popular dish — sweet-and-sour catfish, it looks and tastes like the traditional Peking dish of *"tangcuyu"* (sugar and vinegar fish, usually carp). The restaurant today is a popular place for fine dining. In my opinion the quality of the dishes has met the same standard of good taste over many years. I am certain that ordinary Chinese would not accept it as a Chinese restaurant; it is a European restaurant for non-Chinese diners.

The P.F. Chang's China Bistro is owned and operated by non-Chinese. Before going there to do my fieldwork, some Chinese (born in China) warned me not to expect to eat real "Chinese" food there. I had my first interesting encounter in one of the chain restaurants located in Los Angeles. Although the menu appears to include all the usual dishes one can find in most Chinese restaurant, the food is cooked by Mexican chefs and served by white or Mexican workers. The food is as good as that in any mediocre Chinese restaurant. Some of the California Chinese diners who had eaten there commented on the food by saying that some dishes are quite acceptable to the "Chinese" palate. I shall later further analyze the meaning of this chain restaurant in the evolution of northern Chinese cuisine.

The second type of new fusion Chinese restaurant is what I encountered in a Western (Euro-American) looking restaurant serving authentic northern Chinese cuisine. In the mind of other Chinese the décor and service in this restaurant are too Western to be Chinese. This paradoxical fusion restaurant is known as Mr. Chow of London, New York and Beverly Hills.

As one writer (or promoter) describes the owner — Michael Chow: "This Chinese-born restaurateur, naturalized a British citizen, has spent the past 30 years of his life serving English and American stars and celebrities his subtle Beijing Chinese cuisine — the best and most expensive — in an elegant, stylish setting (Galerie 1999)." He opened his first restaurant, "Mr Chow," in Knightbridge of London in 1968; a second one in Beverly Hills, Los Angeles in 1974; and a third one in New York City in 1978. All three have been and still are very successful (2007).[3]

Diasporic Chinese Restaurant Food

Born in Shanghai in 1940 of the then most famous Peking Opera singer (his father was Chou Sing Fang, stage name Qi-Lin-Tong), Michael Chow attended a "public school" in England at the age of 12. Trained in art and architecture, he ventured into acting, film and decorative design while socializing with famed artists, movie stars and rock singers. His restaurants in London and New York became the gathering places for famous artists (such as Julian Schenabel, Jean-Michel Basquiat and Andy Warhol). His Beverly Hills restaurant has been patronized by Hollywood stars, entertainers, singers, sports stars and other rich customers. Many long-term Chinese residents in Los Angeles I have talked to had never heard of this restaurant.

My wife and I began to dine at Mr Chow's at Beverly Hills beginning in the early 1990s when we visited Los Angeles once or twice a year. We were searching for a good northern Chinese restaurant and discovered with pleasure that Chow serves the most traditional and authentic northern Chinese and Shanghai dishes that we can remember since childhood. These dishes are no longer served in other restaurants in the United States, Taiwan and Hong Kong. However, this restaurant has the appearance of a fancy Western restaurant, with European décor designed by the owner, Mr Michael Chow, himself. The manner of service reminds one of an upscale French restaurant, and the Caucasian waiting staff in white tuxedoes. Mr Chow was proud to say: "My chefs are Chinese, but my waiters are Italian" (Restany 1999: 1). Every time we ate in the restaurant, my wife would spot a Hollywood movie star — emerging new stars as well as old and famous. Legend had it that one day both Elizabeth Taylor and Madonna dined there at the same time with their respective entourages (Restany 1999). The tables were set with fine silverware and European china, but chopsticks are conspicuously missing (provided only upon request). A friend heard Mr Chow commented on his reason for not providing chopsticks: "I want to show 'the foreigners' refined Chinese cuisine of a superior civilization. The foreigners cannot handle chopsticks properly (if they are provided on the table); hence making a mockery of Chinese table manners." Interviews with friends who personally know Mr Chow reveal a man of patriotic and nationalist sentiment, as shown in his explanation of why as an artist he entered the restaurant business. He said he wants to serve authentic Chinese high cuisine in order to educate "foreigners" about the superiority of Chinese civilization.

My Encounters in Australia, Japan and Europe

Australia

I lived in Australia for four years during the early 1970s. My wife and I enjoyed delicious meals at Chinese restaurants in Sydney's Chinatown. We also enjoyed eating at many Australian steak houses and European style cafés. As we lived in Canberra where there was only a small Chinese population, we regularly drove from Canberra to Sydney to shop for "Chinese ingredients" for home cooking. We shopped mainly for tofu and Chinese vegetables that were not available in Canberra, although our usual diet included excellent Australian lamb, beef and fresh seafood.

Canberra in the early 1970s had only two Chinese restaurants. A fancy and expensive one, located at the city centre, was operated by a cook from Taiwan who used to work for the ROC (Taipei) ambassador. The menu showed northern Chinese cuisine. A Cantonese cook from Hong Kong operated another small Chinese restaurant located on the outskirts of Canberra. We frequented this small restaurant that served standard dishes familiar to Australians. It is a sort of the Australian version of chopsuey house. Every entrée ordered comes with a complimentary appetizer — a soup. The customer had the choice of either a "long soup" or a "short soup." This puzzled us on our first visit, but the long soup was actually soup-noodles, while the short soup was wonton soup. We were friendly with the cook and I always by-passed the Australian waitress by going into the kitchen to discuss our order with the cook. He always cooked for us dishes not on the menu but of more authentic Cantonese, which tasted good.

I had the opportunity of discussing Chinese food with others and learned how the topic of Chinese food can be a learning tool about ethnic relations — between Chinese and white Australians as well as between fellow Chinese immigrants who come from different regions of China.

Once we took a close Australian friend to a Chinese restaurant on Dixon Street in Sydney's Chinatown, where ethnic Chinese dined. She asked me to order from the menu posted on the wall and written by brush pen in Chinese calligraphy, not from the printed (dirty-looking and worn) bilingual menu provided by the waiter. She believed that the dishes listed on the wall poster were reserved for Chinese customers, hence more authentic and delicious. She theorized that those dishes were not available to the "foreign devils" who could not read Chinese. In spite of my attempt

Diasporic Chinese Restaurant Food   89

to argue against her theory, she insisted that all her (white Australian) friends knew about this trick of the Chinese who would reserve the best dishes for Chinese themselves.

Another incident involves our visit to a Chinese friend who was teaching at Melbourne University. I had known him in Taiwan, a colleague at the Academy of Science. He was a Beijing native, a graduate of Peking University, and worked in Taiwan prior to immigrating to Australia in the early 1970s. Upon hearing that we were going to Chinatown to have dinner, he warned us not to order roast duck in the restaurant. At that time the Chinatown restaurants were exclusively Cantonese style. He commented that in his opinion "the *shaoya* (Mandarin pronunciation of Cantonese style *siu-up*, or roast duck) of the Cantonese people is not suitable for "our" consumption.[4]

Living next door to our apartment in Canberra was a young German couple. One day the husband told me that they were going to cook a Chinese dinner. I asked if they knew how to cook Chinese food. He answered: "Of course. It is easy. We have leftover food from lunch. We just mix the food with ketchup and heat it up. There we have a sweet and sour Chinese dish." This is a good example of the common stereotypical conception of Chinese cuisine. What I learned from encounters in Australia is the realization that anthropologists have often emphasized in their studies: consumption and choice of food have deep meanings in ethnic identity and ethnic relations. The Australian Chinese population has increased enormously since my sojourn 30 years ago (see Ryan 2003). New Chinese immigrants have arrived from China, Taiwan, Malaysia, and, a majority are from Hong Kong. The Chinese diaspora restaurants in Australia have certainly expanded the range and variety of regional and national cuisines (see Tam 2002).

Japan

My very first experience with Chinese restaurants in Japan was in Tokyo in 1966, on a stopover on my way to the United States. Staying in a hotel which housed a Peking restaurant, three Chinese friends from Taiwan and I enjoyed a familiar and surprisingly authentic Chinese meal that would rival any good restaurant food I had had in Taipei. During the 40 years that followed, in the course of eating out during my visits (once or twice a year) to Japan, I observed widespread acceptance and localization of Chinese cuisine in the Japanese restaurant business. By the late 1970s and during the 1980s, small Chinese restaurants had become common in the scene in every city, big and small. They have become operated predominately by Japanese cooks, not overseas Chinese. Chinese soup noodles (*ramen*), pot stickers (*gyoza*), fried rice, and dishes such as "*mapo* tofu" have entered the Japanese daily diet, and so have Cantonese (or Hong Kong style) *yum-cha* restaurants and refined Cantonese high cuisine (see Aoki 2001, Cheung 2002). The Japanese invention of packaged instant *ramen* (originated from Mandarin *lamian* in north China) is today known around the world as a common Japanese national food. One of my favourite Japanese restaurants in the busy Ginza district of Tokyo, which we frequented almost yearly for the past 30 years, is a *shabu-shabu* place. My gourmet anthropologist friend, the late professor Hiroshi Wagatsuma, explained to me that *shabu-shabu* is a Japanese adoption of northern Chinese hot pot style of eating lamb — *shuan yangruo*. Japanese corrupted the pronunciation of *shuan* — the motion of cooking by swiftly dipping a thin slice of lamb into the soup — as *shabu*, hence the creation of today's popular (and exotic) "Japanese" style eating in Japanese restaurant. It is interesting that the Japanese soup noodle and instance cup noodle called "*ramen*," an adoption and adaptation from Chinese *lamian* (Japanese pronunciation of *ramen* sounds exactly like *lamian* in Mandarin), has become one of the most frequently consumed global food items of "Japanese" food (Billboard advertisement Ramen is today found on the street of Masco, Russia. See Caldwell 2002). Millions of Chinese in China now eat packaged instant "*ramen*" daily, thinking that they are consuming prestigious Japanese food.

Another Japanese invention has to do with the manner of serving Chinese banquet food, especially in up-scale restaurants. Only set menu, instead of *ala carte* menu, is provided to the customers who order the set just like ordering fancy Japanese set meal of "*kaiseki*." The Japanese way of serving Chinese dishes of set menu is similar to set menu in a refined Western restaurants; a set of Chinese banquet dishes are served course by course to each individual diner, whether the diner is dining alone or in a group. One common sense explanation for this practice is that ordinary Japanese are not familiar with the variety of Chinese dishes, especially exotic ones, and would feel embarrassed for not knowing how to order. The Westernized way of serving Chinese high cuisine, or perhaps traditional Japanese way of formal dining, made an important global impact. It spread to Hong Kong and Taiwan in up-scale restaurants during the 1990s. This is an important departure from the ordinary Chinese restaurants in the United States.

Diasporic Chinese Restaurant Food 91

In sum, what happened in Japan in the course of 50 years is a complete absorption and localization of Chinese cuisine, high and low. Two parallel processes occurred at the same time. First, adaptation to local tastes, hence Japanization, of Chinese restaurant food prepared by Japanese cooks that appeals to Japanese consumers [For other Japanese adoption of foreign food see examples in Tobin (1992)]. Second, modification and adoption of Chinese high cuisine of different Chinese regions in up-scale Chinese restaurants operated by either Chinese chefs or Japanese chefs, but served in European-Japanese ways.

Europe

During the 1980s and 1990s, I had many fortuitous encounters with diasporic Chinese restaurants in Europe. Roberts (2003) documents British and other European aversion to Chinese food when Westerners made initial contacts with China before the twentieth century. He also notes how Chinese restaurants became popular in England during the second half of the twentieth century. Watson's classic work on the migration of Hong Kong Chinese from the New Territories to London offers information about how the Chinese started restaurants in London and how these then spread to the rest of England (Watson 1975). Today the British people are used to relying on Chinese restaurants (and more so Indian restaurants) and take-away joints for inexpensive meals, but they also exhibit prejudice against Chinese restaurant workers. A tradition of xenophobia led to continued apprehension of foreign cultures as well as fear of losing limited economic resources to new immigrants. As Roberts (2003) reports, such a mentality was particularly pronounced in England amongst the working class.

A new generation of Chinese immigrants from China and elsewhere (e.g., Vietnamese of Chinese descent) set up restaurants in such big cities as London, Paris, Milan, Geneva, Amsterdam, Brussels, Hamburg and Prague. It could be by chance that my encounters with European Chinese restaurants, in contrast to my early American experience, were very positive. Other than London Chinatown, most of the restaurants I visited in Europe appeared to be up scale, expensive, and had more European diners than Chinese. They served fancy dishes of Chinese high cuisine that catered to more affluent non-Chinese customers of cosmopolitan backgrounds. It is possible that the demand for refined restaurant settings and professional service in these restaurants helped to raise the standard for Chinese food. High quality and good taste in those Chinese restaurants could also be due to the fact that European patrons are willing to spend a comparable amount of money to eat in a good Chinese restaurant just like in a Western one. In the up-scale Chinese restaurants I visited in London, Paris and Geneva, Chinese meals were served in European style. The customers had to order appetizers, entries and deserts, as compared to eating at common Chinese restaurants in the United States where a customer can order, for example, only one soup-noodle dish to constitute a whole meal.

Waves of Transnational Migration and Ethnic Division within the Chinese Cuisine

This section provides further information of historical background in the formation of ethnic divisions within variety of Chinese cuisines we have observed. A common factor explains similar localization and standardization of Chinese cuisines despite many waves of Chinese migration to the United States during the past centuries. Many new Chinese immigrants enter the restaurant business in the United States because they see it as the only means available to them to survive in the new country. It is a common strategy of survival for immigrant families to run a small café or restaurant in order to support a large family (Chan 2002; Wu 2002; Smart 2003). Improvisation, cutting corners to lower the cost and price charged, adaptation to the host population's taste, and hybridization of cooking methods are common in ethnic restaurants in the United States. In such restaurants, food quality and taste may reflect the owners' (and hired chefs') amateurish culinary knowledge and cooking skill. Only when the influx of large numbers of new and demanding (wealthier) migrants continues, such as in the case of Hong Kong immigrants to Vancouver or Toronto in modern times, do good Chinese restaurants keep up with the homeland (Hong Kong) standards. However, my observation of Chinese restaurant cuisine in the Los Angeles area for the past decade contradicts this view. In spite of an obvious increase in the ethnic Chinese population, especially new arrivals from China, many Chinese restaurants continue to serve mediocre and inexpensive food. One visiting Chinese restaurateur who owns several up-scale Peking restaurants in one of the East Coast states told me: "When I see these cheap eating places I feel so sad. Why do fellow Chinese work so hard to provide such cheap and bad Chinese food? Chinese cuisine is superior to Western cuisine. Why can we not elevate our restaurant standards to the level of refined Western style restaurants?" Another Chinese restaurateur, Mr Chow, mentioned in the previous section, shares the same sentiment, as he has established the most expensive Chinese restaurants in London, New York and Los Angeles. However, ordinary Chinese diners seem to shy away from these restaurants, because they appear too Western and too expensive to be "Chinese." When I discussed Chinese restaurant food in Los Angeles with some Chinese diners, both old immigrants and newcomers, some considered themselves lucky to have so many restaurants serving inexpensive Chinese food. To them, cheap is "good."

The Nineteenth-century Migration and Chopsuey Cuisine

For more than a century, until the 1970s, the diasporic Chinese cuisine in North America was dominated by an invented Cantonese peasant cuisine represented by "chopsuey" dishes in chopsuey houses. Until recently, popular image in North America made chopsuey dishes authentic Chinese food (Liu 2009). Chinese new immigrants arrived after the 1950s would not accept chopsuey, or old overseas Cantonese (*lao huaqiao*) cuisine, as "Chinese" and deemed it foreign and unpalatable. It is the American localization of this diasporic cuisine that created the image of a single Chinese food culture. Ironically, chopsuey food since the 1990s was restored and reinvented, and served in a new type of chain restaurants — P.F. Chang's China Bistro. We shall later discuss this ironic twist for a unified chopsuey cuisine, whose signature dishes include *chow mien*, *chow fan*, chopsuey, *moogoo gaipan*,[5] and sweet and sour food.

Sally Chan's (2002) discussion of the British Chinese restaurants takes the food trade, trade marked "Sweet and Sour," as business enterprises of the overseas Chinese for survival. As I have proposed elsewhere (Wu 2001) restaurant trade often is the only means of survival for Chinese migrants overseas. Researchers observed around the globe how small Chinese restaurant owners/chefs raise a family and send their children to the best schools, and they eventually become doctors, engineers, lawyers and professors. However, such food enterprises are predominantly small scale family businesses which would end when the children grow up, while other newcomers will take over the business. We shall continue with the survival and achievement of diasporic Chinese restaurant families.

Pan-China Cuisine (waishengcai) Invented in Taiwan

Since the 1960s increasing numbers of Chinese restaurant in North America coincide with the influx of new immigrants from Hong Kong and Taiwan. I found it interesting that most of the literature about Chinese cuisine and restaurants ignore three important aspects of this immigration that brought new cuisines from Taiwan. The three new developments during the decades of 1960 and 1970 are: (1) the arrival of private chefs from Taipei; (2) Taiwan's entertainment and hotel businessmen came and became restaurateurs; and (3) Chinese graduate students who studied in the United States became chefs and restaurant owners.

First we need to understand the emergence of "*waishengcai*" (cuisines of other provinces) in Taiwan during the 1950s. When the refugee population fled China many talented professional and family cooks from all parts of China brought with them the culinary arts of their home regions to Taiwan. They opened ethnic restaurants (concentrated) in Taipei that represented all the major Chinese traditional cuisines, high or low, to satisfy a clientele of elite social status and gourmets (Wu 2002). By the 1960s the United States major cities saw new type of Chinese restaurants operated by rich refugee Chinese immigrants from Taiwan with their famed private chefs and Taiwanese disciples (e.g., one famed Taipei chef, nicknamed Dwarf Tang, opened a Sichuan restaurant in San Francisco). I would argue that this is the beginning of the pan-China cuisine, or to use a slang of Taiwan, *waishengcai*, which incorporates many dishes of different ethnic cooking developed in Taipei, and which later (after the 1980s) became a standardized new Chinese cuisine in the United States.

Many young members of China refugee and military families (who were known as *waishengren* or people of provinces outside of Taiwan) became business people during the 1960s and 1970s. They dominated the so-called entertainment (and underground sex trade) business [e.g., *wuting* (dance halls), *geting* (singing and cabaret halls), and large restaurants in hotels with cabaret singers]. After acquiring professional experience in managing restaurants and entertainment joints, and saving capital as well, many immigrated to the United States and opened new-style of Chinese restaurants that served an invented and standardized "*waishengcai*".

I shall illustrate the process of how the new pan-China cuisine from Taiwan spread to the United States by telling the story of my friend Mr Cheng's coming to America in the 1970s. Cheng (pseudonym), born in China and went to Taiwan a teenager, was a mid-rank government official

Diasporic Chinese Restaurant Food

whose brother in the mid-1970s had successfully acquired US citizenship after obtaining a graduated degree and permanent employment. His brother sponsored Cheng's entire family, including three children (of elementary school age), to immigrate to the United States in 1974. The majority of the new immigrants like him, including thousands of graduate students who found employment after graduate studies, belonged to the "refugee" families which fled China in the 1950s to Hong Kong and Taiwan. After both Mr and Mrs Cheng confronted with difficulties in seeking work in the United States for lack of special skills, English proficiency and an American degree, they decided to go into Chinese restaurant business. He said: "I had to lower my status to be a restaurant worker for the sake of my children's future." He first worked as a waiter for a Taiwanese-owned Chinese restaurant. In 1980 he invested US$40,000 of his life savings brought from Taiwan to become a partner of a Taiwanese professional chef from Taiwan to take over a failed Chinese restaurant in the Bay Area of California. When they became successful in one year, the chef bought him out. Through his brother's social network Mr Cheng discovered another Chinese restaurant for sale in Texas and decided to move there to open his own restaurant, where he sensed that the oil industry would provide a booming market for eating out. By then his wife had learned the tricks of cooking Chinese restaurant food (she learned by herself from the previous cook-partner) and became the chef herself, while Mr Cheng the cashier trained himself to be the bartender for his new restaurant. They introduced a new menu of pan-China cuisine from Taiwan. It included dishes such as *gongbao* chicken, braised fish, hot and sour soup, smoked chicken and Peking duck; in addition to all the familiar American chopsuey dishes of *chow fan*, *chow mien*, sweet and sour, lemon chicken, beef broccoli and "*moogoo gaipan*." Mr Cheng admits that at first the American customers did not know anything about the new dishes. He had to explain and persuade the customers to order the unfamiliar, new Taiwanese dishes. The restaurant became a big hit in town when the customers got used to the new flavour. With this successful and profitable business they raised two medical doctors and one oil-engineer. They retired in the mid-1990s and worked full time to help raising grandchildren while taking occasional leisure trips, which they never did while running the restaurant.

The story of this Chinese restaurant is so typical and familiar, repeated for hundreds or thousands of Chinese immigrant families who came to the United States during the late 1960s through the 1980s. Among the restaurant owners in Honolulu I have interviewed, there were two pan-

China "northern Chinese" style restaurants which I often patronized since the 1970s. One owner from Taiwan earned a master degree of engineering himself before he opened his restaurant business; and he sent his daughter to the most expensive high school in town (which US President Obama also attended) as well as the Stanford University. The second owner was an engineer from Hong Kong, and his family restaurant specialized in "*shuijiao*" (northern Chinese style boiled *gyoza*). His two sons used to do homework on restaurant tables and helped to serve the customers, but later graduated from MIT and Harvard.

I have reported elsewhere (Wu 2001) how the pan-China (refugee) cuisines emerged in Taipei during the 1950s and 1960s. James Watson (2005: 75) made similar observations for Hong Kong. He recalls the small restaurants and noodles shops in Hong Kong in the 1960s ran by refugee cooks from Mainland China. He observed that for 1 US dollar one could have one's fill. Watson's observation can easily be applied to hundreds of refugee restaurants and sidewalk food stalls in Taipei in the same decade. In a Taipei eatery then one usually spent the equivalent of only US 25 cents for a hearty meal. Income was so low then, so was the living standard, yet I could not afford to indulge in such "luxury treat" more than once in one or two weeks, as sometimes I was sick of the college dormitory food that I paid the equivalent of 3 US dollars for all the meals of an entire month. The comparative high profit and income for cooks and helpers working in Chinese restaurants in America during that period lured the professor chefs or improvised cooks to immigrate, or jump ship, in order to open small non-Cantonese restaurants in Chinatowns. This begins the spread of a new type of Chinese ethnic restaurants in the United States, operated by refugee Chinese or their children from Taiwan, as the case of Mr Cheng above illustrates.

It is important to argue that graduate students from Taiwan who arrived between the late 1950s and 1970s to study in the United States also played a part in the new trend of Pan-China restaurants in America, in big cities and in small towns. Many replaced the old chopsuey houses. Studies of the history of Chinese restaurants in North America often ignore the significant role of overseas students from Taiwan between 1960 and 1980. Also, by the 1990s a new wave of students from the People's Republic of China joined the restaurant business in North America (I also observed its happening in Japan since the beginning of the twenty-first century). When post-modern Appadurai cohorts emphasize the role played by tourist and migrants in the global cultural flows and spread of culinary

Diasporic Chinese Restaurant Food 97

cultural imaginations (Mankekar 2005), they missed this significant episode of international academic exchange in contributing to and circulation of "Chinese" culinary knowledge.

American Chinese Low Cuisine and Foreign Chinese High Cuisine

Chopsuey style restaurant food that dominated North American Chinese cuisine for more than a century represents or misrepresents an image of familiar taste in limited variety of dishes. However, by the end of the twentieth century, a new wave of Chinese restaurants that are owned and operated by non-Chinese but without any Chinese chefs emerged. In the mind of the general public, Chinese restaurants are run by ethnic Chinese, predominantly new immigrants who speak Pidgin English. It is hard for the Chinese to imagine they would face competitions from any "foreigner" restaurateurs and chefs who operate successful "Chinese" restaurants. Many Chinese I have talked to found it inconceivable for any "foreigner" to master Chinese cooking, let alone cooking dishes good enough to be served in a Chinese restaurant. Since 20 years ago, we saw the exception to this rule when Wolfgang Puck opened his Chinois — "Chinese in French" — in Santa Monica, and when in 1993 Paul Fleming incorporated his chain restaurants into a public company — the P.F. Chang's China Bistro. There are now 189 Bistros in 39 states in the United States. The Chinois is no doubt an up-scale "fusion" restaurant that many Chinese (including those who lived in California for decades) have never heard of. While Chinese first-generation immigrants I have interviewed would not accept P.F. Chang's China Bistro as "real Chinese," they also had no desire to eat there. The three P.F. Chang's I visited had no Chinese chefs; they were Mexicans and Japanese. My evaluation of this chain restaurant is quite positive, when taking into consideration of the décor, service and tastes of food, especially in comparison to most of the old chopsuey houses and small Pan-China Chinese restaurants in North America. Just as its original owner claimed, he reinvented the chopsuey house, making each an up-scale Western restaurant with packaged, symbolic "Chinese culture," including stylized Chinese paintings on the wall, replica of Tang glazed pottery horses, and replica of Qin Tomb terracotta warriors. These "foreign" Chinese restaurants with Western service served better chopsuey and pan-China dishes that are already familiar to the American consumers.

As we have discussed, Mr Chow's are the few who still serve old fashioned Beijing and Shanghai dishes of the pre-1950 era. Ironically, because of their Western décor and service, their rich and famous clienteles, and outrageous price charged, few Chinese would consider these restaurants "Chinese." (Most of the customers, after all, would have no idea of what "authentic" tastes of Chinese food of the 1940s or 1950s were like.) I consider these foods traditional Chinese on the basis of my childhood memories of Beijing dishes in Beijing and Taipei, as well as memories of gourmet dishes of the early 1980s in Beijing. I had the privilege in the early 1980s of being treated at exclusive Beijing eateries for state leaders and enjoyed the taste of preserved pre-Communist culinary arts.

I would like to interpret the global meaning of these "foreign" Chinese restaurants, in the context of a "Western" discourse of eating out, class distinction and living in an imagined civilized world. Even though in some up-scale Chinese restaurants we find Western style service, the consumers (or the Western society at large) still hold a preconceived image of Chinese restaurants being at the lower rank of social class. In other words, eating at a Chinese restaurant becomes an expression of lower status in consumption behaviour (Wade and Mastens 2000). Ironically, when "foreigners (non-Chinese)" operate "Chinese" restaurants according to the Western standard, they would be accepted as high-class restaurants serving high cuisine. It may be too strong a statement, but we can argue that the Chinese cuisine in the United States lives under the imagination of Western colonial world. We may judge, for instance, Mr Chow's success by his social status in a white American society. He not only associates with the rich and famous, he himself becomes one. He lives in the most exclusive Bel Air neighbourhood in Los Angeles, in an estate designed by the world-renowned architect Frank Lloyd Wright.

This socio-political explanation also accounts for the conversion from Chinese restaurant business to Japanese. After the 1990s, especially by the beginning of the twenty-first century, many Chinese (actually Taiwanese), along with Koreans, took advantage of their physical resemblance with Japanese (in the eyes of the white Americans), entered the Japanese restaurant business. As the American public regard Japanese food as high class and expensive, it is more profitable to operate Japanese rather than Chinese restaurants. Theodore C. Bestor (2005: 18) reports the story of a Chinese chain restaurant owner in Texas who converted his restaurants to Japanese for the prestige and high price, hence higher profit. The Taiwanese owner maintained that in any case his customers could not

Diasporic Chinese Restaurant Food   99

tell the difference between his Chinese chefs and real Japanese. Behind the counter of the sushi bars in his Japanese restaurants there were even Latino chefs.

Conclusion: Diasporic Chinese Cuisine — No Home to Return to

My encounters around the globe in the past 40 years illuminate expected and unexpected changes in diasporic Chinese restaurant cuisines. It is not just simply economics and culinary skill that governed the appeal of Chinese restaurant food to both the diasporic Chinese populations and the populations of the host countries. I began to realize that four decades of observation of the diasporic Chinese restaurants should be situated in current theoretical discourse on food in anthropology. Ethnic identity, ethnic interaction in diaspora communities, global capitalism and mass media all have played an important role in shaping new developments in the diasporic Chinese cuisines at each location I visited or resided. Furthermore, the recent international flow of cultural influences under global capitalism has created unexpected culinary trends and fusion cuisines that are beyond all imagination. It is not easy to define what Chinese food is. The simple question of what is a diasporic Chinese restaurant could yield a complex answer filled with uncertainty. As I have described above, when in a "Chinese restaurant," the chefs are not Chinese, but are often Japanese, Hawaiian, Mexican, or German, and the consumers are also non-Chinese, how, then, can the culinary art and taste of the restaurant dishes be judged as still being "Chinese?" When we venture one step further by asking the question of who creates the taste, and who determines the quality (or taste), we are then entering an argument beyond simply looking into socially constructed preferences generated by either the consumers or the producers — the chefs (see Smith 2006, Fung 2007).

In the past, many Chinese restaurant chefs or owners in the United States claim to have close contacts with the homeland — Hong Kong, Taiwan, or China, in order to support their claim of maintaining an authentic "Chinese" taste. Today, changes in the "homeland" have become more rapid, more dramatic and more "foreign" than overseas. Globalization and internationalization of cuisines at "home" have become more obvious and visible than what is happening among diaspora communities overseas. James Clifford (1998) argues that a diasporic person is in an ironic situation of "no home to return to," as he or she belongs neither to the home culture nor the host culture. Diasporic Chinese restaurants are certainly in this situation of "homeland no more."

My encounters with Chinese diaspora restaurant food reveal complicated stories of food as cultural commodities that routinely undergo a process of globalization, adaptation, heterogeneity, hybridization, internationalization and complete transformation. The direction and complexity of change in taste and associated social and cultural impacts are both expected as well as beyond expectation. I hope the uncertainty alone will warrant our serious consideration for engagement in further inquiry and research.

Notes

1. In the early days of my life in Taiwan, I attended village wedding banquets attended by almost the entire members of a clan or a village. The largest public banquet I ever attended, for instance, was the celebration dinner for the People's Republic of China's 35th Anniversary held at the Great People's Hall in Beijing. And the largest "home cooking banquet" I participated in was a "One thousand People's Banquet" held in 1995 at the tracking field of the Chung-Chi College, The Chinese University of Hong Kong.

2. With considerable rewriting, the core of this chapter is based on an earlier version of a keynote speech delivered at The 10th Symposium on Chinese Dietary Culture, 12–14 Nov. 2007, in Penang, Malaysia. I write this chapter not only in the capacity of being an anthropologist who applies conventional research methods such as field interviews and participant-observations. This chapter is also a reflexive account which takes advantage of my privileged position as a Chinese, a person in diaspora, a gourmet and a world traveler constantly going around the globe during the past 40 years. While I am privileged in my professional capacity as a socio-cultural anthropologist of food to be able to review and rethink post-modern theoretical issues concerning the cultural politics of food and cuisine around the world, I am exceptionally fortunate also to have since my youth encountered both the high and low cuisines in the Chinese homelands as well as Chinese diaspora communities across several continents. During the two decades (1980s and 1990s) of my yearly field trip to China, for instant, my wife and I often dined at banquets hosted by mayors, governors, or cabinet ministers at the most luxurious eating places (including government guest houses). More importantly, thanks to my wife's social background and exceptional good taste, I was able to explore the most expensive as well as the most "representative" Chinese restaurants wherever we visited (for a few days or weeks) or lived (for a few months or

Diasporic Chinese Restaurant Food 101

years, including Australia, Japan, Papua New Guinea and Singapore). All these experiences have enabled me to write about my global encounters of Chinese restaurant food. I am grateful to the following friends in Australia, Papua New Guinea, Taiwan and the United States for providing insights on Chinese restaurants: George Bi, Chung-min Chen, Francis T.S. Cheung, Winnie W. Hou, Larry Levine, John and Sandra Lau, Francis C.Y. Tu, Ching-hai Tu, Richard H.C. Tu and Charlie Yamamoto. My late wife, Wei-lan Wu, helped me immensely even during the final stage of her illness in collecting website newspaper excerpts of popular food, cuisine and restaurants in Hong Kong and Taiwan for the years 2000 to 2006. Without her encouragement I would not have been able to prepare this chapter.

3. A short-lived fourth one, the Eurochow, opened in 1999 in the Westwood Village near UCLA in Los Angeles and closed in 2006. In 2007 Mr Chow opened a second restaurant bearing his name in New York City.

4. He came from a wealthy family which opened the first "Mongolian barbeque" restaurant in Taipei in the 1950s.

5. For many years, being a Mandarin speaker, I could not figure out the meaning and content of this chopsuey dish of "*moogoo gaipan.*" I knew that it must be Cantonese, but the spelling was creolized, it should be spelled as *mogu gaipin* (Cantonese) or *muogu jipian* (Mandarin). This is sliced chicken meat sautéed with Chinese black mushrooms, a recommended dish nowadays (marked healthy) at the P.G. Chang's China Bistro.

References

Anonymous. 2007. "Dim Sum, Roast Meats Served All Day." *Dining Out*, 5 August, *Honolulu Advertiser Supplement*, p. 20.

Aoki, Tamotsu. 2001. "The Domestication of Chinese Foodways in Contemporary Japan: Ramen and Peking Duck." In *Changing Chinese Foodways in Asia*, ed. David Y.H. Wu and Tan Chee-Beng. Hong Kong: The Chinese University Press, pp. 219–33.

Appadurai, Arjun. 1990. "Disjuncture and Differences in the Global Cultural Economy." *Theory, Culture, and Society* 7: 295–310.

———. 1996. *Modernity at Large: Cultural Dimensions of Globalization*. Minneapolis: University of Minnesota Press.

Beardsworth, Alan and Teresa Keil. 1997. *Sociology on the Menu*. London: Routledge.

Beriss, David and David Sutton. 2007. "Starter: Restaurants, Ideal Postmodern Institutions." In *The Restaurants Book*, ed. David Beriss and David Sutton. New York: Berg, pp. 1–13.

Bester, Theodore C. 2001. "Supply-side Sushi: Commodity, Market, and the Global City." *American Anthropologist* 103 (1): 76–95.

———. 2005. "How Sushi Went Global." In *The Cultural Politics of Food and Eating*, ed. James L. Watson and Melissa L. Caldwell. Malden, MA: Blackwell, pp. 13–20.

Caldwell, Melissa I. 2002. "The Taste of Nationalism: Food Politics in Postsocialist Moscow." *Ethnos* 67 (3): 295–319.

Chan, Sally. 2002. "Sweet and Sour: The Chinese Experience of Food." In *Food in the Migrant Experience*, ed. Anne J. Kershen. UK: Ashgate, pp. 172–88.

Cheung, Sidney C.H. 2002. "The Invention of Delicacy: Cantonese Food in Yokohama Chinatown." In *The Globalization of Chinese Food*, ed. David Y.H. Wu and Sidney C.H. Cheung. Surrey, England: Routledge/Curzon, pp. 170–82.

Cheung, Sidney C.H. and Tan Chee-Beng. 2007. "Introduction: Food and Foodways in Asia." In *Food and Foodways in Asia*, ed. Sidney C.H. Cheung and Tan Chee-Beng. Oxon, England: Routledge, pp. 1–9.

Clifford, James. 1998. *Routes: Travel and Translation in the Late Twentieth Century*. Cambridge, Mass: Harvard University Press.

Fung, Luke Y.C. 2007. "Authenticity and Professionalism in Restaurant Kitchens." In *Food and Foodways in Asia*, ed. Sidney C.H. Cheung and Tan Chee-Beng. Oxon, England: Routledge, pp. 143–55.

Galerie Enrico Navara *et al.* 1999. *Portrait Collection of Mr Chow*. Paris: Galerie Enrico Navara.

Goody, Jack. 1982. *Cooking, Cuisine, and Class: A Study in Comparative Sociology*. Cambridge: Cambridge University Press.

Holtzman, Jon D. 2006. "Food and Memory." *Annual Review of Anthropology* 35: 361–78. Annual Reviews, Palo Alto, California.

Liu Haiming. 2009. "Chop Suey as Imagined Authentic Chinese Food." *Journal of Transnational American Studies* 1 (1): article 12.

Mankekar, Purnima. 2005. "'India Shopping': Indian Grocery Stores and Trans-national Configurations of Belonging." In *The Cultural Politics of Food*, ed. James L. Watson and Melissa L. Caldwell. Malden, MA: Blackwell, pp. 197–214.

Mintz, Sidney W. 1996. *Tasting Food, Tasting Freedom: Excursions into Eating, Culture, and the Past*. Boston: Beacon Press.

Newcomb, Rachel. 2006. "The Social Life of Food: As Nations Unify and Globally Integrated." *Anthropology News* 47 (5): 34–5.

Ong, Aihwa. 1998. *Flexile Citizenship: The Cultural Logic of Transnationality*. Durham, NC: Duke University Press.

Ong, Aihwa and Donald M. Nonini, eds. 1997. *Ungrounded Empires: The Cultural Politics of Modern Chinese Transnationalism*. New York: Routledge.

Pillsbury, Richard. 1998. *No Foreign Food: The American Diet in Time and Place*. Boulder, Colorado: Westview.

Restany, Pierre. 1999. "Mr. Chow's Show." In *Portrait Collection of Mr Chow*, by Galerie Enrico Navara *et al.* Paris: Galerie Enrico Navara, pp. 1–4.

Diasporic Chinese Restaurant Food

Roberts, J.A.G. 2003. *China to Chinatown: Chinese Food in the West.* London: Peakton Books.

Smart, Josephine. 2003. "Ethnic Entrepreneurship, Transmigration, and Social Integration: An Ethnographic Study of Chinese Restaurant Owners in Rural Western Canada." *Urban Anthropology* 32 (3–4): 311–42.

Smith, Monica L. 2006. The Archaeology of Food Preference. *American Anthropologist* 108 (3): 480–93.

Tsing, Anna Lowenhaupt. 2005. *Frictions: An Ethnography of Global Connection.* NJ: Princeton University Press.

Tan Chee-Beng. 2007. "Nyonya Cuisine: Chinese, Non-Chinese Cuisine and the Making of a Famous Cuisine in Southeast Asia." In *Food and Foodways in Asia,* ed. Sidney C.H. Cheung and Tan Chee-Beng. Oxon, England: Routledge, pp. 171–82.

Tobin, Joseph, ed. 1992. *Remade in Japan: Everyday Life and Consumer Taste in a Changing Society.* New Haven: Yale University Press.

Tuchman, G. and H. Levine. 1993. "New York Jews and Chinese Food." *Journal of Contemporary Ethnography* 22 (3): 362–407.

Wade, Alan and Lydia Mastens. 2000. *Eating Out: Social Differentiation, Consumption and Pleasure.* UK: Cambridge University Press.

Watson, James L. 1975. *Emigration and the Chinese Lineage: The Mans in Hong Kong and London.* Berkeley, CA: University of California Press.

———. 2005. "China's big Mac attack." In *The Cultural Politics of Food and Eating,* ed. James L. Watson and Melissa L. Caldwell. Malden, MA: Blackwell, pp. 70–9.

Wilk, Richard H. 1999. "Real Belizean Food: Building Local Identity in the Transnational Caribbean." *American Anthropologist* 101 (2): 244–55.

Wu, David Y.H. 1977. "Chinese as an Intrusive Language." In *New Guinea Area Languages and Language Study,* ed. S.A. Wurm. Canberra: The Australian National University, pp. 1047–55.

———. 1982. *The Chinese in Papua New Guinea.* Hong Kong: The Chinese University Press.

———. 2001. "Cantonese Cuisine (*Yue-cai*) in Taipei and Taiwanese Cuisine (*Tai-cai*) in Hong Kong." In *The Globalization of Chinese Food,* ed. David Y.H. Wu and Sidney C.H. Cheung. Surrey, England: Routledge/Curzon, pp. 86–99.

———. 2002. "Improvising Chinese Cuisine Overseas." In *The Globalization of Chinese Cuisine,* ed. David Y.H. Wu and Sidney C.H. Cheung. Surrey, England: Routledge/Curzon, pp. 56–66.

———. 2008. "All You Can Eat Buffet: The Evolution of Chinese Cuisine in Hawaii." *Journal of Chinese Dietary Culture* 4 (1): 1–24.

PART II

Chinese Food and Foodways in Southeast Asia

CHAPTER

4

The Dragon's Trail in Chinese Indonesian Foodways

Myra Sidharta

Introduction

The Republic of Indonesia is an archipelago consisting of 18,108 islands, large and small, spanning an area of about 1,919,440 square kilometres. Only 6,000 of the islands are inhabited, of which the largest are Java, Sumatra, Kalimantan (Borneo) Sulawesi and the Western part of Papua (New Guinea). Although the island of Java is not the largest, it has become the most important because of its fertility. Over the centuries, it has become an important center of trade and agriculture. The largest city is Jakarta, which is at the same time also the capital of the Republic. Other large cities are Surabaya, Bandung, Semarang and Medan. Ironically the relatively small island Bali is probably the most well known, because of its beautiful landscapes and its rich cultural heritage.

The earlier foreign traders who came to the Archipelago were Arabs, Chinese and Indian traders, who had braved storm and wind and all other kinds of danger in search for spices and exotic merchandise, such as feathers of the bird of paradise, pearls, *trepang*, bird's nest, etc. to bring back to their countries (Purcell 1980: 391). Later on, they also settled on the coastal areas of the larger islands to manage warehouses, set up to store the goods that could not be shipped immediately. They married native women and formed families, which in due time grew to small creolized communities. During the sixteenth and seventeenth century, Europeans have joined the settlers, first the Portuguese and Spaniards, followed by the Dutch, Germans and French. With so many foreigners around, it is not difficult to envision the multi-cultural expressions formed over the centuries.

History of the Chinese Settlers

Archaeological finds points to relations between China and the Archipelago since the Han dynasty. The artefacts found in several parts of the Archipelago were trade objects brought by seafarers or tributary goods exchanged between the two nations. These seafarers and tribute carriers did not settle down, but returned to China after their tasks were done. It was only much later that the Chinese had settled in the Indonesian Archipelago, certainly during the Yuan dynasty, when the Javanese troops betrayed the Mongol troops, who had come to help them to defeat the King of Kediri and to found the kingdom of Majapahit. Many of the soldiers managed to escape and not daring to return to their homeland for fear of severe punishment, had settled in the country where they continued to live and spread Islam as well as introduced technological skills, including culinary skills.[1] According to the present-day Kediri people, the troops had taught the local people to make tofu (Sidharta 2008: 197–8). There is also evidence that the Chinese had introduced certain vegetables to the Archipelago, because in *Yingyai Shenglan*, Ma Huan (1970: 92) wrote that he saw all the vegetables the people had were like those in China. To this day these vegetables are known by their Chinese names, like *bakcoi, kailan*, etc. Also, the indigenous Indonesians in the rural areas seldom have cultivated vegetables on their menu, most of the time they consume leaves, ferns, nuts and gourds. The urban people are more health conscious and have added green vegetables on their menu. The method of cooking applied to these vegetables is also Chinese: *chao* or stir-fry, which may be said to be a Chinese culinary art (Cheng 1955: 42).

The other islands have less Chinese inhabitants and the degree of assimilation into the local cultures is also much lower. However, big cities

The Dragon's Trail in Chinese Indonesian Foodways   109

like Medan and Palembang on Sumatra island, Manado and Makassar on Sulawesi may be exceptions. Being important ports of trade, these places and the environs had a considerable number of Chinese settlers as well. Also the island of Ambon on the island group of Moluccas has many Chinese, because those islands were the ones where the seafarers first came to trade in spices.

When Admiral Zheng He came with his fleet between 1406–23 there were already Chinese communities settled in the coastal areas of Java (Ma Huan 1970: 93). Also settled there, were the Arabs and Indian traders. The Chinese, Arabs and Indians were followed by the Europeans from Portugal, Spain and Holland, who had all left traces of their influence, not the least on food.

It was the Dutch, who colonized the archipelago from 1602 to 1942, who were instrumental in the migration of the Chinese, because they needed labourers to build houses, canals and roads. Craftsmen were also needed to make shoes and uniforms for the soldiers, repair clocks and other goods. Concentration of the Chinese was then in Batavia (presently Jakarta) and on the North coast of Java. Their fate depended on the ruling Governor General. Some had great respect for the hardworking Chinese; others saw them as a threat to the security of the country.

Many Governor Generals regularly consulted the Chinese captains, who headed the Chinese communities. They also consulted Chinese doctors and a certain Master Isaac, a Chinese who had converted to Christianity and was officially appointed as a doctor at the Governor's office in 1635. Since then there were many Chinese doctors on the pay list of the VOC, the East Indisch Company that ruled the archipelago. In 1709 Governor General van Hoorn brought a certain Tjoebitjia (Zhou Meidie 周美爹) to the Netherlands, because he had faith in the healing power of this traditional doctor, who had cured him of his illness. This Chinese doctor was then invited to demonstrate his knowledge before the Mayor of Amsterdam (De Haan 1935: 394).

Chinese opened eating stalls and teahouses, which were also frequented by the Dutch. In one street there were as many as eight teahouses, hence the name *Patekoan* (Hokkien for *ba chaguan* 八茶馆). In 1740 the Chinese population of Batavia had reached around 16,000 and more were trying to settle, when the notorious massacre of the Chinese occurred, killing about 10,000 Chinese including women and children. A small number escaped to the eastern part of Java especially the North Coast and joined Javanese rebels in their uprising against the Dutch.

A few years later life in Batavia returned to normal, businessmen opened their shops and of course there were people who opened food stalls or shops and teahouses again (De Haan 1935: 393).

In the nineteenth century, more migrants came from China and South Asia to work in the indigo and sugar plantations and for the mining companies on the island of Bangka and the coalmines in Sumatra. Later they were also recruited to work in the tobacco, coffee and tea plantations. This group, having kept their own language, was less integrated in the local society. Consequently, the Chinese community was divided into the Peranakans (who were more acculturated) and the Totoks (who had kept their Chinese culture).

The situation became more complicated after the founding of the Tiong Hwa Hwee Koan (Zhonghua Huiguan 中华会馆) in 1900, a foundation which also established schools for the children. As a countermove the Dutch government established Dutch schools for Chinese and native children, while a smaller part of the community was Malay educated. This created three types of Chinese by education, the Malay oriented, the Chinese oriented and the Dutch oriented which persist up to the present day.

In 1945 the Indonesian people became independent and the Republic of Indonesia was founded. New problems arose for the Chinese. In 1959 a decree, known as the PP 10, was announced, prohibiting the traders with Chinese nationality to do business in the rural areas. Many of them re-migrated to the PRC or Taiwan. Others stayed on but were moving away from the rural areas to places in search for more security. Some even moved to other countries, such as the Netherlands and other countries in Europe, some others to the United States and Australia, and even to South America. More followed after the failed coup attempt in Indonesia in 1965, in which the PRC was allegedly involved.

Many of those who preferred to stay in Indonesia settled in the big cities, like Jakarta, Bandung, Surabaya and Semarang, or on the island of Bali. To make a living, they often opened restaurants or eating stalls. This had an enormous impact on the culinary taste in these places, especially Jakarta which had grown into a metropolitan city. Many enclaves of people from different areas were formed and soon eating stalls and houses were opened, offering food from different regions.

Differences between the Foods of the Chinese and the Indigenous Population

The Indigenous People

There is a lack of written sources on the food in the Archipelago in pre-colonial times, but we can resort to the inscriptions found on the world famous monument of Borobudur, located in Central Java, near the city of Magelang. The Borobudur was erected around 800 A.D. when the Indian dynasty of Syailendra ruled the island of Java. Its architect was a certain Gunadharma. According to the sources, it took 75 years to complete the building. The monument comprises six square platforms topped by three circular platforms, and is decorated with 2,672 relief panels and 504 Buddha statues. A main dome is located at the centre of the top platform, surrounded by 72 Buddha statues seated inside perforated stupa.

Most of the 2,672 relief panels depict the life of Buddha Gautama, others are decorative panels depicting the flora and fauna of the environment. These panels inform us about the people's sources of food (Bosch 1929: 179–89). However, we should keep in mind that these sources of food were from the island of Java only.

The panels of the Borobudur shows rice as staple food, next to several other grains, such as *jawawut* or millet (*Panicum viride*) and *gandrung* (*Andropogon Sorghum*). One panel even depicts the *rijsttafel* or a complete rice meal with many different dishes to be served together. Fruits are shown in abundance and we are able to see bananas, mangoes, guava, jackfruit, durians, mangosteens, *majas* (a kind of bitter fruit), coconuts, etc. Of the plants bearing resources for cooking, we can mention coconut and young jackfruit (Bosch 1929: 211–44).

Before Islam was introduced to the Archipelago, pork was consumed, and the natives were especially fond of the wild pigs, which were abundant in the forests. With the advent of Islam, those who embraced the religion refrained from eating pork and other things banned by the religion, such as amphibious creatures. Meat was thus limited to fowl and beef including buffalo meat. Although not all indigenous people became Muslims — some were Catholics or Protestants, Hindus or Buddhists — pork soon became identified with the Chinese. Amongst the Javanese Muslims, however, there are different points of view.

One group, the *santri* referring to the Muslims who practise more orthodox version of Islam, tend to be oriented to the mosque, the Qur'an, and the Islamic canon law (*Sharia*). The second group is the *abangan*, who practise a more syncretic version of Islam than the more orthodox *santri*. Their belief system integrates Hinduism, Buddhism and animist traditions.

The *santri* group shun Chinese restaurants, unless the restaurants display that they only serve 100 per cent *halal* food, which means free of pork and the fowl and cattle used in the cooking has been slaughtered according to the proper Muslim rites. For this group, strange sounding names for dishes would make them shun the eating places that serve them. Linawati, a woman who owns an eating stall in a village in Central Java, told me that she had to change the name of the dish *Fu Yung Hai* (crab meat cooked with egg) because Muslim clients thought that she served pork.

The Chinese

A.G. Vorderman, member of the Department of Health in the Netherlands Indies from 1880 to 1901, conducted many researches on the food consumed by the Chinese as well as the indigenous people here. According to him the food of the Chinese comprised, apart from fish, meat, fowl and fresh vegetables, a considerable number of food products that were imported from China, such as preserved vegetables, salted eggs, winter mushrooms, etc. (Vorderman 1886: 69–75). Bean curd and soy paste were manufactured locally, just as the *arak,* or rice wine which was in the time of the VOC[2] sold to the Dutch, especially the soldiers, who appreciated very much the good yet relatively inexpensive drink (De Haan 1935: 4; Lombard 1996: 248, 255–6).

Vegetables were planted locally, and meat was available in great quantities, and Vorderman mentions pork, beef from cows and buffaloes, as well as meat from reptiles and dogs. The Chinese also made good use of the abundance of fish and other seafood, such as shrimps, prawns, crabs, oysters and seaweed.

The difference is more in the taste of the food and the preparation is thus focused on this aspect. The indigenous people like spicy food with a pungent taste, the preparation of which involves pounding the spices, which are all mixed together for cooking. Today prepared spices can be bought in the shop, which saves the housewives lots of time, but in olden days, when slaves were still part of the household, special slaves were assigned to pound and mix the spices. Interestingly the indigenous people

The Dragon's Trail in Chinese Indonesian Foodways 113

make abundant use of the Chinese condiments like soy sauce, soy paste and often even rice wine.³ Other Chinese ingredients often used in Indonesian cooking include tofu, tofu skin, noodles and rice noodles.

For the Chinese, no elaborate preparing is needed for cooking, except for cutting meat or vegetables into the required shapes or sizes. Next to cutting into the required sizes is skilful cooking. Spices are seldom pounded; they are just chopped or cut. However cooking is more elaborate and there are different methods, such as the above mentioned *chao, men* (焖 braise), and *hong shao* (红烧 braise in soy sauce). Delicacies like *bao* and *siomay* are equally appreciated by the local people, and it is common to see vendors selling these foods along the streets. During the fasting months, the *bao* (Chinese bun) vendors make good business, for quite a few people trapped in a traffic jam would grab a *bao* to break the fast.

Banquets are important events in both cultures. For the Chinese, banquets have to be elaborate and have to include some special dishes such as sea cucumbers (*haishen* 海参) and other delicacies. They have to be prepared with skill to honour guests. New Year banquets have one requirement, which is a fish dish, which symbolizes abundance. The Chinese of Jakarta usually serve the *pindang bandeng,* milk fish cooked into a slightly sour soup. For this, the fishermen cultivate the fish into extra large sizes.⁴

The banquets of the indigenous people are usually traditional, and the same food would be served with different decorations or with different combinations. The main dish is the *tumpeng,* rice coloured yellow by curcuma and made into a cone. This cone is placed in the middle of a large tray and the trimmings are placed around it. Trimmings and decorations are chosen to suit the occasion. Mrs Suryatini Gani, a food expert, told me that a *tumpeng* for weddings is usually very elaborate and colourfully decorated. Meat, fowl and fish are a must and also vegetables, especially string beans. For a funeral two cones are prepared without decoration but accompanied by a black live chicken. These cones are brought to the grave and left there for the poor.

For the celebrations at the end of the fasting month of Ramadhan the Muslims serve *ketupat* (rice wrapped in artistically braided coconut leaves) with chicken, beef, tempe, tofu and vegetables, all cooked in coconut milk, but with different spices, topped with fried onions, ground soybeans and shredded coconut. Although almost all the households serve the same food, it is a treat for the guests to taste the differences in the same dishes. Interestingly, Chinese Indonesians in Central Java serve the same food on *Capgomeh* (Hokkien referring to the festival celebrated on the 15th day of the lunar month). The only difference is that the rice is not wrapped in coconut leaves, but in banana leaves. This dish is then called *lontong capgomeh*.

Variety of dishes around the cut-up *lontong* (rice roll cooked in banana leaves) to make it into *lontong capgomeh*. (Photograph by Aji K. Bromokusumo, February 2008)

Chinese and Indonesian Cooking in the Household

It is not difficult to envision, that in a household of the creolized community, consisting of Chinese and native members, the daily menu is a mixed one. In some households, Chinese dishes may prevail, but in others preference may be given to the more spicy Indonesian food.

First of all, Chinese men must have passed down Chinese cooking, because women did not come to the Archipelago in the beginning of Chinese settlement. However, the native mothers must have given her share in the cuisine. Later when a community was formed the cooking was taught to young girls who were confined to their home during their adolescence time, learning to cook foods for celebrations and religious rites (Tjan Kwan Nio 1992: 157–8). Also important was the making of "wet cakes" (*kueh basah* in Indonesian) used as offerings on the altar table and

The Dragon's Trail in Chinese Indonesian Foodways   115

for special celebrations. On ordinary days these cakes were sold door to door or at the market by vendors.

The daily menu of the average Chinese household which is still China-oriented shows twice the amount of fat and 25 per cent more protein than the Chinese who have settled for generations in the Archipelago. The longer they have stayed, the more the composition of food resembles the Javanese, rather than the immigrant Chinese (Holleman, Koolhaas and Nijholt 1939: 311).

If the husband is more Chinese oriented and educated, he may prefer to eat Chinese food, but his native wife may give preference to her native food. This may vary from area to area. In Palembang in South Sumatra a special dish called *pempek* is a preferred delicacy. This *pempek* is made of fish paste and is actually a preparation for the fish-crackers. But before the entire process is finished, the fish paste is fried and served with a sweet and sour soy sauce. In the area of Manado, this would mean more salted fish spiced with a hot sauce of vinegar and red chilli; in west Sumatra, known for their hot food, more meat is served cooked in a hot coconut milk sauce. However, the Chinese usually alter the recipe and make the dish more agreeable to their taste, by putting less spices, in particular chillies in the recipes. This is in line with Bondan Winarno's finding about Padang food served in Chinese restaurants: In the hands of the Chinese, Padang cooking gets a different, special taste (Bondan Winarno 2007).

Another solution is the *sambal*, a chilli dish that serves as condiment at the dinner table. Different dishes need different condiments and the housewives have learned the best condiments for certain dishes using the right ingredients. The *sambal* also differs from area to area. In the coastal areas, where seafood is plentiful, *sambal*s are made for the consumption of seafood, or may contain seafood products, such as fermented cockles, shrimps or little fishes. Besides ingredients, the makers, too, are important, because certain people are better in mastering this art.

What happened if the husband were Dutch or Western educated and would demand his wife to cook European meals for the family? In that case she would consult foreign magazines or sometimes she could find recipes in local magazines.

One women's monthly magazine *Fu Len*, edited by Ong Pik Nio in the 1940s, featured in the recipe column such dishes as: *Filets de sole à la Colbert, Salad de Homard, Galantine de Poularde, Gateau Normande*, etc. However, on other months they would also give Chinese or Indonesian recipes. The European recipes would certainly challenge the ethnic Chinese housewife to try them out to serve her husband and later brag about it to her friends.

A Europe-oriented culture in pre-war Indonesia was expressed in the entire life-style including the food. Restaurants, too, would advertise that they serve "Delicious Chinese and foreign food." When both husband and wife are Chinese educated, the food would be more genuine Chinese, although this may vary from household to household as well.

A good example of the evolution of the choice of menu is my own family. My paternal grandfather was an immigrant Chinese of Hakka descent, who came to the Archipelago at the age of 14. He married my grandmother who was born in the Archipelago. Although they would eat together he would prefer the Hakka Chinese food like *hongshao* (soy sauce braised) pork, intestines cooked in red wine, steamed chicken, steamed fish and stir-fry vegetables. Sometimes he would be presented with monkey or deer meat which would be cooked in red rice wine and spices. The cook would also cook one or two dishes that came from the Chinese Indonesian menu, like chicken curry, sweet sour vegetable soup. Their sons who ate together with them would eat both kind of food. Daughters and daughters-in-law ate after them and would bring their own fresh vegetables and salted fish and the accompanying *sambal* or other condiments such

Stir fried bean sprouts with salted fish. (Photograph by Myra Sidharta, October 2006)

as fermented cockles or small fish. The men usually ate with chopsticks, whereas the women would eat with their fingers.

My father who was Dutch educated would eat the Peranakan food and the Hakka dishes my mother cooked but would demand European food once a week. He had stayed in a Dutch boarding school where only Dutch food was served, with a *rijsttafel* once a week. My mother would then usually cook Dutch steak, which is tenderloin which after braising would be sliced into thin slices, but sometimes also more elaborate meals such as those from the magazine mentioned above.

My husband who was a Peranakan from Java mostly ate Indonesian food from the menu that he was used to at home, which comprised mostly dishes from the people of West Java, with some Chinese food occasionally. However, over the time more dishes in line with globalization were served. Thus my children are familiar with Dutch, Italian, French, and even Japanese dishes besides the Indonesian and Chinese dishes. In their own families, the menu consists of food from all over the world, including Jewish foods as my daughter is married into a Jewish family.

Chinese Food in the Restaurants and Other Eating Places

At present Chinese foods are available in eating places ranging from five-star restaurants to the most modest and simple push-carts. The first eating places might have been those that served the early settlers who wanted to taste the cooking they were used to at home. Later restaurants were opened for business reason, starting from food stall or pushcart, the business might strive and a larger place had to be opened, sometimes becoming a very big restaurant with many outlets. The cooks were mostly from Shanghai, who moved to safer places after Japan attacked China in 1937. They brought such dishes as *kuluyuk* (咕嚕肉 sweet and sour meat), squid salad known in Batavia as *rujak Shanghai*. They remained in Batavia also during WWII, and counted Japanese among their clients. Also people who became rich during the war were proud to bring their families to the well-known restaurants.

After the war, business started to grow again with the members of the allied forces as the main clients. Judging from the advertisement of one magazine in 1950, there were no less than six restaurants in the Pancoran area, the Chinatown of Jakarta. They were large buildings, some of them three-storey high, all continuations of the pre-war restaurants.

118   *Myra Sidharta*

Soon afterwards there was a decline in restaurants business due to economic and political problems. The big restaurants in Chinatown disappeared, also because of widening of the roads, leaving only a few eating places, simple in style and service. One that remained is *Siauw A Tjiap*, a Hakka restaurant, which was already established in 1923. The owner claimed to have invented the recipe of fried eel cooked with *ku mak*, a slightly bitter tasting green vegetable seasoned with red fermented rice. Another famous dish is the braised fish with soy paste. Now this restaurant has opened branches in several other parts of Jakarta.

New places were opened, small and simple, some by people who had no experience with restaurants at all. They were only equipped with a love for cooking and the hope to make some money for their family. One such place is the noodle house, known as Bakmi Gajah Mada 77, which got its name from the original address of the residence of the owner. Mr Tjhai Sioe Tjhung, a Cantonese, was originally a furniture maker as were most Cantonese in Indonesia. Jobless during the Japanese occupation, he started a restaurant to provide his family with a better living. After the war he returned to his old job, but would serve noodles when there were guests. These guests encouraged him to open a noodle shop. In 1959 when the situation became difficult economically, he started the noodle shop in his own house, putting a few tables and some benches for clients. The lack of good ingredients made him decide to limit his cooking to noodles only, which he topped with sautéed ground chicken. It proved a great success and slowly Mr Tjhai opened new branches, 13 in 2009, in different parts of the growing city. A delivery service has been added as special service to the clients. Many clients have fond memories of the special taste of this noodle. Those who have moved to other countries would always make a visit to the place when they are back in Jakarta. Or when friends come to visit them abroad, they would ask to bring some noodles for them. To make it possible for the public to enjoy the noodles, Bakmi GM shops have remained *halal* and thus do not serve pork. They have added more dishes to their menu, but they insist on not serving pork, for they want to serve all the people and do not want to exclude certain religious groups.

Oei Hong Kian, a dentist, tells how he learned to appreciate good cuisine from a Hakka friend in the 1950s in Jakarta. One place they visited was a small eating place, only reachable after crossing a bridge made of two banana tree trunks. The place was called Angke, after the river they had to cross. Now this restaurant is one of the busiest restaurants in Jakarta. Mr Oei also mentioned a restaurant opened by a former editor

The Dragon's Trail in Chinese Indonesian Foodways

of a newspaper. After the newspaper was closed, he started a restaurant, which served very good crab in oyster sauce (Oei 2001: 224–31).

Another case is the Yun Nyan Seafood Restaurant which was started in the slum area of Tanjong Priok, the port of Jakarta in 1950. Mr Chu was a second-generation Cantonese who came to Indonesia as a young boy with his father who worked as a technician in repairing ships transporting tin ore from the tin company on the island of Belitung. After the war he moved to Jakarta to do the same work at the port of Jakarta, when he saw the fresh shrimps that were available there. He decided to open a food stall and sold shrimps and prawn dishes. His plain dish of steamed shrimps became so popular that he soon had clients from all over Jakarta. The chilli dip for the shrimp became very famous. How the word had spread is not known to him, but amongst his clients were high official such as bankers, diplomats and generals. Because his stall was small, these people would wait for their turn until a table was cleared. In 1976 came an edict to free the land and the restaurant had to move out. A new shop house was found in the Central Jakarta area, where the restaurant is still standing. In an interview with Ms Chu (23 June 2007), daughter of the founder of the restaurant, three more outlets had been opened by the children of Mr Chu in the outskirts,

Mie Belitung without gravy. (Photograph by Myra Sidharta, June 2010)

and a third would be opened soon in a luxurious shopping mall by one of the grandsons.

Other popular places were the roadside places, which usually opened after shops had closed at around 5 p.m. The owner of the shop would then open his restaurant on the sidewalk or he would hire someone to do the cooking. The foods most often served are seafood dishes, which were very popular among movie goers who would enjoy a meal before they go to the theatre or sometimes people would come after the movies.

For more exotic food, one had to go to special places. Snake meat was served in shady restaurants usually called King Cobra. For monkey and dog meat there were stalls in an amusement park called Lokasari. Turtle meat and *swike* (frog legs) were served in the Chinatown area. However, the Chinese are not the only ones serving exotic food, the Bataks also like a good serving of dog meat as do the people from Manado, who are also fond of bats.

Thus in the 1970s the restaurant scene was a mediocre one, with no fancy interior and service. But the food must have been good, because people would line up for a meal. Probably the food was tasty because it was made suitable for the Indonesian palate. In the early 1980s restaurant business started to pick up again. First in the luxurious hotels, which were built to cater for the business people and tourists, later in high-rise buildings which were also starting to serve as office buildings. These restaurants also offered karaoke facilities. Hong Kong style dim sum lunches were offered since the second half of the 1980s. They were popular amongst the ladies who liked to share a lunch with their friends; sometimes they make use of karaoke facilities as well. A dim sum manufacturing place was opened by Mrs Dewi who caters for Chinese restaurants. Having no time to make the dishes themselves, some restaurants would rather order the food from her. Now her husband manages the "factory," while their clients increase by the day because of the popularity of these dishes.

In 1992 diplomatic relations with China, which was frozen since 1965, were restored and so were business relations. Besides the trade in commodities, new restaurants were opened, serving the haute cuisine of China and Taiwan. A novelty was the *lamian* restaurants, where the clients could watch the chef making noodles by pulling and folding the dough. Sometimes this attraction was used as a reason to invite friends to eat out.

Some very chic restaurants offer fusion style food, served with the flair of the international haute cuisine. The choice of restaurants is not

The Dragon's Trail in Chinese Indonesian Foodways   121

limited to southern China food, such as Cantonese, Hainanese, Teochew or Hakka. There are also many Sichuan, Shanghai and Beijing restaurants, and there is even a Hunanese restaurant in the Chinatown, where many kinds of soups are offered. From Taiwan come the special porridge restaurants beside the more luxurious restaurants.

The 1990s is also the time that people moved into apartments and thus adopted a different kind of life style. The kitchen is left clean and people prefer to eat out or bring cooked food home for lunch and dinner. In many small and medium size restaurants we can see the announcement that they have home delivery for the area near their place. Restaurant business is now booming and Indonesians can now enjoy food from all over the world. The so-called Peranakan restaurants, which serve Chinese Indonesian food, are also very popular. Three of the more prominent Peranakan restaurants in Jakarta are: the Dapur Baba (the Baba Kitchen), Kedai Tiga Nyonya (the Shop of the 3 Ladies) and Mira Delima (Red Pomegranate). All three of them serve Chinese foods that are more adapted to the Indonesian kitchen, thus hot and spicy, but each of them has its specialties. Dapur Baba serves a more Dutch menu with Dutch steak, soups and salads. Kedai Tiga Nyonya has a more genuine Chinese Indonesian cuisine with *ayam keluak* (chicken cooked in the *keluak* nut), fried or barbequed chicken Central Java style, and fried or barbecued fish, west Java Style and hot-pot tofu and seafood. The proprietor of Mira Delima which serves more refined Chinese Indonesian food, claims that she has taken the recipe's from her mother-in-law. On top of the list is the ribs cooked in a sour soup. Her fish cake and *lumpia* (spring roll) Semarang style are very popular. In all these restaurants, a long list of *sambal* is included where the customer can choose from.

Conclusion

The influence of the Chinese foodways in Indonesia is evident everywhere at the places where the Chinese have settled. Vegetables, condiments and other ingredients have been adopted by the natives to enhance their own cuisine. Several kinds of food have been accepted by the native Indonesians as their own and these add to their daily menu. Indigenous Indonesians prefer their food to be spicy and pungent and they have many ingredients to make their food to be attractive. The result for the present Chinese Indonesian foodways is a hybrid menu with the style of Chinese cuisine and the taste of the native Indonesian foodways.

Preference for genuine Chinese food is reflected in the opening of many new Chinese restaurants, as well as the continuation of the old established restaurants which have expanded their businesses by opening new branches, not only in the Metropolitan city of Jakarta but also in other cities in the Archipelago.

For the Chinese Indonesians in particular, the foodways is not uniform for all families. The more they have adapted to the Indonesian culture, the more they prefer the spicy Indonesian food, whereas the families that are more oriented to the Chinese culture would prefer more genuine Chinese food. But they all use Chinese ingredients at home, such as soy sauce, soy paste, tofu, Chinese vegetables, and of course noodles in all varieties.

Notes

1. For a history of the settlement of the Chinese in Java, see Fruin Mees, *W. Geschiedenis van Java, dl 1, Hindoetijdperk* (History of Java, part I, The Hindu Era) (Weltevreden: W. Kolff, 1930).
2. Vereenigde Oost Indische Compagnie (Dutch East Indies Company which ruled the Archipelago from 1602–1799, continued later by the East Indies Government).
3. See also the cookbook of the family of R.A. Kartini, *Putri Jepara*, ed. Suryatini N. Gani (Jakarta: Gaya Favorit Press, 2005). R.A. Kartini (1880–1905), also known as Ibu Kartini, was a member of an aristocratic family in Central Java. She became famous because of her thoughts about empowering the women of the Indonesian Archipelago written in letters to her Dutch friends around 1900.
4. *Bandeng* is cultivated in ponds. The owner has thus control over the size of the fish for his own use. For the Chinese New Year the super size fishes can be seen at the market.

References

Bondan Winarno. 2007. "Papi Tiong (Father Tiong)." *Kompas Cybermedia*, 5 July.
Bosch, F.D.K. 1929. "De betekenis der reliefs van de IIIe en IVe gaanderij van Boroboedoer (The Meaning of the Reliefs of the 3rd and 4th gallery of the Borobudur)." *Oudheidkundig verslag*, Bijlage C, pp. 179–244.
Cammerloher, H. 1931. "Wat de Boroboedoer den natuuronderzoeker leert (What the Nature Explorer Can Learn from the Borodur)." *De Tropische Natuur* 20: 141–52.

Cheng, F.T. 1955. *Musings of a Chinese Gourmet*. London: Hutchinson, second print.

Haan, F. de. 1935. *Oud-Batavia*. Bandoeng: A.C. Nix & Co.

Holleman, L.J.W., D.R. Koolhaas, and J.A. Nijholt. 1939. "The Composition of the Diet of the Chinese of Batavia." *Mededelingen van de Dienst van Gezondheid* 28: 306–20.

Jones, Russell, gen. ed. 2008. *Loan-words in Indonesian and Malay*. Jakarta: KITLV-Yayasan Obor, Indonesian edition.

Lombard, Denys. 1996. *Nusa Jawa: Silang Budaya II, jaringan Asia*, translation of *Le Carrefour Javanais II, les Reseaux Asiatiques*. Jakarta: Gramedia Pustaka Utama, in collaboration with Forum Jakarta-Paris and EFEO.

Oei, Hong Kian. 2001. *Dokter Gigi Soekarno* (Soekarno's Dentist). Jakarta: Intisari Mediatama. [This book is also available in Dutch (*Kind van het Land — Child of the Country*) and an English translation is forthcoming.]

Purcell, Victor. 1980. *The Chinese of Southeast Asia*. Kuala Lumpur: Oxford in Asia paperbacks.

Raadt, E. de. 1932. "De afbeeldingen op de Boroboedoer (The Reliefs of the Borobudur)." *De Tropische Natuur* 21: 10.

Steinman, A. 1934. "De op de Boroboedoer afgebeelde plantenwereld (The Plants Represented on the Borobudur)." *Tijdschrift voor Indische Taal, Land en Volkenkunde* 74: 581–612.

Sidharta, Myra. 2008. "Soyfoods in Indonesia." In *The World of Soy*, ed. Christine M. Du Bois, Tan Chee-Beng, and Sidney Mintz. Urbana and Chicago: University of Illinois Press, pp. 195–207.

Tjan Kwan Nio. 1992. "Kisah Hidupku." In *Le Moment "Sino-Malais" de la Literature Indonesienne*, ed. Claudine Salmon. Paris: Cahiers d'Archipel 19.

Torck, Matthieu. 2007. "The Matter of Provisioning in Zheng He's Fleet: A Reconstructive Attempt." In *Chinese Diaspora since Admiral Zheng He with special reference to Maritime Asia*, ed. Leo Suryadinata. Singapore: Singapore Chinese Heritage Centre, pp. 51–9.

Vorderman, A.G. 1886. "Catalogus van eenige Chineesche en Inlandsche voedingsmiddelen van Batavia (Catalogue of Some Chinese and Native Foodstuff)." *Geneeskundig Tijdschrift van Nederlandsch Indie* 25: 103–25.

CHAPTER

5

Acculturation, Localization and Chinese Foodways in the Philippines

Carmelea Ang See

INTRODUCTION

> "Do not look for *lumpiang* (spring rolls) *Shanghai* in Shanghai, or look
> for *pancit* (noodle dish) Canton in Guangdong."

This is a common advice given to Filipinos going to China. Unknowing
Filipino tourists in China sometimes assume these two most popular dishes
in the Philippines to be "China" in origin. In actual fact, these are examples
of how "Chinese" food has transformed and become indigenized, and they
in turn have influenced foodways in the Philippines. Filipino cuisine has
influenced "Chinese food" to the extent that eventually it has evolved
into a localized Philippine version, like the *lumpiang Shanghai* and *pancit*
(Chinese noodles).

With centuries of contact between China and the Philippines, a
two-way intercultural exchange has happened, mutually transforming and
enriching each culture, with influences on food being the most visible. Food
exchange has also become a venue for social interaction. During Chinese
New Year, for example, *tikoy* (sweet rice cake) is given as a gift between

124

Chinese Foodways in the Philippines

friends, employers and employees, colleagues, and even bank managers and their clients to cement relationships. It has also become a "thank you" gift for people who have helped the giver in previous years.

"The global diffusion of Chinese food culture has occurred during the past two hundred years, under the impact of Western capitalism and colonialism. When hundreds of thousands of Chinese left South China, mainly the two provinces of Fujian and Guangdong, and arrived in Southeast Asia, Oceania, and North and South America, they brought with them not only Chinese ways of cooking but also new food ingredients" (Li 2001: xii). One of the most visible examples of this transformation in the Philippines is China's noodles (called *pancit* in Filipino) served in different forms and varieties — Pancit Luglug, Pancit Canton, Pancit Bihon, Pancit Molo, Pancit Malabon, Pancit Habhab, etc. — much the same way that the Ramen in Korea and Japan and the Laksa in Singapore and Malaysia have evolved into their own localized versions of the noodles.

Some fresh produce that are common to the Filipino table have Chinese names, such as *pechay* (白菜 Chinese cabbage), *sitaw* (丝豆 or 菜豆 string bean), *kuchay* (韭菜 garlic chives), *wansoy* (芫荽 coriander), *upo* (葫芦 bottle gourd), *toge* (豆芽 bean sprout), *kinchay* (芹菜 Chinese parsley or Chinese celery); condiments like *hebi* (蝦米 dried shrimp), *kimchamchay* (全针菜 dried lily flower), *ngo hiong* (五香 five spices) and *toyo* (豆油 soy sauce). These food items have become integral parts of Filipino cooking. The names are in the Hokkien dialect of southern Fujian (Minnanhua), where 90 per cent of the local Chinese Filipinos (Tsinoys) hail from.

Perhaps because many early butchers were Chinese,[1] some meat and viscera like *goto* (牛肚 beef tripe), *tito* (猪肚 pork tripe), *kamto* (锦肚 mixed entrails), *paykot* (排骨 spareribs), *kasim* (pork shoulder 甲心) and *kenchi* (腱子 beef tendon) have also retained their Chinese names.

Tan (2001: 126) notes, "Food processing and the culture-specific tastes of food are defined by historical heritage and local experiences, as well as by both local and global processes." This chapter aims to look at how these "Chinese" dishes and foodways have been transformed and localized because of its exposure and interaction with the mainstream Filipino dishes and foodways. The blending of Chinese and local cultures in the Philippines has produced the unique Chinese Filipino food. From such intercultural exchanges in food and foodways, we also get a glimpse of the processes of intercultural relations and transformation.

Brief History

Early Exchanges

The *Song Dynasty Annals* contained the first written record about the arrival of Chinese traders on Philippine shores in the year 982. Throughout the centuries, Chinese merchants frequently arrived in the various islands, bringing their trade wares and exchanging them for native products. According to the early historical documents, the merchants would stay at port for one to two months while waiting for the natives to bring local goods in exchange for Chinese products (Go 2003; Scott 1989). These early seafarers were not just traders but cultural brokers, too. Anthropologist H. Otley Beyer (1979) has written about the early Chinese traders introducing medicinal herbs to the Filipinos. In fact, archaeological evidences have revealed that food and foodways were among the far-reaching exchanges between the early hunters and gatherers from China to Southeast Asia and vice-versa.

Colonial Period

During the Spanish times, the Chinese arrived in the islands primarily as sojourners, much like our overseas Filipino workers of today. They need to work and send money back to China to support their families. Many of these sojourners eventually settled in the country, married Filipinas, and started their families here. With the introduction of the tobacco industry to raise revenue for the Spanish colonial government came food hawkers who catered to the dining needs of factory workers. They offered cheap and ready-to-eat food to hungry labourers.

Soon thereafter, these same hawkers were able to set up their own establishments. They were later called the *panciteria*, the common name for "Chinese restaurants" then. The term itself shows the mixture of Chinese and Spanish. The first word *pancit* is a Tagalog generic word for noodles, the suffix *-eria* refers to a place where something is done as in *accessoria* (dwelling place*)*, *panaderia* (bakery where pan or bread is made), etc. Thus, *panciteria* means a place where noodle is served. They would serve the ubiquitous *pancit* (Chinese noodles) as well as *comida china*, simple Chinese fare but made more "exotic" by its Spanish names in the menu. Fernando (1978) reported as follows:

> A letter of civil servant to King Philip II reports that "the Chinese quarter, the Parian, has many eating houses where the Sangleys

Chinese Foodways in the Philippines 127

(Chinese) and the natives take their meals; and I have been told these are frequented even by Spaniards." Menus in Chinese restaurants even today carry full meals called Comida China. Names of their dishes are in Spanish. Hence the mellifluous Camaron Rebosado Dorado con Jamon (a kind of fried butterfly shrimp stuck to a bit of ham), Lapulapu con Salsa Agrio Dulce (grouper with sweet sour sauce), and Sopa de Nido con Tiburon (bird's nest soup with shark's fin).

The American period is considered by Chinese merchants as the golden era of business. Convenient American food — salads, hamburgers, spaghetti, ham, bacon and hotdogs — were introduced to the Filipino palate. However, Chinese influence in food remained strong with the ubiquitous sari-sari stores (convenience stores) scattered even to the farthest reaches of the Philippine islands. Anything that one needed then could be obtained from these stores, predecessors of the modern 24-hour convenience stores.

Street vendors, with their "portable kitchens," who started plying their food wares during the Spanish period, were still plentiful. The portable kitchen was carried on a long bamboo pole. One end held the huge tin container with tin bowls, the noodles and the condiments. Another end held the smaller tin container filled with soup stock. Noodles were placed on the bowl, condiments sprinkled on top and the soup stock poured into it, and voila, an instant hot meal was provided (Ang See 2005).

Modern Times

The Japanese occupation and the immediate post-war years were difficult times of hunger and deprivation. This is the period when improvised Chinese soy sauce, black bean paste, sweet potato congee and bamboo shoots became staples that helped tide people over hunger. The Pacific War and the immediate post-war era saw China closing its doors to the outside world. Travel to and from China became quite difficult and was eased only in the late 1960s up to the mid-1970s. A fresh wave of migrants from southern China arrived in the Philippines, mostly through Hong Kong. These were immediate relatives of the Chinese businessmen in the Philippines who were cut off in China or left behind in Hong Kong after the formation of the People's Republic of China in 1949. More Chinese restaurants, Chinese drug stores, convenient food outlets selling *siopao* (hot Chinese buns with meat), *siomai*, *E-meng lumpia* (Xiamen spring rolls) and the like sprouted up. Due to the long, continuous and persistent

128   *Carmelea Ang See*

Chinese influence from pre-war era, particular Chinese dishes have been so firmly entrenched in Philippine cuisine that many of them are considered Filipino even through modern times, although their Chinese roots are recognized.

The 1980s saw the rise of fast food establishments and along with it the idea of serving Chinese fast food. They offered typical *panciteria* fare in a clean, well-lighted environment with fast service and value for money. In the twenty-first century, Philippine-style Chinese food is fast spreading to neighbouring countries, especially in areas saturated with overseas Filipinos homesick for "Filipino" food. A Filipino feast, whether held in the Philippines or abroad, cannot be complete without the basic *pancit* and *lumpia*, which many no longer realize are Chinese in origin and bearing Chinese names.

Today, in the twenty-first century era of globalization, and with the influx of new immigrants since the market reform and opening up of China in 1978, many more food items and food varieties are being introduced to Filipino consumers. For example, *lamian* (hand-pulled noodles) and the use of XO sauce (made of shredded scallops) are becoming popular. As Yih-yuan Li (2001: xii) says in his foreword to *Changing Chinese Foodways in Asia*, "New waves of Chinese immigration to foreign countries in the second half of the twentieth century have sparked the introduction of new food ingredients for Chinese cuisine around the world." Whether the new Chinese food items like hand-stretched noodles (拉面) dumplings, hakaw (虾饺) and other fancy dim sum items will also find their niche in Filipino cuisine and become localized and adopted by Filipinos should be the subject of future research. As it is now, innovations and two-way interchange are quite evident in Chinese food that has been part of the Philippine menu in at least the last century. Some of these Chinese food items that have found their way to Filipino staple food are described and elaborated below.

Localization of Chinese Food

Fernandez (2002: 183) has the following description of indigenous Philippine food and foreign influences on the development of Philippine cuisine:

> The bedrock of the Philippine food landscape is indigenous food, drawn from land, sea and air, cooked in simple ways (roasted, steamed and boiled). This includes such dishes as *sinigang*, fish, meat or fowl stewed

Chinese Foodways in the Philippines

with vegetables in sour broth; *laing*, taro leaves in coconut milk; *pinais*, river shrimps steamed with young coconut in banana leaves; *pinakbet*, mixed vegetables steamed in a fish or shrimp sauce and *kinilaw*, seafood dressed in vinegar. Foreign influences came to play upon this matrix which built up the totality now known as Philippine cuisine. The earliest input was Chinese, brought by merchants who, according to historians, have certainly been trading in the Philippines since the tenth century, and quite probably as early as ninth century (from the evidence of ceramic and other trade ware). Later came the Spanish-Mexican food traditions, then the American, brought in by two waves of colonization (1571–1898; 1899–1947).

I shall now describe some items of food which are derived from Chinese cuisine.

Rice

Rice is the staple food in the Philippines. It is eaten for breakfast, lunch and dinner. One can scrimp on viands like vegetables or meat, but never on rice. In this the Filipinos and the Chinese are the same. In fact many Hokkien terms for rice-related products have become basic Filipino vocabulary, as follows:

Am	饮[米汤]	(rice broth)
Biko	米糕	(rice cake)
Bilao	米篓	(round flat woven trays)
Bilu-bilo	米糯	(rice balls)
Bithay	米筛	(rice sieve)

The Filipino terms used in the farming implements are also Hokkien in origins:

Lithaw	犁头	(plow head)
Lipya	犁耙 or 犁把	(back furrow)
Puthaw	斧头	(axe)

Lumpia

The Chinese way of eating is characterized by a notable flexibility and adaptability. A dish is made up of a mixture of ingredients considering their appearance, taste, texture and flavour, not on a single "special" item. Changes in the contents of a dish depend on the availability of the ingredient(s), but changes do not mean a diminishing of the dish's overall quality or desirability. This particular evolution is evident in the centuries of interaction and intercultural exchanges between the Filipinos and the Chinese in their midst. Chinese food has evolved from its original Chinese Hokkien version or Cantonese version to a Filipinized version suited to the Filipino palate. *Lumpia* and *pancit* are the two most classic examples of this evolution. Both dishes are made all over the country, each province or region having its own special way of preparing it. The culinary expert and food critic, the late Dr. Doreen Fernandez, had marvelled about the indigenization of Chinese food into the local cuisine.

The term *lumpia* comes from the Hokkien term *lun bnia* (潤饼 spring rolls). Hokkien spring rolls (E-meng or Xiamen *lumpia* to be more specific) are especially notable and eating *lumpia* to celebrate the coming of spring after the long bitter winter months is not just a gastronomic exercise but a ritual in itself. Both the preparation of the ingredients (which takes more than a day) and the eating of the *lumpia* is an intimate family affair where even the young children are asked to help. The soup stock (usually chicken) is prepared the previous day, while the chicken meat is shredded into strips, and the fresh vegetables are sliced thinly. Using different knives for the different vegetables are observed because the way the vegetables are cut is supposed to keep its original juices and texture intact. The vegetables cooked in the stock are piled into a huge platter, together with other ingredients like crushed peanuts, *ho-ti*,[2] *wansoy* (芫荽 coriander) and crushed garlic. The fresh lettuce leaves are laid out carefully beside the thin *lumpia* wrapper made of ground rice. The lettuce leaves are laid on top of the wrapper, the cooked ingredients piled on top of the leaves and the fresh condiments sprinkled on top and the whole thing is rolled up and ready to be munched upon. The *lumpia* is eaten fresh but the leftovers can be used to make fried *lumpia*, with some more ingredients added if so desired.

In the Philippines though, the *lumpia* comes in a myriad of forms: fresh or fried, meat-filled or vegetarian. *Lumpiang sariwa* (fresh *lumpia*) normally contains bean sprouts, carrots, shredded cabbage, onions, garlic, *kinchay* (Chinese parsley or Chinese celery), *tokwa* (dried tofu), cooked ground pork or shredded chicken. Variations would include cooked shrimp, or ground peanuts. *Lumpiang prito* (fried *lumpia*) is more versatile. It can contain anything from just bean sprouts and sliced carrots and fried.

Potatoes are often added to make it more filling. There are also more elaborate or special (and more expensive) versions that include more vegetables and meat, or even seafood like crab meat. *Lumpiang prito* with just bean sprouts and carrots could be found at any street food stall.

Lumpiang ubod contains sautéed "heart" of coconut palm with garlic, pork and shrimps. *Lumpiang Shanghai*, one of the most popular and common *lumpia*, contains ground pork, minced carrots, potatoes and onions. All ingredients are mashed together with egg and a bit of flour before being stuffed into small wrappers. Unlike the vegetable-based *lumpia* which are full meals in themselves simply because of their size (approximately six inches in length, and two inches in diameter), *lumpiang Shanghai* is a mere half-inch in diameter and two inches in length and this is popularly served to accompany rice.

While most fried vegetable *lumpia* are dipped in vinegar (with or without garlic and the local chilli), *lumpiang Shanghai* is dipped in ketchup or a tomato-based sweetish sauce. Any grilled or fried food, for that matter, is served with its own dipping sauce. On most Filipino dining tables soy sauce, vinegar and fish sauce are available, a signal to the diner that he/she is free to adjust the taste of the food just the way he likes it. It

Lumpiang sariwa.

is rare for a meal to be eaten without even a small taste adjustment. This penchant for dipping sauces has made its way into how the Filipinos eat spring roll.

This evolution from a ritualistic, celebratory meal in Fujian, China, to a simple vegetable dish, then back to various complex meal specialties is primarily due to the availability of many ingredients. Bean sprouts, called *toge* (pronounced toh-geh) in Filipino and *daogge* (豆芽) in Hokkien as testament to its Chinese roots, are among the cheapest vegetables in the market. For very little money, a family could have a feast of a meal with rice and *lumpiang prito*. Other ingredients in "special *lumpia*," added or subtracted by a family or a restaurant that serves it, could often depend on the whims of the cook.

Looking at the *lumpia* phenomenon more closely, we could conclude that it is certainly a poor man's fare. After all, changes in food and food culture do not begin from the top of the economic strata, but from the bottom going up. As the *lumpia* becomes more elaborate, so do the restaurants that serve it. Pat-lin Restaurant in Manila, for example, refuses to serve fresh Xiamen *lumpia* with the sauce because the owners want to educate the consumers that genuine *lumpia* needs no sauce. There are stalls in shopping malls that sell only Pat-lin *lumpia*. Diao Eng Chay is another fast-food outlet in Manila people go to for *lumpia*.

Siopao (烧包) *and* *Siomai* (烧卖)

In the Philippines, meals are not simply divided into breakfast, lunch and dinner. Between the three main meals of the day are two *merienda* or snacks (translated as coffee breaks in offices). *Merienda* is not a simple snack one takes to tide over until the regular meal. It is almost ritualistic where people gather and share their food, and at the same time, their life stories with each other. Hence, the food items served for the snacks should not only be filling, but also a gastronomic delight that could create and sustain friendship. Crackers or cookies simply would not suffice.

Long before dim sum became a byword in Philippine cuisine, *siopao* and *siomai* were regular "party" food items, especially in school or office functions. The Tagalog terms from the word are again derived from the Hokkien terms for these dim sum food, even though they are Cantonese in origin. These two items have evolved into regular snack items found in 7-11 convenience stores, as well as Chinese and Filipino restaurants, and served at all hours of the day.

*Chinese Foodways in the Philippines*133

Siopao and *siomai* are two food items eaten with friends or even in public transport as a quick breakfast meal before arriving at the office. Because they are not easy to cook at home, they have become "specialty" food items. Restaurants and stores vie for having the "best" tasting *siopao* or *siomai*. For *siopao*, more meat and/or other ingredients make the snack more satisfying.

Siopao started with only two versions — *bola bola* (ground pork that looks like a balled up burger patty) and *asado* (minced pork meat). Nowadays, specialty *siopao* has half a salted egg inside the *bola bola*, or a large piece of shitake mushroom inside the *asado*, or *siopao* filled with chicken instead of pork, and there are vegetarian *siopao*, including fried versions.

Siomai is traditionally pork-based. Since the late 1990s, however, specialty *siomai* stores have come out, especially with the popularization of dim sum itself. There are now *siomai* that are purely vegetarian, and there are crabstick *siomai*, as well as *siomai* with quail egg and bacon, ham, or chicken. To continue with the Filipino penchant for dipping sauces, *siomai* is commonly eaten with soy sauce and *calamansi* (Philippine lemon). A new variation that started in the 1990s adds chilli garlic sauce to the soy sauce and *calamansi* mixture.

Pancit

Another poor man's fare that has become a Philippine staple is the *pancit*. *Pancit* came from the Hokkien word *pian-sit* (便食), which literally means fast food or food that can be conveniently prepared. This refers back to the "portable kitchen" discussed earlier, where workers can have an instant ready hot meal (便食) from a food vendor. An alternative explanation is that the term refers to *pian sit* (扁食) which in Hokkien refers to thin and flat rice noodles that look like linguini. While this type of flat noodle is popular in some areas of Fujian province, it was never popularized in the Philippines. Culturally, language-borrowings occur when the word borrowed is commonly used, like *pechay* (白菜) meaning white vegetable, or *mami* (肉麵), literally "meat noodle." Since *pian sit* (扁食) was not popularized in the Philippines, the word could not have crept into the Filipino language, and therefore the term for "fast food" (便食) is a more plausible etymology for *pancit* (Ang See 2005).

Regardless of where the name *pancit* originates, it is generally acknowledged that *pancit* is of Chinese origin. In the past, they were commonly made from flour. Other variations carry a special name like *pancit bihon* (*bihun* 米粉 in Hokkien, which means rice noodle), and *pancit sotanghon*,[3] which refers to both the type of noodle used and the way to cook it.

Through the indigenization process, various forms of the *pancit* dish are now specialties depending on the locale. So thoroughly has this been absorbed into the "local cuisine" that almost every region in the Philippines has its own *pancit*.

Fernandez (2002: 185) describes the various kinds of *pancit* as follows:

> Pansit Malabon, native to the fishing town of Malabon, usually includes shrimps, oysters and squid. Pansit Marilao, from the town of Marilao in Bulacan within the Central Luzon rice-growing area, features rice crisps. Pansit Molo contains noodles but filled with wontons in a broth; it is named after a town in Iloilo in which many Chinese settled. Pansit Guisado (*guisado* being the Spanish word for sautéed) consists of noodles sautéed with tomatoes, onions, shrimp, vegetables and pork. Pansit Luglog (*luglog* being a Tagalog word for "to shake") has noodles shaken in hot broth, and flavoured with a shrimp-based sauce. In Pansit Palabok (*palabok* denoting added flavour or adornment), flaked smoked fish, squid, crumbled crackling, sliced pork skin, etc. are sprinkled over the based noodles.

Another form of *pancit* readily available in most Filipino restaurants is Pancit Canton (literally Cantonese *pancit*), made from egg noodles. A huge phenomenon in recent years is the creation of instant Pancit Canton by numerous instant noodle companies coming in various flavours — hot chilli, *calamansi*, sweet and spicy flavour, and there are also vegetarian ones as well as those with beef or chicken.

Pancit canton.

Chinese Foodways in the Philippines   135

Sotanghon, Lomi, Mami, Misua and Maki

While all these forms of noodles and *pancit* dishes are cooked "dry," there are also soupy noodle dishes that are also very popular among Filipinos, namely *sotanghon, lomi, mami, misua* and *maki*. Everyone knows that the noodles are Chinese in origin, however, everyone also acknowledges that these food items are also truly Filipino.

Mami originates from *ba-mi* (肉面), that is, noodles with pork. The fame and popularity of *mami* is generally attributed to one person — Ma Mon Luk, a Cantonese schoolteacher who had to "make something of himself" before he married. Thus he walked the streets peddling chicken noodle soup. The broth, which Ma made from fat native chickens, is continuously heated in a metal container with burning coals underneath, while the noodles and utensils are in a large basket. Both containers are carried at the ends of a bamboo pole slung over his shoulders. In his older days, Ma continued to walk with one shoulder hanging lower than the other (Fernando 1978).

A more recent form of the *mami* vendor involves a bicycle with a side car attached to it, carrying the separate containers for the broth and the ingredients. These bicycle-riding food hawkers can be found at street corners selling hot *mami* to the working-class people.

As with Pancit Canton, *mami* has had a longer history in the instant noodle business. Home-cooked *mami* or restaurant-ordered *mami* invariably include meat and vegetables, along with the noodles. People would attest to the best *mami* of various restaurants, although when one looks into it, the only differences are the proportions of the ingredients. *Mami* always has egg noodles, meat and vegetables.

Lomi (卤面) is more of a thick stew-like broth seasoned with soy sauce. Thick fat noodles are cooked with meat and vegetables; flour is mixed with the broth to make it thicker. A raw beaten egg is stirred in at the last minute before serving. The name itself indicates the cooking process for in Hokkien *lo* (卤) is to stew or simmer slowly and *mi* (面) refers to the noodles.

Sotanghon can be cooked in a variety of ways: dry as in the *pancit* style, with soup, or as an added ingredient to regular chicken soup. These are thin noodles made from mung beans which become translucent when cooked. The Chinese in the Philippines cook *sotanghon* mostly as soup, usually with vegetables and chicken or seafood. One favourite dish is spicy crab with *sotanghon*. The localized Filipino version is more elaborate because it is consumed during special occasions. As is usual Filipino practice, this noodle has been indigenized into Pancit Sotanghon. The noodles are soaked in water until they are translucent. They are then sautéed with plenty of vegetables and a bit of meat before serving.

Misua (面线) or thin vermicelli is the most popular ritual food among the Hokkien. It is served to relatives who came to visit for the first time. It is also served on other happy occasions like engagements, birthdays and weddings. Filipino home cooking adds *misua* to the traditional chicken soup to make a more hearty meal. *Misua* can also be simply sautéed and cooked as a sort of *pancit*.

Maki (肉羹) is pork rolled in batter and dropped into a broth, while it is boiling hot. The broth is thickened with tapioca starch and could be spicy or just salty. The *maki-mi* (肉羹面) is the dish when noodles are added to the thick soup with the meat. It is undeniable that the inexpensive noodle has pervaded Philippine taste and culture through the centuries. These noodle dishes are considered staples at festivals and parties and are often perfect take-home gifts for the wife and kids.

Soybean Products

Soybean and soybean products are not indigenous to the Philippine islands. As in other parts of Southeast Asia, soybeans were brought in by the Chinese, and thus, still carry their Hokkien term, *utao* (黄豆). All soybean-based "Filipino" food retain the Hokkien nomenclature. From the softest to the hardest, these include *taho* (豆花 bean curd custard), *tofu* (豆腐 bean curd), *tokwa* (豆干 dried bean curd), *tausi* (豆豉 fermented soy beans), and *toyo* (豆油 soy sauce).

With the legendary Filipino sweet tooth, *taho* is eaten with around 5–10 ml caramelized brown sugar and tapioca balls. One can see *taho* sellers with two metal containers slung over shoulder poles. One end of the pole contains plain *taho*. The other end carries a covered bucket with three compartments comprising the liquefied sugar, tiny tapioca balls or sago, and money. Plastic cups, usually put in long plastic bags, are tied to the pole as well.

Taho can be eaten at anytime of the day, usually as a snack, whether one is hungry or not. However, majority of the people eat it in the morning for breakfast when the *taho* has just come out of the factory and is still hot. It becomes harder and harder to find customers as the day grows late because people usually want their *taho* hot and it is too hot to eat it in the afternoon.

Chinese Foodways in the Philippines 137

In recent trips to China, I often find *tokwa* in cafeterias and smaller restaurants, fried or steamed whole and eaten as it is. This form of cooking and eating would be considered truly pitiful if served to a Filipino. As always, there has to be embellishments, the sauce! The result is *tokwa baboy* (*tokwa* and pork), cooked in soy sauce and a little vinegar — a most popular dish in Philippine cuisine. This little dish is good for lunch or dinner or as *pulutan* (any food item or dish eaten with beer).

Toyo or soy sauce is a common Filipino condiment. Go to any Filipino restaurant and instead of salt and pepper shakers at the table, there are *toyo* and vinegar bottles! Filipinos are fond of either fried or grilled food — seafood or meat — and thus, *toyo* is a basic dipping sauce.

Hopia

While the *lumpia* and *pancit* have been changing through more than a hundred years, a recent twentieth century phenomenon involves a little pastry that has Filipinos all over the world salivating for a taste. *Hopia* is the Tagalog word derived from the Hokkien *ho-bnia* (好餅, literally good biscuit). Many Filipinos who leave the country often bring *hopia* to relatives they are meeting abroad. In Fujian, China, *hopia*'s closest relative still looks like what it used to look like 100 years ago — mung bean paste inside a creamy dough skin. The Philippine *hopia*'s closest Southeast Asia relative would be Malaysia's Tau Sar Pia (豆沙饼 mung bean biscuit).

When *hopia* first arrived in the Philippines in the early 1900s, it was a simple pastry made from beans and flour. Like the *taho*, itinerant vendors would carry two flat baskets (*bilao*) full at the end of a pole, and sell the *hopia* as snack food items.

Early Philippine versions sold in Quiapo, a district in Manila, were made from mung beans and flour or red beans and flour. *Hopia* was laid out in large *bilao* (round flat woven trays) and sold for 50 centavos to one peso. More beans than flour in the pastry meant a higher class of product, thus a higher price as well. Curiously enough, these were called Hopiang Hapon or Japanese Hopia, possibly because of the thin, flaky crust that looks like *papel de hapon* or Japanese paper.

Conversations with older-generation Chinese reveal that Hopiang Hapon is named as such because the old *hopia* makers used the Japanese version instead of the Chinese version. It was a more desirable product because it stored well, and was easier to make than the flaky Chinese version. The materials for cooking were also extremely cheap. A simple metal drum as an oven sufficed.

Hopia was a regular snack item for Filipinos, especially within the metropolis. As the years went by though, its popularity was edged out by newer, machine-made snack products, which not only looked more appealing, but were really more hygienic. It was not until 1985 that one desperate *hopia* maker stumbled upon a recipe that propelled his product to *hopia* stardom. Prior to 1985, Eng Bee Tin Hopia's sales were declining rapidly. The main problem, according to third-generation owner Gerie Chua, was the product itself. Their *hopia* was so tough and dry that it would retain its shape even when thrown against a wall. The consistency could not be changed because the pastries had to be strong enough to be stacked one on top of the other as they were transported to the provinces. The almost rock hard cakes were placed inside deep baskets, slung on poles as the seller walked the streets or as they were put aboard trains and boats.

Chua went to a local supermarket and asked a sales person which ice cream flavour enjoyed the highest number of sales. He hit the jackpot with *ube* (purple yam). At that time, the only common food item that came in purple yam flavour is ice cream. A local dessert, *halaya*, is made from purple yam and sugar. However, it is quite tedious to make (involving hours of stirring extremely sticky yam paste, which requires muscles of steel), so it is usually sold as home-made products. Other *ube* products that are made in northern Philippines are jam and milk pastilles.

Purple yam products are traditionally desired because they are nowadays rare. Filipinos love the taste and normally think of it as a special food product to be enjoyed slowly, lest it runs out. Considering this cultural factor is one reason why Chua was able to turn his family business' dismal sales figures to more than 5,000 packs a day. He experimented with different ways of grinding the root crop and incorporating it into the *hopia* pastry. Then, he experimented on various ways of making the *hopia*'s texture more creamy. The end product is a flaky crust with a very sweet and creamy centre.

Eng Bee Tin's sales figures are currently at a staggering 4,000–5,000 packs of *hopia* a day just for two flavours — Hopia Mongo (with mung bean) and Hopia Ube. The rest of the ten flavours' combined sales are also at an average of 3,000 packs a day. Added to those numbers is the year-round sale of *tikoy* (sweet rice cake normally eaten only during the Lunar New Year) and the Chua's innovation — sugar-free flavoured *tikoy* (corn, strawberry and *ube* flavoured).

Chua's desire is to make his *hopia* all-natural. Without preservatives, the pastry would last for around two days. To go around this potential

Chinese Foodways in the Philippines 139

problem, especially now that the product is exported around the world, Eng Bee Tin uses sugar to make the product last for at least four days. While this decision is from a business point of view, it helps that Filipino patrons are traditionally lovers of anything sweet, hence lending to an ever-increasing popularity of the Eng Bee Tin brand over others.

In 2006, Chua took other Filipino favourite flavours whose origins are more Spanish and American than Filipino, and used these to flavour *hopia*. There are now *ube-pastillas* (with purple yam and milk), *ube-queso* (with purple yam and cheese), *ube-langka* (with purple yam and jackfruit) and choco-peanut *hopia*.

CONCLUSION

Through centuries of cultural interaction and exchanges with the Philippine environment, Chinese food and foodways have crept into Filipino cuisine. Just as it has influenced and enhanced Filipino cuisine, Chinese food in turn has also been transformed by Filipino tastes and foodways to evolve into unique dishes in localized Philippine settings.

This experience is similar to what happens elsewhere in the world where the ethnic Chinese migrated to. As Tan (2001: 135) writes, "Changing food heritage of the Chinese living in different parts of the world is the result of Chinese adaptation to local environment, which includes utilizing local ecological and cultural resources. Exposure to local sources of food (ingredients, etc.) and non-Chinese cultural principles of food preparation results in cultural borrowing as well as cultural innovation."

The ease with which this process of transformation has happened showcases the versatility and flexibility of Philippine culture itself. The plural nature of a Philippine mainstream society that has, through the years, been influenced by the early Arab, Indian and Chinese traders and later by its colonial experiences from Spanish and American occupation, gives ample room for smooth intercultural exchanges and transformation. This two-way interchange is reflected in every aspect of Philippine life, but most especially in food because through the years, Chinese influences have become vital threads in the tapestry of Philippine national culture.

Notes

1. There is a popular saying in the Chinese-Filipino community that the early immigrants arrived with three knives "三把刀" — 剪刀 scissors, 菜刀 butcher's knife and 理发刀 scissors for hair to highlight the fact that the early Chinese

did all kinds of services to earn a living. The butcher's knife is used by the cook and the butcher.

2. This ingredient is made of crushed seaweed and fried crispy rice noodles (米粉). Like many Hokkien terms in the Philippines, there doesn't seem to be any corresponding Chinese characters to go with it. Filipinos who know about *ho-ti* usually just refer to it as crispy seaweed when ordering *lumpia*. Some older informants suggested the Chinese characters 好苔 for *ho-ti*.

3. This is 冬粉 in Hokkien, known in Mandarin as *fensi* 粉丝, which is usually translated as cellophane noodle. However, in the Philippines, the Hokkien term used is 山東粉, although it's not really from Shandong. From interviews with some older Chinese, I learned that the noodle dish *pancit sotanghon* was popularized by a restaurant called Shantung Restaurant in the early twentieth century, and that is most probably how the term evolved.

References

Ang See, Teresita. 2005. *Tsinoy: The Story of the Chinese in the Philippines.* Manila: Kaisa Para sa Kaunlaran, Inc.

Beyer, H. Otley. 1979. "The Philippines before Magellan." In *Readings in Philippine Prehistory,* ed. Mauro Garcia. Manila: The Filipiniana Book Guild, pp. 8–34.

Fernandez, Doreen G. 2002. "Chinese Food in the Philippines: Indigenization and Transformation." In *The Globalization of Chinese Food,* ed. David Y.H. Wu and Sidney C.H. Cheung. London: RoutledgeCurzon, pp. 183–9.

Fernando, Gilda Cordero. 1978. "The Mami King." In *Filipino Heritage: The Making of a Nation,* vol. 10. Manila: Lahing Pilipino Publishing Inc., pp. 2592–5.

Go Bon Juan. 2005. "Ma'I in Chinese Records — Mindoro or Ba'i? An Examination of a Historical Puzzle." *Philippine Studies* 53 (1): 119–38.

Li Yih-yuan. 2001. "Foreword." In *Changing Chinese Foodways in Asia,* ed. David Y.H. Wu and Tan Chee-Beng. Hong Kong: The Chinese University Press, pp. vii–xiii.

Scott, William Henry. 1989. *Filipinos in China before 1500.* Manila: De La Salle University.

Tan Chee-Beng. 2001. "Food and Ethnicity with Reference to the Chinese in Malaysia." In *Changing Chinese Foodways in Asia,* ed. David Y.H. Wu and Tan Chee-Beng. Hong Kong: The Chinese University Press, pp. 125–60.

Websites

<http://www.dimsumndumplings.com.ph/>
<http://www.engbeetin.com/products/>

CHAPTER

6

The Chinese Foodways in Mandalay: Ethnic Interaction, Localization and Identity

Duan Ying

The idiom "the masses regard food as their primacy (民以食為天)" shows the primacy of food in human life. Chinese food and foodways are part and parcel of Chinese civilization and they have a long history (see Anderson 1988; Chang 1977). The Chinese foodways in different places reflect their adaptation to local environment ecologically, economically and socio-culturally. They present different local Chinese identities and cultural diversity and mirror the process of globalization–localization, as well as cultural continuity and transformation in the changing world (Goody 1998: 161–71; Tan 2001; Wu and Cheung 2002).

This chapter[1] will describe Chinese dietary culture in Mandalay. Through food and foodways, we get to see Chinese cultural identity, their social interaction and their integration into the local society. I shall also describe the new role and symbolic meaning of Chinese restaurants in Mandalay. The discussion is based on the data which I had collected in Mandalay from August 2006 to July 2007 when I conducted my anthropological fieldwork.

Mandalay: A Historical and Multiethnic City

Mandalay, the capital of current Mandalay Division, is the second largest city in Burma. Located in the geographic centre of Burma and on the eastern bank of Irrawaddy River, its downtown area is about 25 square-miles. The design of the city is like a chess-board. Streets are crossed at right-angle. As the last capital of Burma dynasty, Mandalay was the political, economic and religious centre of Burma before the British colonial war. There are many historical heritages related to Burmese royalty. Unfortunately, almost all the buildings, except the wall and gate towers of the royal palace, were destroyed during World War II. The current architectures in the palace were restored by the military government according to the original state after 1989. The royal palace is still viewed as a landmark of Mandalay, as well as a tour site. Numerous governmental offices and famous restaurants are located around the palace.

Situated at the transportation hub between upper and lower Burma, Mandalay is a distribution centre for all kinds of goods and materials, such as cloth, wood, rice and so on. Moreover, major airlines operate routes from other major cities to Mandalay, which thus has become a busy city with high mobility in terms of human and capital due to its geographical and transportation facilities.

The population of the city is about 1,000,000,[2] comprising Burmese, Shan, Lisu, Chinese, Indian and other ethnic minorities. About 10 per cent are Chinese, who are either descendants of early migrants who have lived in Mandalay since the nineteenth century or are newcomers from mainland China or the mountainous border areas of upper Burma, who came after Burma's independence. There are four sub-groups of Chinese in Mandalay, based on their different regional origins. According to the 2005 records of Regional Chinese Fellow Associations (雲南同鄉會、福建同鄉會、廣東同鄉會、多省籍同鄉會), of the 45,200 Chinese in Mandalay, 66.4 per cent were Yunnanese, 22.1 per cent were Hokkien, 8.8 per cent were Cantonese and 2.7 per cent were Chinese from other provinces.[3]

Eating At Home and Eating Out

Chinese of different regional origins have their respective cuisine. This is reflected not only in restaurant food but also in homemade food. However, in the case of the Chinese in Mandalay, the home cooking has been localized as a result of their interaction with other ethnic groups. For

The Chinese Foodways in Mandalay 143

example, Yunnanese Chinese, the majority of Chinese in Mandalay, still retain the Yunnan style in their foodways. Some dishes, such as minced pork fried with pickled vegetables (酸菜炒肉), stir-fried potato chips (干焙土豆絲) are still common. Pork is the main source of meat, next to chicken, fish and beef. We can see two common Yunnanese food products, namely Yunnanese ham (雲南火腿) and pickled vegetables (腌菜), in almost every Yunnanese family. Some families import Yunnan ham from the border area between Burma and China. Traditional flavours of Yunnan diet are hot and spicy. In Mandalay, local Yunnanese Chinese perceive sourness as one of the main flavours in Yunnanese diet. Similar to other ethnic Chinese in Southeast Asia, Yunnanese Chinese in Mandalay use lemon instead of vinegar as a sour ingredient. Sour-spicy soup made with chilli, ginger, tamarind (酸角) and vegetables is a common home cooked food in Yunnanese families. Many consider this soup as a traditional Yunnanese diet. However, I have never come across this style of soup in Yunnan, where I come from. When my friends in Mandalay invited me to a Burmese restaurant, I found that the soup served at the restaurant was the so-called Sour-spicy Soup. The only difference was that this soup, served free of charge, has no chilli. Obviously, the Yunnanese in Mandalay have created a local Yunnanese diet that combines local flavour with their dietary tradition.

Cantonese are the third largest Chinese sub-group in Mandalay, and have their regional diets too. However, their home cooked food does not follow the traditional Cantonese cuisine. I did not find such famous Cantonese foods in most families, except roasted meat (叉燒) and roasted goose (燒鵝) bought from Cantonese restaurants. Few local Cantonese have the habit of drinking herbal soup before dinner. The home cooking style of the local Cantonese is similar to that of the local Yunnanese, but without chilli. Many Hokkiens do not cook traditional Fujian cuisine because they are more acculturated than the other sub-groups of Chinese. The young generation are especially influenced by Burmese culture and prefer Burmese food to Chinese food. In fact all local Chinese, including the small minorities from Sichuan, Shanghai, Zhejiang, Jiangsu, Hunan, Hubei and others, are quite accustomed to Yunnanese diets as the Yunnanese are the majority among the local Chinese.

We should note that consuming regional food at home does not mean that the Chinese foodways in Mandalay are simple and static. In fact, they choose from numerous culinary traditions, based on their preference. They may also cook Burmese, Indian and Shan food at home. Most of the Chinese merchants in Mandalay hire domestic servants who are usually Burmese, Shan or Chinese from upper Burma. They are trained to cook Chinese food by their hostess. But they also introduce Burmese and Indian foods to the families they work for. Meanwhile, influenced by their friends and servants, most Chinese women can cook Burmese dishes too. Additionally, people of various ethnic groups prefer bringing their own lunch and share with others in the workplace. Thus, they have many opportunities to taste different diets and share cooking experience and recipes.

There are more than one hundred restaurants in Mandalay, which include Chinese, Burmese, Indian, Thai, Muslim and Western. Most of them are Chinese restaurants, followed by the Burmese. These restaurants are perceived as ordinary except the luxurious ones such as Oriental House, Mandalay Hill Hotel and Golden Duck Restaurant. Indian and Muslim restaurants are mostly located in the neighbourhood of Indian and Muslim communities. Local Chinese occasionally go to Thai and Indian restaurants to have breakfast or dinner in order to taste such dishes as *nan*, yogurt and *Tom Yum Goong* soup (Thai-style sour and hot prawn soup). Non-Muslim Chinese normally do not go to Muslim Chinese restaurants except when they want to taste "authentic" beef dishes cooked in Yunnanese style. As to western cuisines, most teahouses in Mandalay offer coffee, milk tea and various snacks, such as cookies, sandwiches and toasts. High class hotels provide formal western-style dinner, but it is too expensive (around US$20[4] each meal) for the general public.

Most Chinese restaurants are Yunnanese. Common dishes include stir-fried chicken with chilli (辣子雞), sour and spicy soup, pickled vegetables stir-fried minced pork, pickled vegetables stew fish (酸菜魚), braised chicken with ginger, chilli, garlic, anise, *caoguo* (草果) and soy sauce (*huangmen ji* 黃燜雞). Most restaurants have their "specialty," that is, their *zhaopai cai* (招牌菜). For example, *da baopian* (大薄片), which is made of pig's ear, is promoted as a typical local dish in the Yunnanese restaurants run by people from Tengchong, a county in western Yunnan. People of Tengchong origin often go to this restaurant for food and nostalgia. Other Chinese restaurants operated by Cantonese and Hokkien serve their respective cuisine, such as roasted meat and goose in Cantonese restaurants, and thin rice vermicelli with meatball (福建面綫) in Hokkien restaurants. There are fewer Cantonese and Hokkienese restaurants, partly because many Cantonese and Hokkien had re-migrated to China or other countries after the anti-Chinese riot broke out in June 1967.

The Chinese Foodways in Mandalay 145

Although the Chinese restaurants express their uniqueness based on regional differences, each restaurant's menu is rather diverse and flexible. For instance, Cantonese restaurants also serve sour and hot dishes for their Yunnanese customers and Yunnanese restaurants provide dishes with less or even without chilli for customers who do not take chilli. Various locally created braised vegetables dishes are found in almost all Chinese restaurants in Mandalay.

Local Chinese often go to Burmese restaurants, too. Burmese diets have become their daily food as a result of localization. The Burmese cuisine is quite different from that of the Chinese one. It takes more than two hours to prepare a meal. Preparing ingredients from garlic, lemongrass, tomatoes and other spices can take much time. Most of foods are stewed with spices prepared beforehand. Curry is the most important condiment in Burmese cooking. An ordinary dinner consists of curry pork (or chicken, prawn or mutton),[5] stewed potatoes, salted shrimp paste and some raw vegetables such as cabbage and cucumber. There is a special dish of sauce made by mashed tomatoes and chilli for eating raw vegetables. Like the Burmese, the local Chinese use fork and spoon, even fingers, to eat Burmese meal. Of course, no chopsticks are offered at Burmese restaurants. Most Chinese in Mandalay, however, prefer eating Chinese food even though Burmese diets are also common in their daily life. There are too many cold dishes in Burmese food, which is contrary to the Chinese dietary habit.

Food and Its Social Meanings in Ceremonies and Rituals

The diversity of Chinese food in Mandalay, including innovation and local adaptation, is reflected much more clearly in wedding banquets. During my fieldwork in Mandalay, I attended more than ten wedding banquets. Surprisingly almost all of them served the same menu, no matter the newlyweds were Yunnanese, Cantonese, Hokkien, or Chinese of other origins. In the case of intermarriage between Burmese and Chinese, usually a Burmese style tea party is held at noon, followed by a Chinese banquet in the evening. In general, the menu consisted of assorted cold dishes (comprising roasted meats, fried cashew nuts and shelled shrimps), steamed chicken with glutinous rice (糯米雞), braised *trepang* (sea cucumber) with sour and hot flavour, stir-fried gingko nuts, boiled prawn with ginger, garlic and chilli, stewed *zhuzhou* (豬肘 upper part of a pig's leg), bean curd custard soup with dried pickled vegetables (酸菜豆花湯), some stir-fried in-season vegetables, and so on. The menu is designed to satisfy the tastes of different groups of Chinese, thus it has Cantonese roasted meats, Hokkien braised *trepang* with sour and spicy style (酸辣海参), and the bean curd custard soup with dried pickled vegetables associated with the Yunnanese. Adopting various ingredients from different regions and eating sour and hot foods not only reflect the localization and adaptation of the local Chinese, they also reflect the communication and interaction between the different sub-groups of Chinese.

Furthermore, Chinese wedding banquet is a social occasion that reveals status and relations. People are fond of discussing the number of people attending a wedding banquet and the dishes served as well as the expensive ingredients used.[6] Wedding banquet is also a lens to examine people's social capital and relationship. It is worth noting that Chinese wedding banquet has been a sensitive issue between the Burmese and the Chinese. Extravagance at Chinese wedding banquets can incur the envy of the local Burmese, reinforcing ethnic tension between them. On the average, a table of dishes at an elaborate wedding banquet costs about

Wedding banquet at the Yunnanese Association in Mandalay. (Photograph by Duan Ying, February 2007)

The Chinese Foodways in Mandalay 147

60,000–80,000 kyat (US$48–64) nowadays, which is about one month's income of a local office worker. In contrast a table of drinks and disserts at a Burmese wedding tea party normally costs no more than 20,000–30,000 kyat ($16–24). A Chinese wedding banquet usually has at least 50 tables of dishes. However, it is rather difficult to put an end to the luxurious style of Chinese wedding although each regional Chinese association has tried to promote thriftiness to avoid the unnecessary envy of the Burmese. Most local Chinese think that a wedding ceremony is the most important thing in a person's life, and they do not mind to be extravagant. Furthermore, a Chinese wedding involves gift exchange, which reflects the social relations among the local Chinese. It will be a breach of etiquette, which can cause the ridicule of relatives and friends, if a family does not hold proper wedding banquet befitting its social status.

As we have seen, Chinese foodways in Mandalay are diverse. In daily food consumption there is no ethnic barrier or religious taboo for most local Chinese, except for the Chinese Muslims. In general, most local Chinese eat sour and hot dishes, partly because of the influence of the dominant Yunnanese and Burmese environments. However, if we pay attention to the food presented at seasonal rites, the scene is remarkably different from that of everyday life. Food offered to deities and ancestors reflects the respective identity of each Chinese sub-group. I shall now use the example of food offered at Qingming festival by the local Cantonese to illustrate the issue of Chinese identities and localization in Mandalay.

The original meaning of "Qingming" is that the weather would be clear and bright during this period. Qingming festival, which falls in April, lasts for a week and it is the time for memorizing ancestors in Chinese culture. The Chinese usually sweep their ancestors' graves and offer food to both the ancestors and the local deity. At the same time, each regional Chinese association, functioning like a lineage in China, organizes a public ceremony at the cemetery and at the association's headquarters. I was invited to one Qingming ceremony held by the Cantonese Association on 5 April 2007.

A few days before the ceremony, the staff of the Cantonese Association had prepared the offerings, such as paper money, joss-sticks, apples, watermelon, bananas, steamed stuffed buns, eggs, etc. In order to keep the food fresh, *sansheng* (三牲), the three cooked animal sacrifices comprising boiled whole chicken, fried fish and roasted pig (烤全豬), were prepared early in the morning on the day of worship. Chicken and fish were prepared at the Cantonese Association's kitchen while roasted pig was

Qingming rite at the Cantonese Association in Mandalay. (Photograph by Duan Ying, April 2007)

ordered from a local Cantonese restaurant. When I arrived at about 9 a.m. at Renji (仁濟) Temple, where the Cantonese Association was located, Mr Zhu, the secretary of the association, told me that the roasted pig was not ready yet, so everyone had to wait. Mr Tan, the president of the Cantonese Association, told me that "roasted pig is a traditional and important symbol for the Cantonese and a public ritual cannot begin without it."

About half an hour later, the restaurant's waiters delivered the freshly roasted whole pig and placed it on the table inside the office. All members then proceeded to the Cantonese cemetery which is about 10 kilometers away from downtown. We arrived at the cemetery around 10 a.m. Some staff started placing the offerings on the altar in front of the Dabogong public grave (大伯公總墳), while some of the others cleaned the graveyard. Mr Peng, the vice-president of the Cantonese Association, said that Dabogong was the first Cantonese in Mandalay. After his death he was honoured as a local deity that protects all Cantonese in Mandalay. Thus Dabogong was the common ancestor for all the Cantonese in Mandalay.

The Chinese Foodways in Mandalay

The sacrifices were offered to him first. There were two rows of offerings on the altar. Facing the tablet of the public grave, the first row was closest to the tablet and the offerings were arranged from left to right. There were five steamed stuffed buns, a piece of *fagao* (發糕 a Cantonese style rice cake), one grapefruit, a boiled whole chicken, a watermelon and three pairs of chopsticks, each of which was placed beside a small cup of wine. The second row consisted of bananas, five apples, five boiled eggs, fried fish and some cakes. Each food offering was placed on a plate. There were one bottle of wine and three bottles of aerated water between the first and the second row.

The ritual began after the staff had arranged the offerings. With the secretary of the Cantonese Association as the master of ceremony, the president, the vice president, the secretary-general and other executive committee members of the association took turns according to their hierarchy to offer joss-sticks, paper money and a cup of wine to the ancestors, and pray for the protection of all the Cantonese in Mandalay. After that, they brought the offerings to the *wan'an* (萬安) grave which honoured all the deceased Cantonese without descendants. They placed the offerings on the ground in front of the tablet of *wan'an* grave and cleaned the graveyard at the same time. The offerings were placed in three rows. In the first row, there were three pairs of chopsticks, each of which was placed beside a small cup of liquor. Beside the three cups, there was a plate of cigarettes, and three bottles of aerated water were placed behind the three cups. The second row consisted of a piece of *fagao*, five apples, five steamed stuffed buns, fried fish, a boiled whole chicken, five boiled eggs and two pieces of cake arranged from left to right. The third row comprised five steamed stuffed buns, one watermelon, and some bananas from left to right. The process of ritual resembled the one performed for Dabogong. The only difference was that the association leaders prayed to these wild ghosts not to harm the living. After the ritual, they shredded the piece of *fagao* and threw them around the graveyard. Such action was perceived as delivering offerings to the wild ghosts.

After a short break at the cemetery's pavilion, Mr Tan called the association leaders in charge of the cemetery affairs together to discuss issues pertaining to the management of the cemetery. Soon after, they returned to Renji Temple. The staff started to arrange a sacrificial altar, a round table, in front of the association. Roasted pig, boiled chicken and fried fish were put on a big rectangular tray and placed at the centre of the altar as *sansheng*. Facing the altar, the first row was a small censer with two joss-sticks. Once again there were three cups of wine with a pair of chopsticks next to each cup in the second row. The third row consisted of the big tray with *sansheng*. On the right side of the tray, there were five apples, five steamed stuffed buns and one watermelon. On the left of the tray, there were a piece of *fagao*, five steamed stuffed buns, bananas and some pieces of cake. The leaders of the association performed the similar rite as they had done at the cemetery. All rituals ended after Mr Tan symbolically cut the roasted pig. The staff then cut it to pieces and separated them into numerous portions. All members who took part in the rite were entitled to a portion. They usually took home this together with other offerings. I was told that these foods could bless and protect their family and descendants.

The secretary of the Cantonese Association told me that variations in offerings did not matter as long as there were *sansheng*, a censer, cups of wine and chopsticks; these formed the most basic offerings at the ritual. In daily life the Chinese in Mandalay may use forks and spoons and sometimes even fingers to eat, they may also drink whiskey, rum and other wine imported from Europe and Singapore. However, during the Qingming festival, chopsticks and Chinese liquor must be used for offering. This practice shows the respect to ancestors and the linkage to the past. Thus the ritual reinforces the Chinese cultural tradition and identity. *Sansheng* were placed at the centre as the primary and most important sacrifices. Other offerings, such as fruits and cakes, could be arranged randomly. Interestingly, the roasted pig was absent at the ritual performed at the cemetery due to a local belief. Mr Zhu, the vice-president of Cantonese Association, explained:

> Actually, we offered roasted pig at the cemetery before. However, right after the ritual, several Cantonese in Mandalay were killed in accidents. We went to a Burmese Buddhist temple and asked an eminent monk why such bad things happened. The monk told us that offering roasted pig was in conflict with the belief of the deity of that particular mountain because he did not eat pork. To avoid such unfortunate events, we decided that we would no longer offer roasted pig at the cemetery; we offered it only at the Cantonese Association.

No doubt not offering roasted pig at the cemetery was in indication of integration to the local society. At the same time, the use of regional foods reflected Chinese cultural characteristics and reinforced sub-group identities. Although I did not have the chance to attend all rituals held by different regional associations during the Qingming festival because of

The Chinese Foodways in Mandalay   151

the over-lapping schedule, I obtained similar description about offerings from some Hokkien and Yunnanese informants. They used typical regional foods as offerings for their ancestors, such as thin rice noodle with seafood and pastries in the case of the Hokkien, and bean-starch noodle in the case of the Yunnanese. This was also true for the other traditional Chinese festivals, such as the Lunar New Year and the ghost festival. Food in the context of offering connects the past and the present, and between the old and the young generations.

Restaurants, Taste and Public Space

There are three categories of Chinese restaurants in Mandalay, namely, the luxurious and famous ones, ordinary ones and those operated by hawkers. Most owners of famous restaurants belong to the second or third generation Chinese who have lived in Mandalay for a long time. These restaurants are old and famous, referred to as *laozihao* (老字號). They have good business, and many owners no longer participate in the daily management, relying on hired managers. They may have other business to run. Most owners of the ordinary restaurants came from other states, such as the Shan state. They migrated to Mandalay no more than one or two decades ago. Running a restaurant is a good choice for them because of the stable income. However, many owners plan to engage in other business after they have accumulated sufficient capital, as running a restaurant is extremely hard work. Most hawkers came from the border or the mountain areas, and most of them still do not have legal status. They usually sell snacks, such as *tangyuan* (湯圓 glutinous rice balls), fried noodle, rice noodle, fried potato chips and sausages at the local market and night plaza to make a living. They may begin to run a snack bar when they have enough money, or take over an ordinary restaurant.

In Mandalay, the well-off Chinese usually go to the Oriental House (東方屋), a luxurious Chinese restaurant, to have Chinese breakfast (*zaocha* 早茶). The breakfast menu consists of more than 20 dim sum, such as *siumai* (燒賣), steamed shrimp dumpling, barbecued pork bun (叉燒包), glutinous rice ball with fillings (湯圓), chicken feet, and so on. I had a breakfast at the Oriental House once. The taste of dim sum was not bad, but it can hardly be compare to the delicious dim sum I had in Hong Kong. I tried five kinds of dim sum and tea, which cost me 3,000 kyat ($2.4), about equal to an office worker's daily income. There are a few luxurious restaurants located around the royal lake in a suburban area in

Mandalay. Five of my friends and I had dinner at the Royal Restaurant there, and the total cost was 38,000 kyat ($30.4). The taste of the dishes was good, but not worth that high price. However, the restaurant's interior decoration and the surrounding scenery were exquisite and beautiful. As Bourdieu has discussed, the more luxurious food's consumption one goes, the more one's taste tends to be aesthetic and formalist (Bourdieu 1984: 196–7). I asked the manager why people would spend money in such an expensive place. He told me that most customers there were Chinese merchants and Burmese senior officers. They usually discussed business affairs during dinner. They were more concerned about the setting and service than the prices. Eating at luxurious restaurants here thus implies a sort of distinction, and Chinese petty capitalists' consumption at these restaurants is not just to taste delicacy, but also to exhibit status, superiority and power.

Besides dinner, drinking coffee, milk tea and fruit juice at teashops is also very popular in Mandalay. Most people in Burma have the habit of having afternoon tea; this might be a legacy of British colonialism. One day, a Chinese friend asked me whether I had tasted the Laomian Tea (老緬茶), Burmese-style tea. He brought me to a teashop. To me, Laomian Tea is quite similar to the milk tea at the tea cafe (茶餐廳) in Hong Kong. The only difference is that the Burmese waitress would offer a cup of free green tea afterwards so that customers can keep on chatting at the teashop. There are various desserts served in teashops, such as cookies, puddings, Indian *nan*, coconut jellies and banana cake, etc. The prices of drinks and snacks at teashops are relatively cheap; a cup of coffee or milk tea costs only 300 kyat ($0.24). Teashop has become a public space where different kinds of people gather and chat as well as exchange information. Friends, colleagues, neighbours and relatives usually spend their leisure time at the teashops after work. Although there is an unspoken rule that people should not talk about Aung San Suu Kyi and political issues at teashops, rumours about military dictatorship often emerge and spread from there (Tosa 2005: 156–7). People know that there are some senior government and military officials as well as secret agents at teashops; some are there to watch out for public opinion. Thus, when people criticize military despotism, they usually use some metaphors which only the members of their circle of friends can understand. This kind of public space has recently extended to the Chinese hot-pot restaurant, where people may spend more than two hours eating, drinking beers, just like at teashops. People get together there and discuss many issues, such as news, literature, government planning, religion, lottery, rumours, folklore, legends, and so on. Teashops and Chinese hot-pot restaurants thus become a kind of social space for articulating cultural politics.

If we compare the scenarios at the luxurious restaurants and those at the teashops, the former are formal, well mannered, elegant and punctilious, whereas the latter are informal, flexible and noisy. This shows that the different way of consuming food expresses the different meanings of life. Although there is no ethnic and religious boundaries on food and foodways in Mandalay, where to eat and what to eat is influenced by social class, economic status and power. In some sense, people make the distinction with others based on the food consumption. Hence, these contrastive scenes and rhetoric at the two distinct places represent the social lives of people in the different hierarchies and relationship between economy and power, and also indicate the imbalance and polarization in contemporary Burmese society.

Conclusion

Overall, this chapter shows the diversity of Chinese food and foodways in Mandalay, and explores how people, environment and culture can be integrated meaningfully. We are what we eat, and foodways link our identity and everyday life together (see Mintz 1986: 187–214). Food and foodways in Mandalay tell us a lot about the Chinese there, including localization, integration, ethnic interaction, social relations, economy, power, and so on. We have also seen that food as a symbol of historical memories and collective representation plays an important role in the year-round rituals. Special regional foods offered at rituals reinforce the cultural consciousness and identity of Chinese sub-groups. At the same time certain places of eating, especially tea houses and hot-pot restaurants, have become places of gathering where the Chinese can exchange information and indeed practise cultural politics, exchanging views about their fate in a country dictated by a military regime.

Notes

1. This study was supported by China Postdoctoral Science Foundation (Grant No. 20100480812). I would like to thank Dr. Wang Danning for reading this article. I am also grateful to Prof. Tan Chee-Beng for his suggestions and encouragement.
2. <http://mandalay.china-consulate.org/chn/mbly/mandalay/t214249.htm>.

3. The number 45,200 refers to those people who have registered at their respective speech group associations. The actual population of Chinese is higher as some people do not register at the associations or do not know how to do it.
4. US$1=1,250 kyat.
5. Beef is not offered in almost all Burmese restaurants because most Burmese are Buddhists.
6. The wedding season begins in early October, after the Thidingyut Festival of Lights, and ends around the Chinese Spring Festival. It is unacceptable to marry during the period of Buddhist Lent according to Theravada Buddhism custom. The Buddhist Lent starts on the first day of the waning moon of the eighth lunar month. It covers a good part of the rainy season and lasts three lunar months. The tradition of Buddhist Lent can be traced back to the early period of Buddhism in ancient India when the holy men, mendicants and sages spent three months of the annual rainy season in dwellings. They avoided unnecessary travel during the period when crops were still new for fear they might accidentally step on young plants. Hence, Buddha decreed that his followers should also abide by this ancient tradition (Maung 2000: 61–3). Most Burmese Buddhists to this day abide by this tradition and avoid holding public activities (such as wedding) during this period; so do the local Chinese, in deference to the local custom.

References

Anderson, E.N. 1988. *The Food of China.* New Haven: Yale University Press.

Anderson, E.N. and Marja L. Anderson. 1977. "Modern China: South." In *Food in Chinese Culture: Anthropological and Historical Perspectives,* ed. K.C. Chang. New Haven and London: Yale University Press, pp. 317–83.

Bourdieu, Pierre. 1984. *Distinction: A Social Critique of the Judgement of Taste,* translated by Richard Nice. London: Routledge & K. Paul.

Chang K.C., ed. 1977. *Food in Chinese Culture: Anthropological and Historical Perspectives.* New Haven and London: Yale University Press.

Goody, Jack. 1998. *Food and Love: A Cultural History of East and West.* London, New York: Verso.

Maung, Kyaa Nyo. 2000. *Presenting Myanmar.* Yangon: Today Publishing House.

Mintz, Sidney W. 1986. *Sweetness and Power: The Place of Sugar in Modern History.* New York: Penguin Books.

———. 2002. "Foreword: Food for Thought." In *The Globalization of Chinese Food,* ed. David Y.H. Wu and Sidney C.H. Cheung. Honolulu: University of Hawaii Press, pp. xii–xx.

Tan Chee-Beng. 2001. "Food and Ethnicity with Reference to the Chinese in Malaysia." In *Changing Chinese Foodways in Asia*, ed. David Y.H. Wu and Tan Chee-Beng. Hong Kong: The Chinese University Press, pp. 125–60.

Tosa, Keiko. 2005. "The Chicken and the Scorpion: Rumor, Counternarratives, and the Political Uses of Buddhism." In *Burma at the Turn of 21st Century*, ed. Monique Skidmore. Honolulu: University of Hawaii Press, pp. 154–74.

Wu Y.H., David and Sidney C.H. Cheung. 2002. "The Globalization of Chinese Food and Cuisine: Markers and Breakers of Cultural Barriers." In *The Globalization of Chinese Food*, ed. David Y.H. Wu and Sidney C.H. Cheung. Honolulu: University of Hawaii Press, pp. 1–19.

CHAPTER

7

Banh Cuon and *Cheung Fan*: Searching for the Identity of the "Steamed Rice-flour Roll"

Chan Yuk Wah

Introduction

Banh cuon (rice-sheet roll) has been my favourite breakfast dish after spending an extended time in Vietnam from 2000 to 2003. As a person who had often eaten *cheung fan* (肠粉) while growing up in Hong Kong, I found *banh cuon* triggered many childhood memories. Eating *banh cuon* in Vietnam helped cure me of my homesickness. To me, *banh cuon* looks like a variant of *cheung fan*. It was later that I became more curious about the origin of *banh cuon* and began to suspect that *banh cuon* actually originated from China and might be a Vietnamese version of *cheung fan*. Is *banh cuon* a dish imported from China? Is it a result of Vietnamese localization of *cheung fan*? As I became more serious about looking into the identities of two of my favourite snacks, I also took on a journey, exploring the Cantonese and Vietnamese cultural identity *vis-à-vis* the so-called "Chinese cultural identity." I began to record my experiences of eating *banh cuon* and *cheung fan* and observing the ways of making *banh cuon* in Vietnam and making *cheung fan* in Hong Kong, Guangzhou and

Searching for the Identity of the "Steamed Rice-flour Roll"

Macau. I have also talked to people who have made as well as eaten *banh cuon* and *cheung fan*.

This chapter attempts to look into the relationship between Vietnamese and Cantonese cultural identities through two breakfast dishes, *banh cuon* and *cheung fan*. No one will refute the fact that much of the Vietnamese culture reflects its roots in Chinese culture. In order to disentangle Vietnamese culture from its sinicized components, many experts in Vietnamese studies have attempted to highlight local Vietnamese traditions and its Southeast Asian characteristics. However this has led to the creation of an imaginary "unified" Chinese culture and neglected many local traditions within the geographical boundary of China which is similar to those of Vietnam.

In terms of food culture, Vietnamese foodways share a number of common features with foodways in China, especially southeast China. However, since China and Vietnam are two separate countries, people tend to draw cultural boundaries in line with national boundaries. In the process of searching for the origins of *banh cuon* and *cheung fan*, I see the problem of drawing cultural boundaries like this. Instead of identifying *cheung fan* as a Chinese food and *banh cuon* as Vietnamese, I argue that *cheung fan* and *banh cuon* are two local traditions of one dish type, the "steamed rice-flour roll." This chapter seeks to redraw the cultural boundaries between Vietnam and the Cantonese region of China and retrieve the historical *Yueh*,[1] the cultural origin of both the Cantonese and the Vietnamese; both have a predominantly rice economy and are experts in the use of rice as food.

Food, Identity, Memory and Tradition

Despite the fact that food and foodways often bear claims to be a part of tradition, food culture, as with culture in general, is never static, but changes constantly. Rao (1986) has studied changing dietary styles and food behaviour among the migrants in India, and he calls these changes "gastrodynamics." Traditional anthropology on food has been keen in exploring the metaphoric meanings of food and food taboos (Levi-Strauss 1969; Douglas 1970). However, much of the burgeoning contemporary anthropology literature on food examines the relationship between food and identity (Scholliers 2001; Wu and Cheung 2002; Watson and Caldwell 2005; Gabbacia 1998) and its changes in the processes of globalization

(Wu and Tan 2001; Phillips 2006; Watson 1997; Roberts 2002; Mintz and Du Bois 2002).

Food is also used for sustaining national and ideological orders. Appadurai (2008) sees contemporary cookbooks in India as a system of class hierarchies in literate civilizations. He argues that the production of new cookbooks has assisted the urban middle class to distinguish regional and ethnic specialization within an overarching national cuisine. Allison (2008) reveals how Japanese mothers' preparation of lunchbox (*obento*) for children conveys deep ideological meanings. By preparing lunchboxes for children and training them to finish all the food in the lunchbox at nursery schools, Japanese mothers help reassert the cultural and aesthetic apparatus of the state and uphold the state's authority and disciplines (Allison 2008).

Although food plays an important role in shaping individuals' cultural, ethnic and national identity, food is at the same time one form of institution that can easily break and transcend cultural barriers. As Watson and Caldwell (2005: 5) observe, "When all fails people will always talk about food." Tan Chee-Beng also asserts this: "Food plays a significant part in ethnic relations. While people may quarrel over ethnic issues, other people's foods are usually adopted or consumed without any problem if they are tasty or good" (see Introduction in this book).

Thus food culture is relevant for asserting cultural identity and ethnic heritage, and it is flexible enough for boundary crossing. One major reason for this lies in the fact that food is essentially a bodily experience. Food is a bodily experience while identity is a mental construct. It is exactly because of this bodily experience of physical enjoyment that the mental construct of "barriers" can be taken away when bodily hedonism prevails.

The relationship between food and identity also has a lot to do with *food memory*. We are what we eat; and we are what we remember what we have eaten. Food memory is less explored by anthropologists, while a large number of literary writings have dealt with narratives of food nostalgia. Holtzman (2006) summarizes food memories into a few typological categories, namely, food as sensuous bodily memory, food as informing ethnic and national identity, food as gastronomic memory of diaspora, food as a marker of social transformation and gender relationships, and food in rituals. Sutton (2001) in his book on memory and food argues that the sensuality of food makes it an overpowering medium for memory. The taste and smell of food easily trigger recollection of past experiences, especially physical experiences. "Bodily memory" is a theme elaborated

Searching for the Identity of the "Steamed Rice-flour Roll" 159

by Connerton (1989) and Lupton (1996). Thomas (2004) also points out that what most easily evokes the emotion of the diasporic migrants is the absence of homemade food.

Food is the embodied experiences of taste and smell. It most easily links us back to situations, events and childhood memories. Thus, nothing is closer to our "embodied" cultural identity than the way we eat. Taste, texture and flavour trigger the senses of taste and smell in the body which further arouse other physical and mental memories.

This chapter examines two varieties of a dish, "steamed rice-flour roll," one from Vietnam, and the other from Guangdong. Through a study of the history of the food and the memories of making and eating it, the chapter attempts to reconsider the boundary between these two foods and the culture of Vietnam and China.

Banh Cuon and *Cheung Fan*: "Rice-flour Roll" Brothers?

Nobody really knows when the Vietnamese started eating *banh cuon*. Known as a light dish traditionally eaten as breakfast, it is sometimes mentioned offhand in novels and television dramas. Some Vietnamese told me that their great grandparents in the second half of the nineteenth century used to eat *banh cuon* as well. That means *banh cuon*, as a breakfast dish, has existed for at least one and a half centuries.

Banh cuon is a steamed rice-flour roll made from rice solution cooked over a steamer mounted with a piece of muslin. The rice solution is spooned evenly onto the muslin and then covered with the steamer lid to allow it to solidify into a white sheet. After it is cooked, the *banh cuon* maker will take the extremely thin rice-sheet out either with their bare hands or with the help of a bamboo stick and place it on an oily surface. She then sprinkles minced meat and chopped mushrooms onto the sheet, and rolls it up.[2] *Banh cuon* is eaten with preserved Vietnamese sausages and Vietnamese herbs as side dishes and is dipped in garlic vinegar sauce or fish sauce.

Banh cuon's counterpart in the Cantonese region[3] of China is *cheung fan*, or *jyu cheung fan*. *Cheung* literally means "intestine" and *fan* "rice noodle." The name *cheung fan* came from the shape of the roll, since the rice sheet is wrapped into a roll like the intestine of a pig. The name *jyu cheung fan* is particularly revealing as *jyu* is the Cantonese word for "pig." While *jyu cheung fan* mainly refers to plain *cheung fan*, *cheung fan* includes different types of rolls with different fillings such as shrimp, roast pork

A woman in Ho Chi Minh City making *banh cuon*. (Photograph by Duong Rach Sanh, 16 May 2011)

A *banh cuon* dish. (Photograph by Duong Rach Sanh, 16 May 2011)

Searching for the Identity of the "Steamed Rice-flour Roll"

and beef. There is no formal record detailing the history of *cheung fan*. Cookery books usually say that it has been a popular snack in Guangzhou since the 1930s. Ouyang (2007: 134) writes:

> *Cheung fun*, other names for it include *gyun fan* and *jyu cheung fan*. This is because its shape is like a pig's intestine. People in Guangzhou also call it *laai cheung*. It was created by the Hoh Sing Teahouse in the district of Buhn Tohng, Guangzhou while the Chinese were fighting the Japanese. Today, it is one of the most popular snacks provided by snack shops, teahouses, tea restaurants, and hotels. The most famous *cheung fan* place in Guangzhou is the Ngahn Gei on Mahncheung Road. Before China's liberation, it was run by Ngh Ngahn whose skill was imparted by a famous cook. Her most famous *cheung fan* dish was beef *cheung fan* in supreme soy sauce dip. Her *cheung fan* was famous because it was thin, chewy, smooth, and had a special flavour.[4]

Today, the Ngahn Gei *cheung fan* shop has developed into a chain restaurant in Guangzhou run by different companies. Only the oldest shop situated on Mahncheung Street belongs to Ngh Ngahn's family and is run by Ngh's daughter. Chinese and foreign tourists alike crowd into the shop for a taste of traditional *cheung fan*.

In another cookbook, Xu (1998) suggests that *jyu cheung fan* was actually a street snack sold by mobile hawkers in the 1930s. But it was later picked up by restaurants and became famous and new varieties were added, such as the shrimp roll, beef roll and roast pork roll (Xu 1998: preface).

Cheung fan, like *banh cuon*, is made from rice solution which is steamed into a sheet. The traditional way of making *cheung fan* begins with lining the steamer with a piece of wet muslin. The cook then spreads the rice solution on the muslin, and covers it with the lid to let it steam for three to five minutes. After it turns into a rice sheet, it is taken out together with the muslin and turned upside down. The cook then removes the muslin by pulling it off from the rice sheet (see Xu 1998: 26). It is because of this "pulling" procedure that local people in Guangzhou nickname the dish as "*laai cheung*" (*laai* in Cantonese means "pull"). Today, not many *cheung fan* shops still make *cheung fan* in the traditional way. Instead, many have turned to modern steamers which do not require wet muslin to make the rice sheet.

Compared to *banh cuon*, the rice sheet of *cheung fan* is thicker and bigger in size. One experienced *cheung fan* maker in Hong Kong said that if the rice sheet is too thin, it is too hard to pull off the muslin. Both *cheung fan* and *banh cuon* are rolled with fillings. *Cheung fan* is bigger in size and has a larger meat filling while *banh cuon* is smaller and filled with minced meat and mushrooms. The ricesheet of *banh cuon* is thinner and is dipped in a sauce mixed with vinegar, fish sauce and chopped garlic and turnip before eating. *Cheung fan* on the other hand is dipped in soy sauce.

Although *cheung fan* and *jyu cheung fan* are best known as a breakfast dish, teahouses in Hong Kong and Guangzhou sell this as one popular type of dim sum (snack). Many people in Guangzhou also like to eat *cheung fan* at night in *cheung fan* shops as *siu yeh*, night-time supper. *Banh cuon* on the other hand is mainly eaten for breakfast. Good *banh cuon* must be soft while good *cheung fan* should be smooth.

Is *Banh Cuon* Chinese? Is *Cheung Fan* Vietnamese?

In the process of researching the identities of the two snacks, I have found that specific dishes often convey specific past meanings. The two rice-sheet rolls discussed in this chapter are two similar street snacks, and both are made from rice solution steamed into a rice sheet, and both are still eaten as a breakfast dish. *Cheung fan* often provokes nostalgia from Hong Kong people since it was once sold on street corners by hawkers pushing trolleys piled high with steamers.[5] After these mobile hawkers were banned by the government, buying *cheung fan* on street corners became a thing of the past.

Having learned how the Vietnamese have incorporated Chinese culture into their own culture throughout their history, and having supposed that the Chinese possess much more sophisticated cooking skills, I previously suspected that *banh cuon* might have been a Chinese import. That was why I used to introduce it to my Hong Kong friends as *yuht naam cheung fan* (Vietnamese *cheung fan*). I asked a number of elderly *banh cuon* makers: "Is *banh cuon* a copy of Chinese *cheung fan*?" "Was it imported from Guangdong or Guangxi?" Taking an ethnocentric view, I was like many others who take it for granted that anything in Vietnam which looks like something found in China may probably be a Chinese import.

I have never thought of the possibility of the reverse situation until I started to appreciate how sophisticated the Vietnamese are in making rice snacks — they have a vast array of rice cakes and dumplings. The steamed rice-sheet roll as a snack has existed for a long time in Vietnam. While I heard informants saying that *banh cuon* first appeared as early as

Searching for the Identity of the "Steamed Rice-flour Roll"

the mid-nineteenth century, I have yet to find evidence that says *cheung fan* is over a century old. Cantonese traders had been trading and doing business with the Vietnamese for many centuries. It is highly probable that such a dish could have been brought by traders to Guangzhou, where local people modified it into something slightly different, *jyu cheung fan* and then *cheung fan*. The Chinese version of *banh cuon* became a thicker and tougher rice-sheet roll.

This new version of *cheung fan*'s origins may offend many Chinese, who may find it hard to entertain the idea that such a popular local snack (full of nostalgic memories) could be a foreign import. While I put the question "whether *banh cuon* is originally a Vietnamese or Chinese dish" to an experienced *banh cuon* maker, who has Vietnamese and Chinese parents and learned how to make *banh cuon* from her Vietnamese mother in the 1960s, she answered as follows:

> There is no book talking about this. This is something pass down from the past through generations. This is developed by the skill of the people here, both Vietnamese and Chinese.

One problem in the manner I compare the two snacks previously lies in the way I distinguish between the Vietnamese and Chinese cultures. I have taken it for granted that things from places we call China today belong to the category of "Chinese culture," while those within the national boundaries of Vietnam belong to "Vietnamese culture." It is problematic to try to distinguish Chinese and Vietnamese cultures within today's national boundaries as this assumes both cultures are distinct entities physically enclosed within specific national territories.

Sinicized Vietnamese Culture and Vietnamese Local Traditions

From an ethnocentric view of a Chinese person, it is tempting to say that *banh cuon* is just a variety of Chinese (actually Cantonese) traditional rice-sheet roll. After tasting *banh cuon* and *cheung fan* in many different places and trying to rearticulate the history of both dishes, I began to doubt if there is a formal answer for the origin of this dish. Instead of seeing them as two different dishes belonging to two different cultures, I would rather see them as local variations of the same dish.

It is acknowledged that Vietnamese culture has long been Sinicized. A portion of present-day northern Vietnam was under Chinese direct control for ten centuries (111 BC to AD 939). In AD 939, a Vietnamese general, Ngo Quyen, defeated Chinese troops and proclaimed kingship. Many historians take this as the end of Chinese rule in Vietnam and the beginning of an independent Vietnam.[6] However, independence did not hinder Vietnam from taking in Chinese cultural models. In the following centuries, Vietnam was under China's overall cultural influence. It imported China's court rituals and court ideologies, as well as Confucian tradition. Woodside (1971: 7) has pointed out, "Vietnamese people were sinicized centuries before Chinese culture had even been definitely consolidated in areas that are today considered part of China proper." For example, the Vietnamese elite incorporated the Confucian gentry and lineage system much earlier than the Cantonese in Guangdong. David Faure (1996) has written about the "acculturation" process of the Cantonese. He suggests that it was not until Ming times that Cantonese lineage families began to acculturate themselves into the larger Confucian cultural system of imperial China.

Though acknowledging the deep sinicization of Vietnamese culture, many scholars have paid much effort to disentangle Vietnamese culture from Chinese culture in order to "rescue" Vietnam from being "overshadowed" by China. This is mainly done by highlighting the local traditions of Vietnam and by identifying the so-called Southeast Asian characteristics within Vietnamese culture. As Woodside (1971: 1) argues, "One of the arts of Vietnamese studies lies in being able artificially to disentangle the Chinese or Sino-Vietnamese characteristics of Vietnamese history and society from the Southeast Asian characteristics." For example, some argue that Vietnamese culture has followed general Southeast Asian traditions and allows a higher status of women (O'Harrow 1995). Others stress that Vietnamese culture has incorporated hybrid cultural attributes drawn from the Chams and the Khmers (Wolters 1999: 22). The local tradition of *nom* words ("southern characters") and *nom* literature has also been used to illustrate Vietnam's cultural distinctiveness (Nguyen 1987).[7]

This way of arguing for the distinctiveness of Vietnamese culture is problematic since it assumes a static and unified Chinese culture with which to contrast Vietnam. As argued by Evans (2002), "The efforts in bestowing Vietnam with a distinctive local culture different from that of China inevitably assumes a counter object of a static and unified Chinese culture ... the counterposition of a hybrid Vietnam to an allegedly pure 'China' becomes less and less convincing" (2002: 154).

Searching for the Identity of the "Steamed Rice-flour Roll"

Local Traditions in China

This way of arguing for Vietnamese distinctiveness ignores the fact that many places in China carry very local traditions, too. Guangdong, a place in the far south, hosts many local traditions, especially in their foodways, which are distinguishable from central and northern China. Within the Chinese study of culture and religion, there has been a continuing effort to explore the local traditions of different areas in China so that a re-examination of "Chinese culture" is possible. This effort has reflected on the traditional scholarly assumption of a unified Chinese culture (see, for example, Liu and Faure 1996). Through examining the case of the Hmong (Miao) of Gongxian in Southwest China, Tapp (1996) argues for a specific notion of ethnicity and a local culture different from that of the Han Chinese culture. Ching (1996) also writes about the unique Guangdong culture by examining vernacular Cantonese literature and song lyrics.

The argument for "Southeast Asian" characteristics embedded in Vietnamese culture also assumes that within China's borders, there is no such cultural attributes. Chinese places that are close to mainland Southeast Asia or that are close to the coastal region (which allows more contact through sea voyages) actually have throughout history entertained shared cultures. For example, in southwest China, Yunnan province is home to many ethnic groups who have been living side by side with other ethnic groups which are also found in Southeast Asia. They either shared the same ancestral traditions or had similar ways of life (Fan 1999; Zhang 1999). Furthermore, what does "Southeast Asia" mean anyway? Emmerson (1984) has elaborated on the constructed notion of the term "Southeast Asia" since the term made its appearance. Rather than representing a unified and homogenous entity, Emmerson argues that it should be seen as a product of a constructive process through diplomatic policies, historical events and world politics.

To me, one acute problem in this argument about culture is the tendency to line cultural boundaries with geographical national boundaries as if culture stops at border checkpoints. If national borders shift, should cultures change identity too? In my past experiences in Vietnam, I was amazed to learn that many of those practices claimed by both Vietnamese scholars as well as laypeople to be distinguishingly Vietnamese appeared to me very "Chinese" too. As a person growing up in a Cantonese culture and having Chaozhou[8] parents, I particularly feel at home when experiencing

Vietnamese local foodways. For example, despite the fact that *nuoc man* (fish sauce) is seen to be typically and prevalently a Vietnamese tradition, I grew up in a home in which my mother put fish sauce in almost every dish that she cooked. Fish sauce is also used more than soy sauce in Fuzhou, Fujian (Simoons 1991: 349; Anderson 1988: 143, 164). Other fermented fish products also have had a long history in south-eastern China (Simoons 1991: 349). Another typical Vietnamese flavouring, fermented shrimp paste, is also popularly produced and consumed by Chinese in the far south, including many coastal people living in Hong Kong.

Selling Vietnamese rice noodle and cakes in Hanoi. (Photograph by Duong Rach Sanh, 16 May 2011)

Re-establishing the *Yueh* Cultural Area

In order to establish more refined cultural comparisons between the so-called Chinese and Vietnamese cultures, we need to first eliminate the rigid concept of classifying cultural boundaries along national boundaries. We need to "downsize" China in order to know what exactly we are comparing. Within China, there are a number of different cultural areas. In terms

Searching for the Identity of the "Steamed Rice-flour Roll"

of food culture, Simoons (1991: 45) classifies Chinese cuisine into four regional types: northern, eastern, western and southern. The eastern region, unlike the northern region, plays a major role in China's rice economy and culture. While northerners rely on wheat as their staple food, southerners depend on rice (Simoons 1991: 65–7). Wheat is made into all sorts of noodles and wheat pastry. Rice can be eaten in the form of steamed rice and various sorts of rice noodles. Thus, there is a common saying in the Chinese language: "the northerners' diet is mainly noodle-based while the southerners' is rice-based."[9] In Vietnam, there is a similar idiom: "Chinese eat noodles, Vietnamese eat rice noodles."[10] This idiom stresses the fact that Chinese mainly eat noodles made from wheat while Vietnamese eat noodles made from rice. The Vietnamese are actually contrasting themselves with the Chinese in a way similar to how the Chinese southerners contrast themselves with the northerners. In this sense, the Vietnamese and the southern Chinese are of "one" culture (contrasting to that of the northern Chinese) as they both live in rice-cultivating regions.

Besides being predominantly a rice culture, the Vietnamese as well as the southern Chinese regions historically belong to the *Yueh/Viet* culture. A large part of the southern part of China including Zhejiang, Fujian, Guangdong and part of Guangxi is called the "land of the hundred *Yueh* (*Viet*)." However, cultures in these areas are today rarely considered in the *Yueh* cultural context. As pointed out by Simoons, there is "scanty reference to what the *Yueh* contributions to Cantonese cuisine might have been, or indeed to the more general question of the evolution of Cantonese cuisine" (1991: 54). He also states that Cantonese cookery, in Tang and Song times, was not recognized as a cuisine of distinction and thus not worthy of consideration. Even during Ming times, there seemed to have no awareness of a distinctive Cantonese-cooking style. The land and culture of the *Yueh* were far too remote and barbarian to deserve attention from central China; this is also why records are so scanty.

Today, Cantonese culture is largely seen as a member of the big family of Chinese culture. Cantonese cuisine has surely become an important component of Chinese foodways, and it is not considered in the context of *Yueh* culture, which can include large parts of southern China and part of northern Vietnam. As this *Yueh* origin has been taken away, Vietnamese (food) culture is separated from Cantonese (food) culture, and they fall into the national orbits of the Vietnamese and Chinese states. By pushing *Viet* (Vietnam) and *Yueh* (Cantonese) cultures back to the limits of the geographical boundaries of Vietnam and China, we somehow artificially create a (national) boundary between cultures which actually share many similarities and a common origin.

Conclusion: The Rice-flour Roll in Rice Economies and Cultures

Cultures do not stop at border crossings. The local food cultures of the Cantonese and Vietnamese may share a lot of similarities since they are both predominantly rice cultures with similar climatic conditions. By unveiling the misconceptions of classifying cultures according to national boundaries and by redrawing cultural areas, I begin to see *banh cuon* and *cheung fan*, my two favourite breakfast dishes, not as popular dishes belonging to two different cultures, but two varieties of one typical dish, the rice-sheet roll, which is an embodiment of a rice-based economy and culture. It does not matter who, Cantonese or Vietnamese, first "invented" the rice-sheet roll. Both cultures are experts in making rice-sheet, and thus rice noodle and rice roll.

Both the Cantonese and the Vietnamese could have been the originators of the rice-sheet roll. Both peoples share *Yueh/Viet* traditions and are experts in eating rice and making rice food products and dishes. They have invented foodways that fit local habits and suit local needs. This research has delved into the two similar snack dishes of the Cantonese areas and Vietnam and has re-examined the habitual way of linking cultural boundaries to national boundaries. It calls for "downsizing" China from one monolithic entity when we start to compare cultural practices between China and Vietnam.

Notes

1. *Yueh* refers to the ancient cultures and peoples in southern China and northern Vietnam. It appears as *Yue* in Chinese Pinyin system, as *yuht* in Yale Cantonese system, and as *Viet* in Vietnamese.
2. In Vietnam, I have only encountered female *banh cuon* maker. I have never seen men making *banh cuon.*
3. Cantonese areas mean areas where the residents speak Cantonese. These include most places in Guangdong, Macau and Hong Kong.
4. Names of person, shop and street in this paragraph are translated in the Yale system of Cantonese.
5. A number of popular Hong Kong writers have described such scenes in their essay writing (see, for examples, Li 1988: 95).

Searching for the Identity of the "Steamed Rice-flour Roll" 169

6. Vietnamese and Western scholars tend to see this time as the birth of an independent Vietnam while views of Chinese scholars vary.
7. *Chu nom* (southern characters) appeared in Vietnam around the eleventh century as a native script or demotic system of writing. It involves combinations of Han characters to create new words. It was used in private documents, deeds and contracts, as well as in popular literature such as poetry and verses, until its demise in the early twentieth century (Nguyen 1987: 22).
8. Chaozhou is a part of Guangdong province. It often appears as "Teochiu" in academic literature.
9. In Chinese Pinyin, the line appears as "*bei fang ren yi mian shi wei zhu, nan fang ren yi mi shi wei zhu*" (北方人以麵食為主，南方人以米食為主). A simpler version is "*nan mi bei mian*" (南米北麵) (rice in the south and noodle in the north). A snack chef claims that "the snacks in northern China are mainly noodles and pasta, but rice-derived items prevail in southern China" (see Xu 1998: preface). Some say that the Guangdong people did not begin to have the habit of eating wheat-made food until the Song times (Han 1990: 45).
10. The idiom in Vietnamese reads, *nguoi tau an mi, nguoi Viet Nam an pho.*

References

Anderson, Eugene E. 1988. *The Food of China.* New Haven: Yale University Press.

Allison, Anne. 2008. "Japanese Mothers and Obentos: The Lunch-box as Ideological State Apparatus." In *Food and Culture: A Reader* (2nd ed.), ed. Carole Counihan and Penny Van Esterik. New York: Routledge, pp. 221–39.

Appadurai, Arjun. 2008. "How to Make a National Cuisine: Cookbooks in Contemporary India." In *Food and Culture: A Reader* (2nd ed.), ed. Carole Counihan and Penny Van Esterik. New York: Routledge, pp. 289–307.

Chang K.C., ed. 1977. *Food in Chinese Culture: Anthropological and Historical Perspectives.* New Haven: Yale University Press.

Ching May-bo. 1996. "Literary, Ethnic or Territorial? Definitions of Guangdong Culture in the Late Qing and the Early Republic." In *Unity and Diversity: Local Cultures and Identities in China*, ed. Tao Tao Liu and David Faure. Hong Kong: Hong Kong University Press, pp. 51–66.

Connerton, P. 1989. *How Societies Remember.* Cambridge: Cambridge University Press.

Douglas, Mary. 1970. *Purity and Danger: An Analysis of Concepts of Pollution and Taboo.* Harmondworth: Penguin.

Douglas, Mary, ed. 1984. *Food in the Social Order: Studies of Food and Festivities in Three American Communities.* New York: Russell Sage Foundation.

Emmerson, Donald.1984. "'Southeast Asia': What is in a name?" *Journal of Southeast Asian Studies* 15 (1): 1–21.

Evans, Grant. 1995. "Between the Global and the Local There are Regions, Culture Areas, and National States: A review Article." *Journal of Southeast Asian Studies* 33 (1): 147–62.

Fan Honggui (范洪貴). 1999. *Yuenan minzu yu minzu wenti* 越南民族與民族問題 (The Vietnamese Nationality and Ethnic Issues of the Vietnamese). Guangxi: Guangxi People's Publishers.

Faure, David. 1996. "Becoming Cantonese, the Ming Dynasty Transition." In *Unity and Diversity: Local Cultures and Identities in China*, ed. Tao Tao Liu and David Faure. Hong Kong: Hong Kong University Press, pp. 37–50.

Gabbacia, D. 1998. *We Are What We Eat: Ethnic Food and the Making of Americans.* Cambridge, MA: Harvard University Press.

Goodman D. and M. Watts, eds. 1997. *Globalizing Food: Agrarian Questions and Global Restructuring.* London: Routledge.

Han Boquan (韓伯泉). 1990. *Yuecai wan huatong* 粵菜萬花筒 (A Kaleidoscope of Cantonese Cuisine). Hong Kong: Zhonghua Press.

Holtzman, Jon D. 2006. "Food and Memory." *Annual Review of Anthropology* 35: 361–78.

Lévi-Strauss, Claude. 1969. *The Raw and the Cooked* (translated by John and Doreen Weightman). New York: Harper & Row.

Li Bihua (李碧華). 1988. *Bai kaishui* 白開水 (Boiled Water). Hong Kong: Hong Kong Weekly Press Ltd.

Lupton, Deborah. 1996. *Food, the Body and the Self.* Thousand Oaks, Calif.: Sage Publications.

Mintz, Sidney W. 1985. *Sweetness and Power: The Place of Sugar in Modern History.* New York: Penguin.

Nguyen Dinh Hoa. 1987. "Vietnamese Creativity in Borrowing Foreign Elements." In *Borrowing and Adaptation in Vietnamese Culture*, ed. Truong Buu Lam. Honolulu: Southeast Asia Program, Centre of Asian and Pacific Studies, University of Hawaii at Manoa, pp. 22–44.

O'Harrow, Stephen. 1995. "Vietnamese Women and Confucianism: Creating Spaces from Patriarchy." In *"Male" and "Female" in Developing Southeast Asia*, ed. Wazir Jahan Karim. Oxford: Berg Publishers, pp. 161–80.

Ouyang Fuzhong (歐陽甫中). 2007. *Guangdong cai* 廣東菜 (Cantonese Cuisine). Hong Kong: Wan Li Books.

Phillips, Lynne. 2006. "Food and Globalization." *Annual Review of Anthropology* 35: 37–57.

Rao, M.S.A. 1986. "Conservatism and Change in Food Habits among the Migrants in India: A Study in Gastrodynamics." In *Food, Society, and Culture: Aspects in South Asian Food Systems*, ed. R.S. Khare and M.S.A. Rao. Durham, North Carolina: Carolina Academic Press, pp. 121–40.

Roberts, J.A.G. 2002 *China to Chinatown: Chinese Food in the West.* London: Reaktion.

Searching for the Identity of the "Steamed Rice-flour Roll"

Scholliers, Peter, ed. 2001. *Food, Drink and Identity: Cooking, Eating and Drinking in Europe Since the Middle Ages.* Oxford: Berg.

Simoons, Frederick J. 1991. *Food in China: A Cultural and Historical Inquiry.* Boca Raton: CRC Press.

Sutton, David E. 2001. *Remembrance of Repasts: An Anthropology of Food and Memory.* New York: Berg.

Tapp, Nicholas. 1996. "The Kings Who Could Fly without Their Heads: 'Local' Culture in China and the Case of the Hmong." In *Unity and Diversity: Local Cultures and Identities in China,* ed. Tao Tao Liu and David Faure. Hong Kong: Hong Kong University Press, pp. 83–98.

Thomas, Mandy. 2004. "Transitions in Taste in Vietnam and the Diaspora." *Australian Journal of Anthropology* 15 (1): 54–67.

Watson James, ed. 1997. *Golden Arches East: McDonald's in East Asia.* Stanford, CA: Stanford University Press.

Watson, James L. and Melissa L. Caldwell, eds. 2005a. *The Cultural Politics of Food and Eating: A Reader.* Malden, MA: Blackwell.

Watson, James L. and Melissa L. Caldwell. 2005b. "Introduction." In *The Cultural Politics of Food and Eating: A Reader,* ed. James L. Watson and Melissa L. Caldwell. Malden, MA: Blackwell, pp. 83–98.

Wolters, O.W. 1999. *History, Culture and Region in Southeast Asian Perspectives* (Revised edition). New York: Cornell Southeast Asian Program.

Woodside, Alexander. 1971. *Vietnam and the Chinese Model: A Comparative Study of Nguyen and Ching Civil Government in the First Half of the Nineteenth Century.* Cambridge: Harvard University Press.

Wu, David and Tan Chee-Beng, eds. 2001. *Changing Chinese Foodways in Asia.* Hong Kong: The Chinese University Press.

Wu, David, and Sidney C.H. Cheung, eds. 2002. *The Globalization of Chinese Food.* Honolulu: University of Hawaii Press.

Xu Chen Fenyu (許陳粉玉). 1998. *Xianggang tese xiaochi* 香港特色小吃 (Distinctive Snacks of Hong Kong). Hong Kong: Wan Li Books.

Zhang Youjun (张友隽), ed. 1999. *Bianjie shang de zuqun* 邊境上的族群 (Ethnic Groups at the Borders). Guangxi: Guangxi Peoples' Publishing.

PART III

Beyond Southeast Asia

CHAPTER

8

Transnational Cuisine: Southeast Asian Chinese Food in Las Vegas

Jiemin Bao

In less than 15 years, Las Vegas has been transformed from "a dining wasteland," or a place where "money could buy anything except a good meal" to one of the top restaurant cities in the world (Apple 1998: F1, F6). In her description of the wide-ranging selection of restaurants clustered within a few blocks, food columnist Heidi Rinella captures the diversity of the local dining scene:

> I was stopped in front of the parking lot for a Vietnamese restaurant and was thinking about the Indian restaurant across the street. If I had parked my car in the lot and taken off on foot, I could've easily reached two more Indian restaurants, an Ethiopian restaurant, a Brazilian restaurant, a derivative Spanish restaurant, a Japanese restaurant, a Chinese restaurant, a Caribbean-style restaurant and a couple of Italian restaurants, not to mention a handful of American restaurants in different styles (2007: 40).

This setting can be read as an index of Las Vegas dining culture. Some restaurants offer exotic food, others gourmet fare, still others comfort food and good value for the money. One can dine at Chinese, Japanese,

Korean, and Indian restaurants, of course, as well as a range of Southeast Asian restaurants including Thai, Vietnamese, Laos, and Filipino.

In the Las Vegas Metropolitan Area, Southeast Asian restaurants, like Mexican or Indian eateries, often are referred to as "ethnic restaurants" and their cuisines as "ethnic food." Southeast Asian cuisines only *became* ethnic food when they crossed certain borders. For instance, French cuisine is rarely conceived of as ethnic food but rather as bourgeois cuisine. These Southeast Asian restaurants, on the one hand, do bear ethnic markers and distinctive cultural characteristics; on the other hand, classifying them as "ethnic restaurants" reproduces and reinforces ethnicity as a category, which tends to be negatively applied to immigrants. The discourse on food reflects hierarchies embedded in the presentation of food in Las Vegas in particular and the United States in general. Moreover, associating the category ethnic food with "authenticity" has had a profound impact on the operation of ethnic-themed restaurants. By emphasizing authenticity, a cuisine becomes frozen in time and space. I argue that we need to pay special attention to the creativity of the chef, not the origin of the dish.

To challenge the category ethnic food and the notion of authenticity, I treat Las Vegas Southeast Asian Chinese food and Chinese Thai food as transnational cuisine. Southeast Asian cuisines had absorbed Arab, Chinese, Indian, French, or Spanish influences long before arriving in the United States.[1] Thus, foodways can serve as markers of deterritorialization and reterritorialization. In other words, foodways can be uprooted in one place and then take root somewhere else. For example, spring rolls and noodles from Guangdong and Fujian in China were carried to Southeast Asia by Chinese traders and (im)migrants, took root in Southeast Asia, and then were transformed into Vietnamese spring rolls, Filipino *lumpia*, and Thai *kway teow*.[2] At the same time, foodways are "powerful markers of territories and places" (Avieli 2005: 283). They capture local flavours, ingredients, and styles. The processes of deterritorialization and reterritorialization are intertwined (Inda and Rosaldo 2002: 12).

In the following, I will analyze the ways in which the local dining culture has shaped the cookery introduced by (im)migrants, and how the emerging fusion cuisine, in turn, reshapes the local dining and food culture. It is crucial to understand the connection between migration and food. Migration contributes to global change not just in terms of labour but also in the movement, adaptability, re-creation, and transformation of cuisines.

Reterritorializing Chinese Food in Southeast Asia

For centuries, the Chinese, who travelled to Southeast Asia to trade or to work, brought their cuisine with them. They operated food stalls, or opened restaurants, or sold dishes and snacks along the street as vendors, for such occupations did not require advanced language skills or much capital. Chinese (im)migrants have introduced new foods, noodles for example, and cooking techniques, such as stir-frying, throughout Southeast Asia. Salted soy beans, bean curd, and bean sprouts also have been integrated into a variety of local cuisines (Ho 1995: 10; Hutton 2004: 12–3). Soy sauce, a Chinese ingredient, has reshaped Southeast Asian cuisine, in which fish sauce had been the primary salty condiment.

The distribution of Chinese cuisines in Southeast Asia is underscored by the routes of Chinese (im)migration, which were organized along regional, lineage, or dialect lines until the mid-twentieth century. For instance, Teochius tended to migrate to Thailand, Laos, and Cambodia; Hokkiens tended to migrate to Malaysia, Singapore, Indonesia and the Philippines. Hainanese, Hakka, and Cantonese scattered throughout Southeast Asia. The food they brought to Southeast Asia often reflected their hometown cuisines which could vary greatly due to differences in local economies and ecologies, access to rivers or oceans, the amount of rain, and so on. Even though Cantonese and Teochiu both dwelled in Guangdong Province, each speaks a different language and has a distinctive cookery.

Although Chinese cookery is made up of distinctive regional flavours, styles, and dishes, the cuisine of the most dominant Chinese dialect or regional group in a particular Southeast Asian country is often called "Chinese cuisine" by the locals. Moreover, the dialect name of a particular dish often enters the local vocabulary. The Teochiu term *kway teow* (rice-flour noodle) has become part of the everyday language of Malaysians, Singaporeans, Cambodians, Laotians, and Thais. The Hokkien word *lumpia* has been absorbed into Indonesian and Tagalog (Yap 1980: 101–2).

Over time, these dishes became an important part of the local diet. *Kway teow* has become a favourite dish, which people in Thailand, Laos, and Cambodia eat for breakfast, lunch, and dinner or as a snack. *Lumpia* (Chinese spring rolls) and *pancit* (fried noodles) are popular dishes in the Philippines. Different towns and regions developed their own style of *pancit*, such as *pancit* Malabon, *pancit* Marilao, and *pancit habhab* of Lucban (Fernandez 2003: 61). Hainanese Chicken Rice, which was invented by the Hainanese in Malaya (now Malaysia and Singapore), spread throughout Southeast Asia and then was introduced back to China.[3] The chicken is boiled in chicken broth and various spices and tends to be very tender and moist (Vinning and Crippen 1999: 87). The rice is usually shiny and soft but does not stick to the teeth.

Kway teow, spring rolls, and Hainanese Chicken Rice are prepared with a local twist. In Thailand, Laos, and Cambodia *kway teow* often is flavoured with lime, chilli, fermented fish sauce, and palm sugar. Vietnamese use rice paper wrappers instead of wheat-flour wrappers for spring rolls, since Vietnam is a big rice-growing country. Vietnamese spring rolls are made with local herbs and tend to taste sweeter than the Chinese version. Hainanese Chicken Rice is also cooked with local ingredients. In other words, Southeast Asian Chinese cuisines are constantly changing, in the process of being remade, reinvented and reterritorialized.

Southeast Asian Chinese cuisine continues to change by inspiring experimentation among both locals and transmigrants. *Nyonya* cuisine is a good example of this. It was invented by the local Baba Chinese, whose earliest Chinese ancestors married Malay and other Southeast Asian women (Tan 1983: 59–60); it is a fusion of Chinese and Malay cuisines created by selectively combining distinctive ingredients and cooking techniques (Hutton 2004: 14; Hyman 1993: 114; Vinning and Crippen 1999: 121). Nyonya refers to female Babas, while the term Baba refers to the community and the men (Tan 1983: 58). While Malaysia is a Muslim country, Baba and Nyonya eat pork in a "kind of chilli paste sambal" (ibid.: 63).

When Southeast Asians and Southeast Asian Chinese immigrated to the United States, they also brought Southeast Asian Chinese food with them.[4] Since the 1970s, as increasing numbers of Southeast Asian immigrants and refugees have come to Las Vegas, the number of Filipino, Indonesian, Malaysian, Thai, and Vietnamese restaurants has grown. As of this writing, Las Vegas has more than 50 Thai restaurants, and at least 27 Vietnamese restaurants, 6 Filipino restaurants, 6 Indonesian restaurants, 2 Malay restaurants, and 1 Laotian restaurant.[5] So Las Vegas has more Thai restaurants than the number of other Southeast Asian restaurants combined. Many of these restaurants are owned and operated by ethnic Chinese who immigrated from Southeast Asia. Southeast Asian Chinese food, which combines southern Chinese and Southeast Asian flavours and ingredients, differs from typical Chinese food in the United States, which was first introduced by Cantonese from the Taishan area, and later by Chinese from Taiwan, Hong Kong, and mainland China.

Before addressing Southeast Asian food in Las Vegas, I will first discuss Las Vegas casino food culture which has transformed from providing cheap, all-you-can-eat buffets, to promoting gourmet food, including Southeast Asian food.

Las Vegas Casino Food Culture

In 2007, the Las Vegas Metropolitan Area was home to 386 hotels, including 14 of the country's 15 largest, over 100 casino-hotels, 132,947 hotel rooms, over 780 full-service restaurants, and entertained a record 39,196,761 visitors, 12 per cent of which were foreign.[6] Various "exotic" transnational cuisines are available; buffets, in particular, provide super-abundant food and a wide variety of choice at a fixed price. Restaurants and buffets have become sites where the local meets the global. Diners in the restaurants and the buffets include international and domestic tourists and locals. Locals can pay less at "early bird specials," especially during the week in the off season. Gamblers, tourists or locals can join the player's club and accumulate points to spend on free or discounted meals, and line passes for two for one buffets.

The city's first all-you-can-eat buffet, the "Buckaroo Buffet," was opened in 1946 at the El Rancho as a tactic to keep hungry gamblers from leaving the casino.[7] Others followed suit. The inexpensive buffet became ubiquitous. 1992 marked a turning point, when Wolfgang Puck opened Spago Las Vegas and grossed nearly 12 million dollars in his first year (Apple 1998: F1). (Puck was later honoured as a culinary visionary and voted into the Las Vegas Gaming Hall of Fame.[8]) Inspired by the huge demand and the incredible money to be made, some of the world's most renowned chefs, including Alain Ducasse and Joel Rubuchon from France, Emeril Lagasse, Charlie Palmer, and Bradley Ogden from the US, Nobu Matsuhisa from Japan, and others, opened restaurants in Las Vegas and utterly transformed the dining landscape.[9] Today, Las Vegas boasts 24 of the 100 highest grossing non-chain restaurants in the United States, second only to New York, which has 32.[10]

At present, foodservice is no longer a loss leader but a money maker for the Las Vegas gaming industry. According to casino consultant John Engor, from 15 to 20 per cent of a casino's overall revenue may now come from foodservice operations (Levin 2006). As more visitors come to Las Vegas in search of high-end food, buffets at the Bellagio, Paris, Mirage, and Venetian, among others, have gone upscale. The cheap food strategy, quantity over quality, has shifted to emphasizing quality food.

180   *Jiemin Bao*

Some casinos promote Asian and Southeast Asian food as part of this new trend to satisfy the needs of the dramatically increasing numbers of Asian American patrons and visitors from Asia and Southeast Asia. Tao — a "Pan-Asian" fusion restaurant and nightclub that opened in 2005 at the Wynn — has been "lauded on many fronts and features influences from China, Japan, Thailand, and Korea" and was the highest grossing restaurant in the United States in 2006 and 2007.[11] Tao has become a must visit for well-to-do adventuresome culinary tourists. Transnational dishes such as Japanese sushi, Chinese chow mein and dim sum, Korean kimchi, Vietnamese spring rolls are on the menu at many hotel buffets, especially on the Strip. In 2005 the Bellagio buffet drew more than 1.5 million patrons who were willing to pay as much as $34.95 to dine on dishes such as eggplant-tofu salad and game hen (Jones 2005). Many buffet patrons sample new dishes with an adventurous spirit and a pleasure-seeking attitude. For some, sampling unfamiliar food is almost like tasting flavors of different cultures.

Since 2004, approximately 80 per cent of the biggest gamblers in Las Vegas, the high rollers, or "whales" are from Asia (Rivlin 2007; Will 2008). The Wynn, Bellagio, Venetian, and MGM Grand have invested an enormous amount of money to attract and keep these Asian whales gambling at a particular property. Casinos have even hired *fengshui* masters to give advice on the design and placement of decorations (Friess 2007: A14). In 2007, the Wynn imported super-expensive seafood such as abalone and bird's nests for special Chinese New Year's dinners (ibid.). In February 2008, to celebrate the Chinese New Year, the MGM Grand went so far as to fly in the entire Diaoyutai State Guest House culinary team (including the tableware) for a weeklong culinary extravaganza of special dim sum, lunches, and dinners.[12] These highly sought after customers, then, can eat their preferred food and gamble in a familiar cultural setting, while they are in Las Vegas.

Noodles, a restaurant at the Bellagio, is a good example of how many casinos feature Asian dining as an important part of an overall marketing strategy. The legend is that an Asian high roller loved to eat noodles so much that, to keep him gambling at the Bellagio, the casino built this noodle shop. This story might be apocryphal but its spirit is true. This restaurant offers a variety of Asian-style noodles and dishes including Mandarin noodles, sweet and spicy noodles, *pad Thai*, Penang Fried Kway Teow, Hong Kong egg noodles, Singapore curry rice vermicelli, and *yaki udon*. It also offers "old time favourites" such as Nyonya curry, a dish integrating both Chinese and Malay ingredients. In targeting Southeast Asian Chinese, the restaurant's attempt to associate food with memory and place is clear. Virtually all of the upscale casinos, including Bellagio, Wynn, Mirage, Mandalay Bay, and the Venetian, now feature a noodle restaurant among its food offerings. The Palazzo too serves noodles and dim sum at an Asian-themed restaurant.[13] Meanwhile, the relatively inexpensive but plentiful food buffets still draw lots of customers. The Circus Circus buffet, for example, includes a small sampling of Chinese dishes and was serving as many as 12,000 people a day in 1998 (Apple 1998: F1). Moreover, casino buffets, to a certain extent, influence how Southeast Asian restaurants are operated in Las Vegas.

Reterritorializing Southeast Asian Chinese Food in Las Vegas

Southeast Asian restaurants tend to be located off-the-Strip, put the spotlight on their cuisines, and emphasize authenticity, bold flavours, and seasonal ingredients to attract adventurous diners (Whitely 1999: 1E). Southeast Asian restaurants strategically conform to the expectations of ethnic food by highlighting authenticity. At the same time, they also offer a wide range of food that transcends ethnic boundaries to attract both local customers and tourists. Such seemingly contradictory practices might be read as the ways in which they play politics with authenticity while engaging with casino food culture. Satay Malaysian Grille describes itself as a purveyor of "authentic Malaysian cuisine in Las Vegas." However, its menu covers a range of dishes known throughout Asia: *pad Thai*, Indian-style *roti canai*, Filipino *lumpia*, Singaporean fried rice noodle, Malaysian mixed vegetables and tofu curry, Hokkien Mee (a kind of Chinese Malaysian prawn noodle) and Cantonese chow fun with gravy, as well as Chinese sweet soy sauce whole fish.[14] Similarly, Lotus of Siam, which food critic Jonathan Gold called "the single best Thai restaurant in North America" (2000: 58), offers Japanese miso soup, Vietnamese butter shrimp, Panang[15] fish, Sichuan eggplant, Singapore noodles, and a Vietnamese rice noodle bowl. The chef creatively integrates East and West in a dish called "Crab cheese wonton," in which cream cheese is blended with crabmeat and green onions. The restaurant also features an inexpensive all-you-can-eat lunch buffet to attract customers. By the same token, Thai Place uses American ingredients offering "Hawaiian curry," in addition to Thai red, green, and yellow curries. Other Thai, Filipino, Laos, and Vietnamese

182   *Jiemin Bao*

restaurants also operate this way, catering to patrons who hail from a variety of backgrounds.

In Las Vegas, we can find Hainanese Chicken Rice at the Satay Malaysian Grille and the Penang Restaurant. However, one restaurant deep fries the Hainanese Chicken to meet the taste of patrons who are used to fried chicken. *Tofu nyonya* (Nyonya tofu) is now listed as a "healthy vegetable" dish at the Penang Restaurant and also is available at casino restaurants. *Lumpia* with a variety of different fillings is served at virtually every Filipino restaurant. Various styles of *kway teow* are not only available in restaurants but also at Thai and Laotian Buddhist temples. All these restaurants, to varying degrees, modify their ingredients and flavours according to local expectations. One Thai American explained to me that this is just like global chain restaurants such as Kentucky Fried Chicken modifying its dishes in Thailand, for example, "Thai-style" chicken wings.

In a study examining authenticity and culinary tourism at Thai restaurants in the Dallas Metropolitan Area, Jennie Molz pointed out that the Thai restaurants are significantly shaped by their customers' taste, from the arrangement of space to the flavourings of specific dishes. Nevertheless, Molz tends to focus on just one side of the coin — the ways in which the Thai restaurants are being influenced by the locals such as "cater[ing] to their customers' desire for an authentic experience" (Molz 2005: 6) — without examining the ways in which Thai restaurants actively introduce Thai cuisine to the locals. Molz represents Thai restaurants as though they are engaged with two types of authenticity, the real one among themselves and the staged one for American patrons:

> Rather than displaying *true* Thai culture, the Thai restaurant plays out the American perceptions of Thai culture…. [T]he restaurant owners and designers are constructing a new definition of authenticity, one that is based on an American perception of Thai culture rather than a *purely* Thai point of view (Molz 2005: 60, 62. My emphasis).

What Molz means by "true Thai culture" or "a purely Thai point of view," however, is never made clear. Thai foodways are fluid. Each generation continuously creates and recreates its cuisines. Even within a generation, the taste of the food is different. One Hainanese Thai told me that he preferred Thai cuisine in the United States, because he shared similar tastes with Thai restaurant owners, who, like him, immigrated here more than 30 years ago. Thai cuisine in Bangkok, where he came from, now "adds too many new herbs." His experience reminds us that changes take place both in the United States and in Thailand. Therefore, the concept of authenticity, similar to the category of ethnic food, fails to serve as a useful analytical tool in understanding and studying transnational food.

Making and Remaking Chinese Thai Cuisine in Las Vegas

In contrast to the mainstream discourse in the United States which categorizes Thai cuisine as ethnic food, the Thai state represents Thai food as part of a world cuisine. In 2006, Thailand's Minister of Foreign Affairs, Kantathi Suphamongkhon, pointed out that "We were once known as the Rice Bowl of Asia. People are now referring to us as the 'Kitchen of the World'."[16] According to Kantathi, there are more than 9,000 Thai restaurants worldwide with about 4,000 of them in the United States.

Kantathi and Molz represent two different discourses. The former takes pride in Thai cuisine having gone global, providing food to people far beyond Thailand's national boundaries; the latter emphasizes authenticity in relation to ethnic food and how American customers have influenced Thai restaurants. Despite their differences, the two share one thing in common: minimizing the heterogeneity of Thai cuisine. If we take a closer look, we will find that not only is the cuisine diversified but utensils differ depending on the situation, and that the name, ingredients, and flavour of the same dish can vary greatly depending on the region.

Wendy Hutton beautifully summed up the diversity of Thai cookery in relation to region: "The cuisine of Thailand is probably the most varied in Southeast Asia, ranging from the generally hot, sour food of the north, through the simple yet striking dishes of the poor northeast, down to rich coconut-milk dishes in the south, with sophisticated royal cuisine found in the capital" (2004: 13). In Las Vegas, Thai restaurants are similarly diverse. Some restaurants are known for their northern or northeastern style cuisine, which has a strong Laotian influence and often includes sticky rice and dishes flavoured with limes; others are known for central region cuisine which was in part influenced by southern Chinese cooking, the style with which Americans are most familiar; and some are known for southern Thai cuisine, which often includes curry dishes and is especially popular among Muslims who came from Asia. Thai cuisine reflects these ethnic, regional, and religious differences.

In any given city, town, or hamlet in the United States, Thai restaurants are usually established before a Thai Buddhist temple, even though a temple is the most influential institution among Thai Americans. In Las Vegas, the first Thai restaurant was established in Chinatown in 1973, but it was not until 1986 that the first Thai temple was founded. Building a temple requires significant human and economic resources. Restaurant owners often play a crucial leadership role in the course of building a temple by raising funds, making donations, regularly offering food to the monks, and inviting monks to conduct rituals. Thus, the Thai restaurant plays a vital role in the creation, support, and maintenance of the Buddhist temple.

Las Vegas' first Thai restaurant has prospered over the past 35 years. Its name is displayed in three different languages — "Thai Teochiu Restaurant" (Chinese), "Kungfu Thai & Chinese Restaurant" (English), and "Thai Kungfu Restaurant" (Thai) — on the menu and outside over the main entrance. The Chinese name highlights its Teochiu origin, distinguishing it from the other restaurants in Chinatown. The name Kungfu was used to connote China to an American audience. These multiple names for a single restaurant capture the owner's transnational practices.

The agency of a restaurant owner and/or chef is expressed in different forms and can be the decisive factor in a restaurant's success or failure. Archi's Thai restaurant opened in 2002 and in less than six years has

A Chinese Thai Restaurant in Las Vegas with names in English, Thai and Chinese. (Photograph by Jiemin Bao).

Southeast Asian Chinese Food in Las Vegas   185

expanded to three locations. At the centre of the cover of Archi's menu, the restaurant's logo, "100% Authentic Thai," is printed in extra large bold type. However, Archi's also offers several Thai-style Chinese dishes including a Mongolian dish, chow mein, egg rolls, and deep fried tofu. The owner explained to me that he found Chinese dishes to be "too light" and generally lacking flavour. He "added more flavours" (*tumlot*) to make these dishes "Thai-style." Moreover, he repeatedly emphasized that cooking is an "art" that requires creativity, passion, and imagination. For example, his Mongolian dish was prepared with extra chilli and dry shrimp sauce. Besides adding different sauces to Chinese chow mein, he gave the dish a smoky flavour by cooking it over a burner set on high so that the flame slightly singed the noodles. Authenticity, for him, meant modifying the ingredients of a dish or using different cooking implements or techniques to have it come out with a "good smell and a good taste." In these Chinese dishes, he tried to mix and balance sour, sweet, salty, creamy, and spicy, the five "Thai flavours." Instead of conceiving of authenticity as something pure, he emphasized the skill of the chef who makes the dish rather than the origin of the dish. Chinese Thai cuisine is not frozen in time or rooted in its so-called origin but rather reinvigorated by the chef who prepares it.

In comparison, the Thai Kungfu restaurant offers some Teochiu dishes such as Chinese *ong choy* (water spinach), pork hock, chopped chicken and mushroom soup and so on. But what really struck me was the variety of noodles, and the extent to which Chinese Thais and Thais know which type and shape of noodle to use in a particular dish; most local diners are unaware of the nuanced selection of the appropriate noodle according to the dish. *Kway teow* is made with a mildly sweet slightly salty wide rice-flour noodle. It can be seasoned with oyster sauce, fish sauce, garlic, chilli, and mixed with a wide variety of meat including barbequed pork, beef, and chicken. While wide rice noodles are used to make *kway teow*, flour noodles are used for wonton noodle and chow mein. The restaurant also offers *pad Thai* and *pad si eiw*. In Thai, "pad" means stir-fried. "Si eiw" is Teochiu for soy sauce. While both dishes are stir-fried, each has different ingredients and a distinctive taste. *Pad Thai* noodles are flat rice noodles that are sautéed in the restaurant's special sauce and stir-fried with bean sprouts, green onion, meat, and sprinkled with crushed peanuts. *Pad si eiw* uses much wider rice noodles and is seasoned with oyster soy sauce or a sweet dark-coloured soy sauce. It is often stir-fried with Chinese broccoli (*gailan cai*) together with meat.

The complexity of a "simple" noodle dish further demonstrates the ways in which a noodle can be renamed and combined with local ingredients in the process of remaking it in a new location. *Khanom chin* is a good example of this. In Thai, "*khanom*" means dessert; "*chin*" refers to China or Chinese. But together these two words become the name of a rice noodle dish. *Khanom chin*, which is made of thin and more rounded shaped Chinese-style soft rice noodles, usually goes with fresh herbs, raw vegetables, and a flavoured sauce or a soup. The northern style sauce is called *nam ngiu*, and it often contains tomatoes ("*nam*" refers to water); the central style *nam ya* sauce is much sweeter than the northern style and often contains curry; northeastern styled sauces, or *namya pa* ("pa" refers to forest), are considered country style; in contrast, the southern style is usually much hotter and sweeter. The Teochiu noodle dish Chinese migrants brought to Thailand was supplemented with various Thai regional flavours and was called "Chinese dessert." Now it has been re-named "Thai spaghetti" in the United States. What diners appreciate is the variety of noodles they can choose from rather than swallowing whole the notion of authentic Chinese noodles.

Any good bowl of *kway teow* or *khanom chin* is made up of well-integrated sweet, sour, salty, and spicy flavours. Nevertheless, lime, chilli, fermented fish sauce, and palm sugars — which were added to the "light" noodle dishes that the migrants brought from southern China to Thailand — have been toned down in Las Vegas. Such a transformation symbolizes a transnational twist: a Teochiu noodle dish that was first remade in Thailand now is being remade again in the United States. And not just the noodles, but all the other dishes are much less spicy. Fish sauce, one of the most important ingredients in Thai cooking, is sometimes replaced with salt or soy sauce. The amount and kinds of herbs also are reduced. Some chefs substitute instant curry for fresh, because instant curry has a much milder flavour and takes less time to prepare.

The variation and complexity are also expressed in the ways utensils are used. In the past, many Thais ate with their fingers, especially in the north and the northeast, in part because their primary food is sticky rice. They take their fingers and knead glutinous rice to make it chewy. Then they dip the little ball of rice into a sauce or into a dish in which meat, fish, or vegetables are finely ground or chopped. (Today in private settings — especially in rural Thailand — many still eat with their fingers.) However, due to new table manners promoted by the Western-educated Thai elite, Thais have gradually changed to using forks and spoons, especially in the

Southeast Asian Chinese Food in Las Vegas   187

urban areas and among young people. Holding the spoon in the right hand and the fork in the left, the fork is used to push the food onto the spoon and then eaten. They rarely use knives, because the meat is usually already chopped. Interestingly, Thais often switch to chopsticks when they eat *kway teow* and *khanom chin*. Fingers, forks, spoons, and chopsticks are all used in everyday life. The key is to know which style is considered "proper" according to the circumstances.

In Las Vegas, Thai restaurants usually provide forks and spoons, distinguishing themselves from Western and Chinese food culture. However, some Euroamericans do ask for chopsticks (Bao 2005: 175; Molz 2005: 56). This may reflect an assumption they make about chopsticks and Asian foodways. So some Thai restaurants lay out not only forks and spoons, but also chopsticks. This reminds us of the Thai saying: "When you move to a city of cross-eyed people, you also have to become cross-eyed" (*khaomuang tariu, tong riuta tam*). More recently, however, fewer Thai restaurants lay out chopsticks as many American diners have learned that Thai table manners are different from those of the Chinese, Japanese, Korean, and Vietnamese. The owner of Archi's opined that Americans now know much more about Thai food than they did just five years ago, because so many of them now know how to order. Thai restaurants serve as a public space for introducing and educating people about Thai foodways. Many Americans first learn about Thailand not through Buddhism or the arts, but through Thai cuisine. An American-born college student said to me, "When people find out that I'm Thai, they usually ask about food. Because, you know, that's the first thing people think of. But I always like to tell them that I play [Thai] music, I dance, I go to Thailand to perform with my temple [ensemble]." Without Thai restaurants and chefs, Americans would have many fewer opportunities to imagine what Thai cuisine and culture are like.

Conclusion

Foodways are connected from country to country and continent to continent. When we conceive of Southeast Asian Chinese food as transnational food, we are thinking big, connecting food with transnational migration and mobility; we see food as a subject of adaptation, a subject of change, and a subject of re-creation. I coined the term transnational cuisine to challenge the category "ethnic food," the notion of authentic food, and the links between these two, because a cuisine is neither bounded by ethnicity

188   *Jiemin Bao*

nor national boundaries. I concur with Raymond Grew, "Recognizing foodways as part of large-scale patterns of historical change makes it possible to relate the food practices of one place at one moment to theories about global change" (1999: 22).

In Las Vegas, southern Chinese food has gone through a process of de/reterritorialization twice over: first in Southeast Asia, then again in the United States. The spirit of transnational food is articulated through making and remaking by those who cook the dishes. Recipes are flexible in responding to the local conditions and the customers' taste. What had been added to southern Chinese dishes in Southeast Asia can easily be toned down or modified in the United States. We should never overlook the agency of the restaurants, chefs, and cooks, for they are the key players in facilitating cultural and dietary diversification.

Notes

1. By foodways I am referring to the culinary practices of different peoples and regions, and not only their food, but the entire complex of histories, behaviors and ideas related to its preparation, serving, and consumption. See <http://www.georgiafoodways.org/> [Electronic Document] [accessed 28 Sept. 2008].
2. There are various English spellings for a single dish. I have chosen the spelling most frequently used.
3. I would like to thank Tan Chee-Beng for this information.
4. I chose to use the term "Southeast Asian Chinese" to reflect their connections with the region that they settled down in and the country that their ancestors came from.
5. My restaurant survey is drawn from information taken from websites and telephone directories as well as personal visits. Many Mom and Pop restaurants are not listed in the phonebook and do not advertise online. The number of restaurants fluctuates as new ones open and old ones close. Therefore, this data should be used for reference only.
6. "2002 Economic Census," Accommodation and Foodservices, Las Vegas-Paradise, NV Metropolitan Statistical Area, Geographic Area Series, <http://www.census.gov/econ/census02/data/metro2/M2982072.HTM> [Electronic Document] [accessed 19 Mar. 2008]. "Historical Las Vegas Visitor Statistics (1970–2007)," Las Vegas Convention and Visitors Authority, <http://www.lvcva.com/press/statistics-facts/index.jsp> [Electronic Document] [accessed 19 Mar. 2008]. "About Clark County," Public Communications, <http://www.co.clark.nv.us/Public_communications/About_clark_county.htm> [Electronic Document] [accessed 30 Mar. 2008]. "Tao Las Vegas Restaurant & Nightclub Repeats as the Highest-Grossing Restaurant in the U.S.," 15 Apr. 2008,

Restaurants and Institutions Magazine. <http://www.rimag.com/archives/2008/04b/sr-top100-ranking.asp> [Electronic Document] [accessed 15 Apr. 2008].

7. See "Fifty Years of Dining on the Las Vegas Strip," UNLV Center for Gaming Research, <http://gaming.unlv.edu/dining/early.html> [Electronic Document] [accessed 25 Mar. 2008].

8. See "Gaming Hall of Fame," UNLV School of Gaming, <http://gaming.unlv.edu/hof/index.html> [Electronic Document] [accessed 20 Apr. 2008].

9. Much has been written about the celebrity chef phenomenon in Las Vegas. One of the earliest and most prescient articles is by Apple, "In Las Vegas, Top Restaurants are the Hot New Game," pp. F1, F6.

10. "Tao Las Vegas Restaurant & Nightclub Repeats as the Highest-Grossing Restaurant in the U.S.," 15 Apr. 2008, *Restaurants and Institutions Magazine* <http://www.rimag.com/archives/2008/04b/sr-top100-ranking.asp> [Electronic Document] [accessed 15 Apr. 2008].

11. Ibid.

12. Pearl Chinese Restaurant website, <http://www.mgmgrand.com/dining/pearl-chinese-restaurant-diaoyutai.aspx> [Electronic Document] [accessed 1 May 2008]. Diaoyutai State Guest House in Beijing is China's prestigious state guest house.

13. Jade Noodle Dim Sum Restaurant online menu, <http://www.palazzolasvegas.com/jade.aspx> [Electronic Document] [accessed 17 Mar. 2008].

14. Satay Malaysian Grille website, <http://www.sataygrille.com/Staff.php> [Electronic Document] [accessed 10 Feb. 2008].

15. Panang curry paste is very popular; it is often used to season river fish, seafood, pork, beef, and chicken as well as vegetables.

16. H.E. Dr. Kantathi Suphamongkhon, "Remarks," 12 July 2006. The quote comes from a speech by the Minister of Foreign Affairs of Thailand at the Thailand Grand Reception on 12 July 2006 in Battery Park, New York <http://www.mfa.go.th/web/1839.php?id=17061> [Electronic Document] [accessed 4 Jan. 2008].

References

Apple, R.W. 1998. "In Las Vegas, Top Restaurants are the Hot New Game." *New York Times*, 18 Feb. 1998, pp. F1, F6.

Avieli, Nier. 2005. "Roasted Pigs and Bao Dumplings: Festive Food and Imagined Transnational Identity in Chinese-Vietnamese Festivals." *Asia Pacific Viewpoint* 46: 283.

Bao Jiemin. 2005. *Marital Acts: Gender, Sexuality, and Identity among the Chinese Thai Diaspora.* Honolulu: University of Hawaii Press.

Fernandez, Doreen G. 2003. "Culture ingested: Notes on the indigenization of Philippine food." *Gastronomica* 3 (1): 58–71.

Fimrite, Ron. 2000. "Eating Las Vegas." *Via Magazine: AAA Traveler's Companion,* Sept. 2000, pp. 1–3 <http://www.viamagazine.com/top_stories/articles/eating_las_vega00.asp> [Electronic Document] [accessed 15 Apr. 2008].

Friess, Steve. 2007. "Las Vegas Adapts to Reap Chinese New Year Bounty." *New York Times,* 21 Feb. 2007, p. A14.

Gold, Jonathan. 2000. *Gourmet Magazine,* Aug. 2000, p. 58.

Grew, Raymond. 1999. "Food and global history." In *Food and Global History,* ed. Raymond Grew. Boulder: Westview Press, pp. 1–29.

Ho, Alice Yen. 1995. *At the South-East Asian Table.* Kuala Lumpur: Oxford University Press.

Hutton, Wendy. 2004. *Green Mangoes and Lemon Grass: Southeast Asia's Best Recipes from Bangkok to Bali.* Singapore: Periplus Editions.

Hyman, Gwenda L. 1993. *Cuisines of Southeast Asia.* New York: John Wiley & Sons, Inc.

Inda, Jonathan and Renato Rosaldo. 2002. "Introduction: A World in Motion." In *The Anthropology of Globalization: A Reader,* ed. Jonathan Inda and Renato Rosaldo. Malden, MA: Blackwell, pp. 1–34.

Jones, Chris. 2006. "Las Vegas Buffets: Step up to the Plate. Longtime tradition of Self-serve Restaurants Still Big Business for Casinos." *Las Vegas Review-Journal,* 5 Feb. 2006 <http://www.reviewjournal.com/lvrj_home/2006/Feb-05-Sun-2006/business/5539048.html> [Electronic Document] [accessed 19 Apr. 2008].

Levin, Amelia. 2006. "Casino E & S: High Rollin." *Foodservice Equipment and Supplies Magazine,* 1 July 2006 <http://www.fesmag.com/archives/2006/07/es> [Electronic Document] [accessed 15 Apr. 2008].

Molz, Jennie G. 2005. "Tasting an Imagined Thailand: Authenticity and Culinary Tourism in Thai Restaurants." In *Culinary Tourism,* ed. Lucy M. Long. Lexington: University Press of Kentucky, pp. 53–75.

Rinella, Heidi Knapp. 2007. "Las Vegas Offers World Tour of Cultural Cuisine." *Las Vegas Review-Journal,* 25 Mar. 2007, p. 40 <http://www.reviewjournal.com/bestoflv/2007/rinella.jsp> [Electronic Document] [accessed 19 Mar. 2008].

Rivlin, Gary. 2007. "Las Vegas Caters to Asia's High rollers." *New York Times,* 13 June 2007, Travel Section <http://travel.nytimes.com/2007/06/13/business/13vegas.html> [Electronic Document] [accessed 11 Feb. 2008].

Tan Chee-Beng. 1983. "Acculturation and the Chinese in Melaka: The Expression of Baba Identity Today." In *The Chinese in Southeast Asia: Volume 2, Identity, Culture, & Politics,* ed. L.A. Peter Gosling and Linda Lim. Singapore: Maruzen Asia, pp. 56–78.

Vinning, Grant and Kaye Crippen. 1999. *Asian Festivals and Customs: A Food Exporter's Guide.* Kingston, Australia: Asian Markets Research, Rural Industries Research and Development Corporation, Project No. AMR-3A, Publication

No. 99/60 <http://www.rirdc.gov.au/99comp/glc1.htm> [Electronic Document] [accessed 31 July 2008].

Whitely, Joan. 1999. "In Search of Ethnic Cuisines." *Las Vegas Review-Journal*, 15 Sept. 1999, p. 1E.

Will, George. 2008. "He banks on high rollers." 2 Apr. 2008 <http://www.tampabay. com/opinion/columns/article440993.ece> [Electronic Document] [accessed 3 Apr. 2008].

Yap, Gloria Chan. 1980. *Hokkien Chinese Borrowings in Tagalog*, Pacific Linguistics, Series B, No. 71. Research School of Pacific Studies. Canberra: The Australian National University.

CHAPTER 9

Four Dances of the Sea: Cooking "Asian" As Embedded Australian Cosmopolitanism

Jean Duruz

> [Cheong] came up with four small islands of seafood on a bare white plate. There were tiny fillets of soused snook (pike) on avocado slices with a wasabi mayonnaise, thin slices of raw cuttlefish with squid-ink noodles, slices of poached octopus tentacles with a garlic mayonnaise and spiced prawn sushi with glutinous rice. ... The result is a constant on the Grange's menu. It cannot be taken off. As a creation, it is myriad flavours and textures all in magnificent balance ... Perhaps it is the greatest of Australian dishes. (Downes, 2002a: 72–3)

At the time when Chef Cheong Liew first conceptualized Four Dances of the Sea, he was no stranger to celebrity. The year was 1995; the place, Adelaide, Australia. Cheong had already established his reputation for innovation ("the first to open other chefs' taste buds to Asian possibilities") (Ripe 1993: 20) through his legendary restaurant Neddy's (1975–88). This reputation was further enhanced by Cheong's years of teaching at the Regency Hotel School, arguably Australia's leading centre of hospitality training. Now he was about to take up the position of consultant chef to the Adelaide Hilton International Hotel's restaurant, the Grange (Downes 2002a: 51, 78–80). In that same year, his book *My Food*, written with

Cooking "Asian" As Embedded Australian Cosmopolitanism

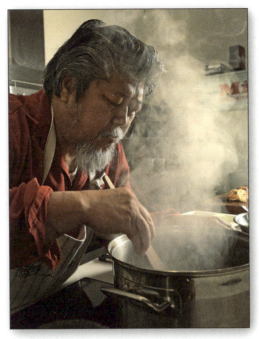

Chef Cheong Liew. (Photograph by Tony Lewis)

Liz Ho, was published. In its foreword, Barbara Santich, Adelaide food historian, was to declare "Cheong is a culinary magician, a sorcerer of the kitchen" (1995: xiii).

While Cheong's celebrity status might be considered unrivalled in the history of Australian cooking, this chapter is not primarily concerned with charting this history or assessing Cheong's contribution as such. Instead, it offers a different "take" on changing food and social identities in the region — the embedding and fusing of foods that, in the process, retain echoes of their Chinese origins — through an exploration of Cheong's more "homely" attachments. Conceptually, the argument aims, in part, to undo the conventional distinction between the archetypal opposing figures of chef and the cook (Gunders 2009) — between the practised professional with an eye global trends, and the experienced home cook rooted in the rituals of his/her community. Likewise, the argument is not so concerned with identifying "Chinese food" as a diverse and distinctive set of "ethnic" cuisines in Australia, despite their continuing historical presence.

Instead, this alternative tour explores some of the grey spaces in between, spaces where the boundaries of professionalism and immigrant

194 *Jean Duruz*

home-making become somewhat blurry ... spaces in which food reflects the complex, tangled histories of those who cook and those who eat it. In charting such spaces, we'll encounter childhood memories of Cantonese family's shophouse and farm, together with memories of a Malay *kampong* (village) nearby ... a long table in an Adelaide garden ... moments of forensic prowling through Adelaide's Central Market ... opportunities for convivial eating with the chefs of the city's Chinatown. In the process, the analysis, taking a narrative route through multi-layered meanings and sites of belonging, rubs against issues of identity, globalization, hybridity and cosmopolitanism (Highmore 2002: 159) — issues framing current "tastes" for Chinese (and other "Asian") food in Australia and issues negotiated within, and through, the dynamics of these "real" spaces. Reaching its destination in the final section of the chapter, the analysis positions this cumulative narrative of Cheong's "grounded" and nostalgic/imaginative practice within debates of the "new cosmopolitanism" — conceptions of cosmopolitanism in which difference, rather than universalism, plays a critical role (Werbner 2008).

Meet the Gastro-Father of "Asian" Australia ...

To set the scene for this "other" story, however, it is necessary to understand how the celebrity account became *the* Cheong Liew story. Magical or not, Cheong's unique cooking "style" emerged five years earlier than Ken Hom and Jeremiah Tower's official launch of "East-meets-West" cuisine in California in 1980 (Ripe 1993: 13). Furthermore, it was a "style" that proved formative in shaping Australia's culinary imaginary. According to Downes (2002a: 79):

> Neddy's revolutionized what Australians believed the best restaurant food amounted to. ... [T]his occurred when gastronomy in other parts of the world was almost entirely ignorant of South-east Asian ingredients, when Asian culinary techniques were thought to be exercised only in the mud of the kampong, and acceptable restaurant food was chained at least stylistically to the new French cooking (nouvelle cuisine).

From the opening of Neddy's restaurant to that moment of Four-Dances-dreaming in front of the computer, and beyond, the accolades have continued. Cheong has been celebrated as "one of the most innovative, untraditional chefs of the world" (Scarpato 2000: 47), and as "the godfather of East-meets-West food" (*Good Living* 2007: 3); the banquet he and Philip Searle prepared in 1984 for the First Symposium of Australian Gastronomy

Cooking "Asian" As Embedded Australian Cosmopolitanism

has become "the most important meal ever cooked in Australia — a quirky and exotic ... [feast that] ... ignited Australian cooking" (Downes 2002b: 29). In 1999, Cheong was listed by the American food media's *Food and Wine* as one of the ten "hottest chefs alive" (cited in Downes 2002a: 71), and in the same year awarded the Medal of the Order of Australia in recognition of his gastronomic contribution to the nation.

The Four Dances of the Sea is undoubtedly part of a larger narrative about the "Asianisation of the Australian palate" (Ripe 1993: 7–21). Certainly, there is much debate of the cultural and historical threads woven through this narrative and the relative significance of these (Ripe 1993: 11–3, 72–4; Symons 1993: 7–11, 52–3). Nevertheless, whatever the contributing elements — immigration, travel in the region, globalization of food products, rise of the food media — no-one would deny that something quite fundamental had taken place to change the tastes of the Australian nation (Santich 1996: 14). Even the Two Fat Ladies (of the British television cooking series of the same name) noticed this. As Clarissa prepares a fillet of beef with a sauce of ginger, garlic, spring onions, coriander, chilli, coconut milk, dark soya sauce and lemongrass, Jennifer asks, "What is this — what nationality?" Clarissa replies: "Thai, well it's sort of Pan-Asian — the sort of thing that's coming out of Australia at the moment" (*Two Fat Ladies* 1997: Episode 2). This, of course, begs the question: how does the taste of chilli, coconut milk, ginger, coriander and garlic — classic Southeast Asian spice and flavour combinations — become "the sort of thing that's coming out of Australia?"

While this will continue to be an intriguing question (and one I've addressed elsewhere in relation to *laksa*, a now-iconic "Australian" dish) (Duruz 2007: 195–7), here my curiosity demands the mapping of a different geography. So, I don't intend to follow the relatively well-trodden route of charting Australian cuisine's coming-of-age — from its Basic British but Chinese-influenced roots during early years of white settlement (Shun Wah and Aitken 1999: 11–9) to its contemporary designations as "Asian," "modern," "fusion" etc. Neither do I want to construct a hagiography for one of its "stars," or even to develop — as others have done substantially — a critique of adventurous cosmopolitan eating as instances of greedy grazing on the "exotic" (Hage 1997: 118–20; Cook, Crang & Thorpe 1999: 230–1; Probyn 2000: 81–2; Heldke 2003). Instead, this chapter approaches issues of changing Australian food cultures and social identities from the oblique direction that I indicated earlier. Inspired by Chef Liew's signature dish, Four Dances of the Sea, and paying particular attention to its biographical resonances rather than those of finesse and breath-taking artistry, the chapter will unravel a few threads of the web of affective relationships that might "embed" a chef, (even one whose reputation is prized by an international hotel chain) within the gastronomic everyday. Here, with a gaze both intimate and microcosmic, we might explore meanings of "place" as intersecting global-local relations, and the significance of spaces for negotiating cultural exchange, reciprocity and belonging through food. In the process, we might also catch fleeting glimpses of "new" hybrid forms of Asian-Australian culinary citizenship, and forms in which — at least, in this narrative — Chinese food is implicated.

Places of Memory: Hawkers on the High Street ... The Farm Near the Kampong

In his cooking, Cheong has a habit of returning to his roots. Four Dances signifies this return in its circular arrangement of "islands" on the plate, each indicating a critical place, person or moment within Cheong's culinary biography. The waiter instructs you to begin by eating the morsels directly in front of you and to proceed in a clockwise direction. This is in order to appreciate increasing intensity of flavour (McCabe 2004: 8). The strongest flavoured "island" is spiced prawn with glutinous rice, "a salute to home" (Downes 2002a: 72) — to Malaysia, particularly to those years associated with childhood, family, growing up.

The imagery of "crossroads" pervades Cheong's memories of his early years. The shop house from which Cheong's family initially operated a wholesale chicken business, and later a Cantonese restaurant, stood on the busy Jalan Bandar (High Street) in the outskirts of Kuala Lumpur. The shop house was close to a central bus station and market with a plethora of food stalls (Liew 1995: 1–2). "My favourite stall was that of the Indian *kachang* man," says Cheong. "He sold *kachang puteh*, roasted white beans ... and a variety of fried beans and lentils." "Just across the road," he continues, "were numerous restaurants — Malay, Indian, Chinese — including the Chinese barbecue stalls with the most basic of tables and chairs, selling the equivalent of fast food" (1995: 1). Nearby were Hokkien tea traders and noodle restaurants, and a Teochiu restaurant serving congee with "a master stock full of duck and chicken, offal, pork ears and intestines, bean curd and pickles" (1995: 1–2). Hence, the shop house is sited in Cheong's memories not only near a transport junction (from which point buses departed to elsewhere in Malaya) but also at the

Cooking "Asian" As Embedded Australian Cosmopolitanism   197

"crossroads" of taste and ethnicity — where proximity of different ethnic groups and their cuisines encouraged eating across the borders (providing cultural and religious rules permitted this) (Tan 2001: 146–8). Here, in the hybrid spaces of ethnicity and food cultures that constituted Malaya in the 1950s, it was possible for a child from a Cantonese family to acquire, for life, a taste for the Indian *kachang* man's "fried beans and lentils" or Hokkien snacks such as "fried prawn and pumpkin patty ... [like] a frisbee" (Liew 1995: 2).

The ritual appearance of hawkers throughout the day in the street below adds further layers to this narrative of cross-cultural eating. Their appearance serves as a timely reminder that cooking across borders occurs as well:

> At around eight the breakfast sellers would arrive. One of the first temptations was rice vermicelli cake with palm sugar. Then a Chinese lady would come with her nonya sweets, and around ten, the laksa man. ... At noon the yong tow fu man would come on his tricycle, bearing the vegetables and bean curd stuffed with fish farce.
>
> At three or four in the afternoon the rojak seller would enter the scene, and at five, the soup man with red bean soup, peanut soup, black rice soup, and sesame soup, all eaten with coconut milk (Liew 1995: 2).

While there is insufficient space to unravel each of these dishes' complex histories however fascinating, there are hints enough that these are stories of global migration (soups and stuffed bean curd, from China, for example; *rojak*, a spicy salad from Indonesia), of local adaptation (the ubiquitous local presence of palm sugar and coconut milk) (Holuigue 1999: 146), of culinary fusion and cultural exchange. (Here, *laksa* performs as the archetypal example. A traditional dish in Nyonya/Peranakan cuisine, *laksa* combines Chinese ingredients, such as rice-flour noodles with Malay spices and coconut milk. Historically, this dish is grounded in the marriages of Chinese traders and Malay women in the Straits' Settlements of Malacca, Penang and Singapore, chiefly during the eighteenth and nineteenth centuries [Brissenden 1996: 185–6].) Such a childhood as Cheong's then — its tastes, smells, textures and sounds — gives new, or rather returns us to older, meanings of "fusion" foods and "cosmopolitan" eating (Goldstein 2005: iv). These are nostalgic meanings formed within dynamic intersections of global movements (of people, goods and cultures) and locally produced meanings (of time, place, tastes and ethnicities). This, of course, is an inherent reminder, if one were needed, that global movements of people pre-date twenty-first century forms of globalization and that "vernacular cosmopolitanism" is not the exclusively property of the "west" (Werbner 2008).

In this definition, "fusion" becomes a deeply embedded phenomenon, bearing the imprint of history and memory. At the same time, born of perpetual movement at the "crossroads," it is, obviously, subject to change. This enables culinary cultures to resonate with not only flavours and textures of the past, but also with those of the present and the imagined future. A salad of Moreton Bay Bugs [small, saltwater crustaceans] and toasted salted fish, for example, which Cheong remembers as "one of the first Oz fusion dishes ... I created ... at ... Neddy's" (Liew 2006a: 19), becomes homage both to his Malaysian heritage and to the Australian coast and its bounty. Meanwhile, Cheong's Christmas turkey with glutinous rice, saffron and turmeric, drawing on memories of "the kerosene-fuel oven that my aunty used for this creation," imaginatively references the flavours of childhood. At the same time, this recipe is reworked (with advice in regards to local ingredients and providores) for readers of Cheong's column in *The Adelaide Review*: "My gift to readers is this nostalgic recipe from past cultural crossroads," he announces (2006b: 22).

When Cheong was 14 his family and four other families of relatives moved to their farm while maintaining the shop on Jalan Bandar as a restaurant. As well as raising chickens, the families worked vegetable plots, planted fruit trees — star fruit, mangosteen, *rambutan* — grew crops of sugar cane and farmed fish. Cheong describes the farm as "a paradise for those old expatriates [in the family] who had suffered near starvation in China." Nearby was a Malay *kampong*. With the extended Liew family invited to village celebrations, Cheong's culinary biography now included the festive foods of *kampong* (1995: 3–4). Reflecting on *kampong* life and food production in the 1960s, especially having seen it close at hand, Cheong paints this in glowing terms:

> You look at their food style ... way of cooking. I mean their lifestyle is fantastic ... an idyllic lifestyle, really. They like to live in a place ... where everything is there for them. There's always a river where they can net a few fish, a few chooks in the yard. ... The forest provides a lot of the herbs, you know ... [to] ... make their salads, and fruits — wild fruits in the forest, and there's always coconut trees, so everything is actually within their reach. ... Half the time they would just buy the rice and everything [else] is already provided ... [so] why do they need to work so hard [laughter]? (Liew: Interview Transcript)

Cooking "Asian" As Embedded Australian Cosmopolitanism   199

It would be easy to dismiss these memories as nostalgia for childhood as a time of more freedom, less responsibility, open spaces to explore, intense sensual delight in eating, and the companionship that growing up with 20 or so cousins of similar ages produces. Furthermore, the Malay *kampong* itself is subject to intense romancing, perhaps in ways reminiscent of those permeating the genre of writing known as "villa books" (Falconer 2000: 5). In these books and their accounts of self-transformation, westerners (usually jaded British or Americans) desire a return to an "authentic" lifestyle of food production and community relations. And so they flee global cities like London and Los Angeles or San Francisco to buy a villa in Tuscany or a Mexican casa in a charming village with a lively food market. Typically, they renovate their ancient farmhouse, engage their neighbours as cheerful workers in this enterprise, pick olives, delight in local produce, attend village festivals, all the time while writing books and producing films to sustain their "authentic" back-to-the land existence (Duruz 2004).

Nevertheless, the Malay *kampong* has a more specific and immediate history of loss than the urban west's more generalized yearning for pre-industrial landscapes of the eighteenth and nineteenth centuries and "peasant" modes of living (Symons 2007: 20–1; Gabaccia 2002: 177). *Kampongs*, particularly in Singapore, have all but disappeared, and very recently as well. In Malaysia, since the ethnic riots of 1969, programs in response to increase industry and hence employment throughout all states and ones to eradicate poverty have resulted in more young people moving to cities to seek employment and increasing numbers of women in rural areas finding work on nearby industrial estates (Andaya and Andaya 2001: 304). Meanwhile, in Singapore, with the movement of much of the population to state-built high-rise apartment blocks as part of "a national public housing programme [instigated in 1963] to accommodate residents of overcrowded urban areas, villages and *kampungs* (Chua 1995: 228)," this has left behind, in living memory, a legacy of regrets.

Such regrets are expressed in terms of loss of time, space and "community" (1995: 228). Chua, interestingly, re-works this nostalgia as a strategy of critique of the present:

> [I]nvoking the relaxed life of the *kampung* is not about desiring to go back to the *kampung* with all its material disadvantages. Instead it points to an alternative construction of "what life can be" in the presence of improved material conditions (1995: 238).

Ghassan Hage develops a similar argument in relation to Lebanese migrants in Australia who express deeply nostalgic feelings for their homeland: "[T]he aim," Hage says, "is not to go back. It is to foster these homely intimations so as to provide a better base for confronting life in Australia (1997: 108)." In other words, it is a form of bringing the desired meanings of "home" and the "past" with you, across space and time.

So, does Cheong bring the values of his Cantonese family farm and its neighbouring Malay *kampong* to the city of Adelaide, born "modern" under the planning of Surveyor-General Colonel William Light in the 1830s, and established as a gracious urban centre for a British colonial settler society (Whitelock 1985: 27–33, 180)? There are "intimations," certainly, in Cheong's description of Adelaide (Liew 2001: 6–7), particularly for the "Neddy's years" from the mid-1970s when the city was regarded as "cutting-edge" in relation to radical politics and food cultures (Downes 2002a: 320). Of his adopted city, Cheong says:

> Adelaide gave me the space to be revolutionary. ... Every morning we'd go to the East End markets to pick up our ingredients, and then over to the Central Market to pick up the fish and meat, and then we'd come back to the restaurant and write up the chalkboard menu for lunch. ... (Liew 2001: 6–7)

> I'm proud to be an Australian, especially in Adelaide. ... The countryside is fantastic. Twenty minutes and you're at the beach or in a vineyard in the hills. But the beauty of Adelaide is in its ingredients. If I want to cook Indian, Malaysian, Chinese or Vietnamese, I can go to the Central Market. And there you'll find one of the best food halls in all of Australia. ... Here people actually care [about their cooking], which I think is wonderful. (Liew 2001: 7)

There is no turning back to the farm or the *kampong*. After race riots broke out in 1969 (Andaya and Andaya 2001: 298), Cheong and his family dispersed. He and his brother set out for Australia, to Melbourne and Adelaide respectively. Now, 40 years later, the entire family lives in Adelaide — parents, the nine Liew siblings, partners, children and grandchildren (Liew: Interview Transcript). Family gatherings, for new generations and initially a new place, must be not unlike those years of five families living together on the farm. Furthermore, in Cheong's description of Adelaide, there are echoes of his earlier memories of the shop house, the *kampong*: once again we find "crossroads," "fusion," the fresh produce of the countryside, the community who "cares" about their food. While Adelaide will never be the *kampong* (and would we want it to be?), a

Cooking "Asian" As Embedded Australian Cosmopolitanism　　　201

ghostly criticism lingers in the imagery of Cheong's *kampong*-as-utopia: "So why do they need to work so hard?" The image of "what life can be" returns to haunt even the idealized past and even the most satisfying of adopted homes.

Long Tables: In the Courtyard ... In the Garden

Adelaide, with its "Mediterranean" climate, predominantly low-rise architecture and tradition of green spaces — parklands and private gardens — is obviously suited to outdoor dining. Certainly, there are critics of the city's increasing attempts to create spaces for European-style "café society." Michael Symons (2007: 324) complains that these have often translated simply into furniture cluttering up footpaths outside cafes while the coffee remains of poor quality; Susan Parham (1990: 219) points to the dominance of the car in shaping contemporary Adelaide and the ways "unsympathetic building and road design" reduce possibilities for conviviality.

At Neddy's, however, the ideal of marrying alfresco dining with an imaginative take on cosmopolitan cuisine seemed achievable. The courtyard behind the restaurant, under the shelter of its grapevine "gnarled and almost a century old" (Liew 1995: 45) provided a further space for "embedding" one's identity as a chef, experimenting with new identities, culinarily speaking, and for creating a sense of community:

> [T]he courtyard at Neddy's often gave us inspiration. We could have been anywhere. We dreamed in the Land of Dreaming ... and the courtyard led us to the Middle East along the spice routes, to the Greek Islands, to Tuscany, Provence, Singapore, Sichuan and last but not least to the Australian back garden. ... [The courtyard] was urbane or homely depending on your needs — you could breastfeed there, or play politics, or both. Australian bluestone lined the walls giving it a very provincial feel and yet the food was beyond traditions, which Australians relished. (1995: 45)

The homeliness of Neddy's courtyard, in particular, is recalled by Cheong's daughter, Gina, now in training as a chef in the Grange kitchen: "[As a child] I slept at the restaurant a lot, podded peas, peeled potatoes, generally hung around and I recall courtyard dinners we had there with big long tables of family and friends with kids running amok and waterfights" (quoted in Fleming 2008: 14). Interestingly, Cheong himself had a similar childhood of "growing into" cooking within the extended family's kitchens (both home and restaurant) (Liew 1995: 2–3).

Under the eye of his grandmother and later his aunts, Cheong acquired many skills, such as "preparing sour dough buns, cleaning shark fin, removing the young shoots from lotus seeds ... making chilli sauce, and grinding rice to make flour." When older, he was to work in the family restaurant during school holidays. Obviously, this tendency of blurring the boundaries of the familial and the commercial, typical of small food businesses, was to continue in Neddy's courtyard, where the line between family, friends, staff and restaurant patrons, became a somewhat thin one. ("Christmas in the courtyard was celebrated at the long table — friends and relatives gathered and it was a time for the staff to relax and enjoy ... the friendship") (Liew 1995: 46). There are other ways, too, that dining in the courtyard contained intimations of homeliness. In keeping with Cheong's personal history (belonging to a Cantonese family business with rural connections — a business involving pigs being spit-roasted at the back of the restaurant and chickens provided from the family's own farm), Neddy's (illegally) maintained its commitment to freshness through the keeping of live chickens in the cellar and live pigeons "at the back" (1995: 46). Just as the vine-shaded courtyard might provide a microcosmic glimpse of family and community, so too can it call up nostalgic images and tastes — of freshness, seasonality and "rootedness" in the landscape.

Cheong, however, sketches an imaginative geography that releases the courtyard from its grounding in the "homely" and moves it in the direction of the "urbane" ("the courtyard led us to the Middle East along the spice routes ..."). These places of fantasy — their names alone constituting an excess of meaning — together promise journeys of escape from the everyday into the realm of the "exotic" ... Greek Islands, Tuscany, Provence. ... The "Land of Dreaming" becomes an almost magical domain of mystery and wonder. Nevertheless, as in fairy tales, it also guarantees a return to the familiar — the mythical back garden of the nation's "suburban dream" (Allon 2008: 136). Such "dreaming" might seem overly fanciful, of course, and riddled with clichéd travel destinations of lifestyle prose. As well, the outcome of such "dreaming" might appear politically dubious. So, rather than courtyard "dreaming" performing as a "[a reflection of] the multicultural mood of Australia in the 1970s" (Liew 1995: 46), it might indicate instead the commodification of difference on behalf of greedy cosmopolitan consumers (Heldke 2003). At this point, it is salient to recall the courtyard's promise as a haunted place (de Certeau 1984: 108). Drawing on the courtyard's tension of homely-urbane, I want to suggest

Cooking "Asian" As Embedded Australian Cosmopolitanism   203

that Cheong's "Land of Dreaming" is not simply a space for free-ranging consumerism across places and products, and nor is it lacking in anchorage points or moments of exchange.

The reference to the Greek Islands, for example, takes Cheong back to his early days of cooking in Adelaide when he worked in a Greek restaurant and learnt much from the chef who also lent Cheong books on Greek food (Liew 2001: 5). One of the "dances" ("poached octopus tentacles with a garlic mayonnaise") is a tribute to this period and to this mentor while a further one of snook with wasabi and avocado acknowledges a Japanese friend and colleague who conducted fish-pickling classes for Cheong's students at Regency Hotel School (Downes 2002a: 72). The sources of knowledge then are varied — exchange with colleagues, learning from books and observing other cultures ("'Who are the Australians? ... How do they think? ...What do they cook in their kitchens?' This intrigues me still," says Cheong) (2001: 5). These sources are in addition to those gained by drawing on one's own memories and stores of pre-existing knowledge.

Perhaps, for Cheong, evoking place through the senses — through an imaginative act of self-transportation and empathy — is one of the most critical paths to cross-cultural understanding:

> I like to get as close to the temperament of a culture as I can and to feel as if I'm one of them. For example, beef stroganoff — I want to make sure I am cooking stroganoff as if I'm close to that place in Russia where it originated. ... Other than the sour cream everything is like the northern Chinese style of stir-frying. There's a similarity which is how you relate to those dishes. ... If I'm cooking Greek, I'm dreaming about the Greek Islands and I want to be there. Of course when I started out I couldn't afford to go there ... But [in] cooking from the heart ... [y]ou have your own touch ... You draw all your senses into it to form something unique. ... (Liew 2001: 7)

The products of this dream travel are unlikely to be exact reproductions of heritage dishes. Rather than attempts at replication, they are imaginative re-interpretations that are in keeping with the spirit of the dreamed-of places and cultures. Furthermore, for Cheong, the need to discover points of connection (for example, the "similarity" of stir-frying) is imperative. At the same time, there is space to create "something unique," even with familiar dishes such as Hainanese Chicken Rice (the latter I ate at a banquet staged by Cheong in 2002; the dish was complex, exquisite, refined, and yet deeply nostalgic of its hawker version).

From the remembered courtyard at Neddy's, it is a short step to one of the spaces it references — the Australian backyard. Don Dunstan, who was (I think) the first State Premier to publish a cookbook, claims the popularity of the barbecue and eating outdoors was an attempt to address gender inequality: "If a man is to ... [cook], he likes it to be associated with his rugged outdoors ideal. Dad can be encouraged to take charge of making a fire outdoors ... and happily sling some chops and snags [sausages] on to a piece of chicken wire suspended over coals..." (1976: 36).

While barbecue equipment has increased in sophistication, and likewise its (hopefully not burnt) offerings, traditions of collective outdoor cooking and eating in the privacy of one's own garden persist in Australia, and are firmly established in its cultural iconography (Duruz 1994: 199). Imagine it is the day of the Liew family's "giant annual backyard Barbie" (Liew 2007a: 25). For all Cheong's readers, the household preparations are endearingly predictable: "we sweep the brick paving, clean down the barbie table, give the lawn a mow and get ready to grill for family and friends in the warm evening glow of summer" (2007a: 25). The sense of place, however, is even more palpable as Cheong describes the smells, flavours and textures of the feast. Lingering in the air are the aromas of fruit prunings thrown on the fire, the burning of wood from olive, pear, apple, persimmon, plum and orange trees and grapevines suggesting the seasonal abundance of garden and countryside. Meanwhile, a giant lobster is roasted in the embers, a ritual tribute to the sea, particularly that of the South Australian coast (to which Cheong pays homage in his fourth "dance" — a portion of cuttlefish with squid ink noodles) (Liew 2007a: 25; Downes 2002a: 73).

A procession of dishes follow, together calling on a hybrid mix of places and times, diverse cuisines and individual preferences. These include a salad of "mango, banana flower, Vietnamese mint, red chilli, cucumber and Spanish onion" and "earthy Italian sausages and super jumbo quails," favourites of Cheong's children. The menu also features packets of Kingfish with spices and mung bean noodles seasoned with fish sauce, brown sugar and young coconut juice, all wrapped in banana leaves and grilled. While this recipe is reminiscent of other forms of preparation that involves wrapping food in leaves (for example the Nyonya snack, *otak-otak*, or even Greece's *dolmades*) Cheong adds an Australian touch by encouraging readers to use the leaves of fig, persimmon or mulberry trees (trees commonly found in Adelaide gardens) as substitute for banana leaves. Grilled legs of suckling pig, seasoned with five-spice salt and Cheong's

Cooking "Asian" As Embedded Australian Cosmopolitanism

daughter, Alice's "wonderful salad of tomato, roasted capsicum, cucumber and watercress" complete the "giant" spread (Liew 2007a: 25).

The point of this hunger-making description of a backyard family occasion is not simply the celebration of Cheong's expertise transferred from the courtyard to the home garden. One would expect chefs who are inventive in professional contexts to display their skills in domestic settings as well, particularly in preparing meals-writ-large that extended family gatherings demand. Instead, the back garden becomes a place with its own nostalgic associations — perhaps of "earthy Italian sausages" nodding in the direction of Dunstan's "chops and snags" but adding European inflections; perhaps of traditional Adelaide gardens drowsing through summers of ripeness and fecundity, yet the leaves of grapevines and fruit trees suggesting new possibilities. The garden offers space for creativity in other senses too. While clearly the leader in this enterprise, the chef is not the only person to experiment with tastes, ingredients, cooking methods; other family members develop their own "special" dishes. (See also Cheong's account of a Liew Christmas [2006b: 22].) In quite complicated ways then this garden re-invents Neddy's long-gone courtyard with its tension of homely-urbane, its potential for remembering and dreaming ("the aromas of Chinese pork and European venison, the romance of provincial France in the stone walls and the bouquet of big Australian reds [wines]") (Liew 1995: 46). In grilled suckling pig and "earthy" Italian sausages, the ghosts of Neddy's and the ghosts of family spit-roasts at the back of the shop, together with Proustian-style remembrances of Australian gardens past, haunt the Liews' "giant annual backyard barbie." Such hauntings, in turn seem to re-affirm, for Cheong, the pleasures of the "barbie" as a suburban ceremony, including "the sheer happiness of family and friends around you" (2007a: 25).

Melting Pots, Cooking Pots: Meeting at the Market ... Eating in Chinatown

Like all Australian cities, Adelaide is marked by its patterns of migration. In the post-war years, in addition to British-origin migrants, large numbers of Greek and Italian migrants settled in Adelaide suburbs, to be followed, from the 1970s onwards, by migrants from Asian countries in the region and more recently, by those from African nations and the Middle East. Meanwhile, Adelaide's gastronomic heart is indisputably its Central Market, literally at the centre (almost) of the city's original mile and operating continuously on that site since 1869 (Murphy 2003: 20–2). Much-lauded in tourist literature, food media, the local press and particularly in collective remembering (Murphy 2003: 12), the Market reverberates with images of cornucopia, sensory pleasure, sociability and diversity — of ingredients, people, cultures. The following description is typical:

> The Central Market is a mouth-watering melting pot of local and ethnic produce. Brilliant colours, intoxicating scents and animated camaraderie among the stallholders and customers make it a favourite meeting, eating and shopping spot. Wandering up and down the aisles it's easy to be transported to South-east Asia, Italy, Spain or Greece — anywhere that great food and *joie de vivre* are in abundance. (Gerard 2004: 51)

Leaving aside the much-disputed term "melting-pot" (with its overtones of racial assimilation) (Giroux 1998: 181), the market performs as spectacle — a diverse array of tastes, textures, sights, sounds and encounters. For sheer sensuousness, its description vies with ones found in guides to ethnic neighbourhoods of New York that aim to encourage gastrotourism, whether of locals or visitors. ("[T]he colors, sounds aromas will tell you much ... You are the adventurer," they are wont to say.) (Chantiles 1984: xxx; see also Berman 1999; Parker 2005).

Certainly, Cheong describes his regular visits to the Market as explorations in the gastronomy of specific ethnic communities. Nevertheless, for him such adventuring is aided by a fortuitous conjunction in urban planning: "One of the main attractions of working for the Hilton Hotel ... is having the Central Market right next door. ... You've got virtually the whole world — from Eastern European and Germanic to Mediterranean, from Vietnamese to Thailand to Malaysia to China" (Cheong, quoted in Murphy 2003: 121). Here, the Market, with its beguiling possibilities for global travel and its intense differentiations — in ethnic groups and cultures, in seasons and in geographies, in food products and their modes of preparation — echoes the courtyard's "Land of Dreaming." Nevertheless, the fulsome "world-on-a-plate" imagery, threading through Cheong's comments and the typical Central Market description above, has disturbing connotations (Cook and Crang 1996: 136–7). Is this a case of specific food products taking centre stage, and performing to excess? Are these products fetishised — as taste "experiences" — to a point where the people who've traditionally produced and consumed these foods are simply shadows in the background? In Hage's words, is this an example of "multiculturalism without migrants" (1997: 118)?

Cooking "Asian" As Embedded Australian Cosmopolitanism 207

I want to argue against this, and claim that Cheong's relation with the Market is "grounded" in significant ways. His accounts of market visits do not contain an exclusive focus on celebrity products or celebrity chefs. Instead, these are peopled with everyday figures, satisfying eating rituals and instances of cross-cultural exchange. Crucially, these stories take shape firstly, through the poignancy of memory, and, secondly, through accumulated everyday interactions.

Cheong has a long history of market-going. As a child of about 11 or 12 years in Kuala Lumpur, Cheong would accompany his grandmother almost every day to a local market. Leaving home before dawn, they would walk several kilometers to reach this destination; on the return journey, Cheong would carry their purchases. Despite the scoldings Cheong received from his grandmother if purchases were dropped en route, this market of childhood was a continuing site of sensory satisfaction:

> I like going to the market because it's bustling and it's still dark [outside] and it's bright lights [inside] and I like looking at all the vegetables and the chooks, even when I was young and … the reward is to have my early bowl of porridge. … This is congee … and well, a lot of people would be put off by this, this is a porridge of mixed pigs' offal. (Liew: Interview Transcript)

Breakfast at home with Cheong's mother, on the other hand, might be "bread and jam and a cup of tea" to help him last until 11 o'clock "and then you get your *laksa* man come around." Alternatively, the local *kopi tiam* [coffee shop], food stalls and hawkers guarantee such breakfast delights as *nasi lemak*, the traditional Nyonya rice dish with condiments; Indian *massala dosai* [thin pancakes of rice flour with curried vegetables]; Chinese [Teochiu or Hokkien] radish cake and [Hakka] *yong tow fu* (Liew 2007b: 24).

Like Hage's Lebanese migrants, whose store of homely intimations assists their place-making in suburban Sydney's alien landscapes, Cheong uses his own market memories (with all their familiar rush of excitement and exploration) to connect with markets elsewhere. Hence, not only the market of childhood and the Central Market next door to the Hilton Hotel but all markets become transformed into homely places. ("I love the [Central] Market. I just have some affiliation with any market," Cheong says) (Interview Transcript). More precisely, all markets are invested with nuances of the homely-exotic. Paradoxically, this allows the incorporation of the "strange" into the comforts of the everyday (Highmore 2002: 16). ("I walk into the Market to get inspiration. … You've got virtually the whole world. ...") (Cheong, quoted in Murphy 2003: 121). Here, this strong sense of connection, rooted in everyday memories and practices, is sufficient cultural baggage to face the adventure of the less familiar and to take pleasure from this.

Furthermore, connections across place and time can also ensure a cycle of return: "I can still be known to turn up for a traditional bowl of *laksa* at Asian Gourmet in the Central Market on an early shopping expedition. I guess it is those Malaysian yearnings bringing me back to my spoilt-for-breakfast childhood" (Liew 2007b: 21). These cycles, of embracing new places to the point that these become familiar ones while still remembering the old, continue to create complex spaces of belonging from which to venture forth into the unknown. And, in time, the ritual bowl of *laksa* at the Asian Gourmet acquires its own nostalgic baggage of "embedded" hybrid citizenship. Interestingly, this is not only for Cheong but for Anglo-Australians as well, in spite of their very different histories — of eating and remembering — from his. ("On Friday nights customers still queue for tables ... [at Asian Gourmet] where they first tasted authentic Asian food") (Murphy 2003: 130).

Cheong's Central Market is not only furnished with the tastes of the "world" or of the "past" but also with a rich body of characters — stallholders, customers, providores — and a density of daily interactions. As a young chef, he was part of a professional network that engaged with stallholders in ways marked by reciprocal respect for the Market's flourishing cosmopolitanism:

> In the days when all the chefs were running round in the Market, we were in a learning process. We'd be looking for artichokes or we'd read a cookbook that mentioned a "salsifier" and if you didn't know what it was you could go into the Market and ask a couple of European ladies who'd say, "Yeah, but it's very hard to grow in Australia. We get it sometimes." There was a mutual learning process going on between stallholders, some of whom were very food savvy and the chefs, who were asking for different varieties of herbs, vegetables and fruit. (Cheong, quoted in Murphy 2003: 122)

Such exchanges reverberate with the excitement of discovery and the satisfaction of collaborative effort. No doubt there is a frisson too that very differently-positioned groups (chefs, providores, stallholders) are collectively participating in the project of food adventuring. This spirit of collaboration extends to assisting fellow market goers and potential customers ("I just treat [going to the Market as if] ... I'm just a normal person doing my

Cooking "Asian" As Embedded Australian Cosmopolitanism   209

shopping," says Cheong, "and ... if [people] come up to me [and ask questions] ... I'm quite happy to give advice") (Interview Transcript). Leaving aside the question of the "normality" of having a celebrity chef on hand to answer cooking queries, it is precisely the delightful serendipity of such exchanges that is part of the nostalgic attraction of contemporary markets:

> The modern public loved these powerful moments of local life which gave them a taste of types of social interaction, sociability, that had more or less vanished. In the cold world of market rationality, markets offered a little extra soul. (de la Pradelle 1996: 2)

However, it would be unwise to assume that relations in these spaces of "local life" are always harmonious and unproblematic. Such an assumption would run counter to stallholders' imperatives — to *market* their goods — and increasingly, to market the market's symbolic meanings ... its "soul" — in a competitive context.

Obviously, selling one's "soul," the unsellable, is a contradictory enterprise. Gerard's effusive description of the Central Market at the beginning of this section continues with hints of the delicate balance required for maintaining social relations — managing the tensions and ambivalences of different groups sharing space. "Most people have a good relationship here [at the Market]. There's a bit of healthy rivalry but most people are willing to help you if you run out of stock," says Say Cheese Manager and co-owner of Dough Bakery, David Mansfield (2004: 51). "Most people are willing" suggests, conversely, there are some who aren't, and, although the rivalry may be "healthy" (at least, not destructive), there is no doubt that traders are competing for business.

Cheong alludes to this contradiction somewhat obliquely. Initially he lists some of the "name" providores in and around the Market (especially fishmongers like Michael Angelakis, the Cappo Brothers and Samtass Seafoods, and poultry sellers such as Merlin's) some of whom he has known professionally "for about twenty or thirty years now." At the same time he expresses some diffidence about developing close relations with many of the market traders and their staff:

> I've seen some of them working for one stall or another. ... I don't have that sort of intimacy with them ... because I do a lot of purchase around there so I have to keep a little bit of distance so I don't want [them] to say "You have to buy this from me" or "You have to buy that from me." I keep a bit of distance so I just choose what I like. I don't want to be tied down to buy from one shop ... specially [as] they know I work for the Hilton. (Interview Transcript)

The interesting image to offset Cheong's comment about "distance" and not having "that sort of intimacy" is the one of Cheong as a ubiquitous figure in the Market. As a "regular" myself, I have made countless sightings on a Saturday as Cheong potters from stall to stall examining ingredients or sits outside at one of the nearby Gouger St cafes. In fact, all the Market "regulars" probably recognize him but are far too "cool" to acknowledge this. Even *The New York Times* has noticed his presence. In one of its articles, partly reprinted in the local Adelaide press, the following observation is included:

> Everyone, from the guy deep-frying ... fish and chips made from local King George whiting at Paul's café ... to the Grange's celebrity chef, Cheong Liew, whom I spotted in Adelaide Central Market examining a kangaroo sausage as if he was diffusing a bomb, seems to have an obvious passion to live up to the cornucopia of fresh products that is ... [South Australia]. (Quoted in Jory 2008: 18)

When, during our interview, I comment on the lack of privacy that labels like "celebrity chef" must engender and Cheong's generosity in responding to shoppers' queries, he replies, "Well ... that's what life is, you know. I'm not a person [that] I have to be a really private person. I'm a market person, that's what I am! " (Interview Transcript)

The "market person" is an appealing identity for Cheong he trawls the stalls looking for "finds" and chats with the providores and curious cooks. Like the shop house on the High Street, the Malay *kampong*, Neddy's restaurant courtyard and the Liews' Australian backyard garden, the market provides Cheong with an additional site for "grounded" everyday interactions. However, these interactions are not without inflection from other identity tracings. The figure of the chef haunts that of the cook as he offers advice, or keeps his "distance," accordingly. Cheong is no "normal" shopper, after all. However, neither is he a "normal" "celebrity." The spirit of the market demands a sense of knowledge sharing, of belonging to an "embedded" community and of pleasure in ritual, although the romanticization of this, together with the privileges and responsibilities of celebrity, must be negotiated within these relations. The "warm fuzzies" of networks that I had anticipated among traders are tinged with a complicated mix of "willing to help" and "distance," after all.

A similar unsettling of expectation occurs when Cheong and I make a narrative move from the Market's main hall to Gouger St, on its southern boundary. Gouger St has been subjected to similar hype in the popular press as the Market itself:

Cooking "Asian" As Embedded Australian Cosmopolitanism

> [Gouger St is] a gastronomic smorgasbord of diverse cuisines ... It's the culinary equivalent of the Bermuda Triangle, a powerful vortex sandwiching Adelaide Central Market, Chinatown and 40-plus licensed restaurants along a 500m strip. ... This delicious evolution [migration from 1950s] continues today with a healthy dash of Asian influences extending the blend. (Andrews 2007: 42)

Cheong is delighted by this expansion, particularly the numbers of Southeast Asian and northern and southern Chinese restaurants, clustering along the street and in the side lanes of Chinatown. For him, one of the positive outcomes of Gouger St becoming *the* Asian food street of Adelaide is the development of a strong network of Chinese chefs who meet together regularly to exchange ideas ("Well, I'm not a restaurateur over there, but I do know virtually all the chefs ... [Once] in a while everyone will bring a bottle of red wine and everyone will bring one dish to somebody's restaurant and they'll gather round and have a chat") (Liew: Interview Transcript).

None of this is surprising. As I indicated earlier, Cheong is a regular patron in many of the Gouger St restaurants. As well, I've noticed how frequently he refers to local chefs in his column in *The Adelaide Review*. (His article "Duck Walk," for example, is virtually a walking tour of businesses in Gouger St (2007c: 24); "In Praise of Goat" provides the opportunity to draw attention to winter dishes in his "favourite Gouger St restaurants" (2008b: 35); "Chiew Chao Feast Tour" takes Cheong's readers on a tour of "the province of one of my favourite restaurants in Adelaide, T-Chow," and he concludes by thanking Chef So for the contribution of his regional "style" to the Adelaide food scene) (2008a: 27). However, when I comment on the generosity of this form of professional acknowledgement and of the evident camaraderie among the Gouger St chefs, Cheong counters with:

> Among the chefs there is a sense of competition ... undercurrent. There'd have to be! There's always a sense of competition, you know. On the surface they all sort of love each other as brothers ... [laughter] [but] I think I'm in a fortunate position ... They all consider me as the outsider because I'm working in a hotel, you see ... I'm not part of the strip. (Interview Transcript)

Here, Cheong's "outsider" status is predicated on being a waged worker in an international hotel chain in contrast to the chefs who, presumably, own their own local businesses. This would appear place him "somewhere else" in relation to the mythology of "lov[ing] each other like brothers" while "undercurrents" of competition intervene. Like the Market's stallholders with their "healthy rivalry," the Chinese chefs of Gouger St are faced with negotiating the tension of shared and competing interests. And of course, in a similar way to Cheong's imagining himself as a "normal" Market shopper, his self-designation of "outsider" contain ironic overtones. These are vested not exclusively in the binary of business owner/paid worker or even small restaurant/hotel dining room but more properly in that of international celebrity/local entrepreneur. I can only guess that competitiveness might attain new heights when celebrity intervenes in the mix.

Unravelling memories and everyday practices, this account of cooking, eating, shopping and talking in a city's acclaimed gastronomic spaces has become a hybrid one that challenges simple binaries. While certain figures dominate (or at least, resonate) at points within the narrative — the celebrity chef versus other professionals, for example, or the migrant who carries market meanings as personal baggage versus a group of chefs' professional excitement in discovering "new" produce — none of these figures are uncomplicated by other identity meanings. The figure of the migrant, for example, bleeds into that of the celebrity chef and vice versa. Hence the title of Downes' chapter on Cheong's contribution to Australian cuisine ("Refugee to Gastro-Father") (2002: 71) might need re-working. Remembered traces of Chinese heritage, of childhood and family life in Malaysia, of migration and re-settlement in Australia are ever-present in Cheong's gastronomy while experiences of celebrity and a profound sense of place shape his past, present and future imaginings. The refugee is not left behind as a defined stage in his culinary biography, or gastro-father status positioned as its pinnacle of achievement. In other words, Cheong's Four Dances are not choreographed as linear progress from the farm or the *kampong* to the stoves of the Hilton and beyond but, together, map a continuing cycle of return and re-embedding.

Grounds for Belonging: "Grounded" Cosmopolitanism and Hybrid Citizenship

Much debate has focused on the need for a "new cosmopolitanism" that addresses the task of living together in an increasingly globalized world in which people, goods and cultures appear constantly on the move (Werbner 2008). The problematic at the heart of many of these debates is shaped by a critique of western-centric forms of liberal humanism to be found, for example, in Martha Naussbaum's work where, critics claim, "universal

Cooking "Asian" As Embedded Australian Cosmopolitanism   213

liberal values are privileged above family, ethnic group or nation" (Werbner 2006: 497, citing Naussbaum 1994; see also Bhabha 1996: 193–4). Approaching questions of nation, Malay identity and cosmopolitanism from the opposite direction to critics of universalism, Joel Kahn (2006) similarly complains of identity privileging, though this time privilege is not associated with the figure of the cosmopolitan. Instead, argues Kahn, locally situated identity representations, "fixed," at the same time, normalised — the mythical *kampong* dweller, for example — ignore the complexity of people's identity positionings and the (literal and figurative) mobility of members of the modern Malay nation.

Our narrative of Cheong has deliberately trodden a path that takes heed of such debates. "Grounded" in everyday spaces, the analysis has sought to privilege neither the global nor the local, neither the chef nor the cook, the immigrant nor the celebrity, the *kampong* dweller nor the cosmopolitan. At the same time, like Kahn, and like Naussbaum's critics, I want to produce more complex figurings of cosmopolitan sensibilities and of the cuisines that nourish these. So, "cooking Asian" and "eating Asian" (with "Asian" here including inventive fusions of Chinese and other "tastes") in the city of Adelaide, Australia (a nation that continues to function as a colonial settler society, and one ambivalently sited in the Asia-Pacific) (Moreton-Robinson 2003: 37–8; Liddle 2003: 23) becomes an exercise in hybridity. In other words, this cooking, this eating, represents a series of strategic moves in border crossing rather than a dissolution of boundaries. Of course these moves across borders are not always successful or without their losses (Cheong's interview narratives range from the dark days of escape from racial conflict and the struggles of living in diaspora to survival in a competitive industry and its inevitable disappointments — his proposed venture for a neighbourhood commercial kitchen was rejected by a local council, for example) (Liew: Interview Transcript). Nevertheless, his "I'm a market person" not only serves as an *aide memoire* for nostalgic travel to the past and for future encounters but also underlines the significance of space itself — spatiality — and of "real" spaces for negotiating difference and belonging.

Writing of the postcolonial city, Jane M. Jacobs calls for a refocusing on "real space" within a dynamic conception of space in which "material and imagined geographies ... [are not] neatly separate ... [but] one constitutes the other" (1996: 5). Space, conceptualized in this way — as "grounded" social relations of doing, living, interacting, eating, feeling — does not become merely the setting for activity but part of its impetus. According to Jacobs, this dynamic view of space might be linked with

Said's "a geography that struggles" (Said, quoted in Jacobs, 1996: 5). Jacobs continues:

> These spatial struggles ... are formed out of the cohabitation of variously empowered people and the meanings they ascribe to localities and places. ... These struggles produce promiscuous geographies of dwelling in place in which categories of Self and Other, here and there, past and present, constantly solicit one another. (1996: 5)

From these perspectives, it seems that practices of "cooking Asian" are never completely and finally bedded down into conceptions of cosmopolitan citizenship — in utopian intimations of "crossroads," collective sharing, respect for "nature," awareness of diverse cultures and pleasure through sensory embodiment, for example. Instead, within relations of "real places," these practices, with their productive potential, require continual courting and re-embedding.

To write large Cheong's story of "real places" (despite the specificities and, at times, unusualness of his narrative) might be to say that Chinese food in Australia is constantly on the move. In the process, it undergoes transformation — a transformation resulting from a multiplicity of engagements with different cultural meanings and practices of belonging. At the same time however, through the poignancy of memory and creative encounters with other people, places and ingredients, this food — persistently, nostalgically — conjures up the ghosts of ancestral homes encircled by the breath of the wok. This complex cycle of moving, re-grounding and re-invention (of "bringing home with you" while re-inventing "home" anew) makes it possible to imagine "cooking Asian" in Australia as a sign of embedded, hybrid citizenship. Meanwhile, back at the Grange, Chinese-origin tastes, in skilful "mix" with other tastes to produce resonant fusions of the homely-urbane, continue to define Four Dances of the Sea as "[p]erhaps ... the greatest of Australian dishes" but also as an evocative example of the "new" Australian cosmopolitanism.

Postscript

Cheong was interviewed for this chapter in December 2008. In late 2009, the Grange closed its doors and, after a few months' "retirement" of travel and hosting food events, Cheong took up the position of Executive Chef at the Botanical Dining Room, an iconic Melbourne hotel restaurant. There he continues his tradition of innovative cooking, though in a more casual setting.

References

Allon, Fiona. 2008. *Renovation Nation: Our Obsession with Home*. Sydney: University of New South Wales Press.

Andaya, Barbara and Leonard Andaya. 2001. *A History of Malaysia*. Basingstoke, Hants: Palgrave.

Andrews, Graeme. 2007. "Grazing on Gouger." *Scoop Traveller South Australia* (May–Dec.): 42–6.

Bhabha, Homi. 1996. "Unsatisfied: Notes on Vernacular Cosmopolitanism." In *Text and Nation*, ed. Laura Garcia-Morena and Peter C. Pfeifer. London: Camden House, pp. 191–207.

Berman, Eleanor. 1999. *New York Neighborhoods: A Food Lover's Walking, Eating, and Shopping Guide to Ethnic Enclaves throughout New York City*. Guildford, CT: Globe Pequot Press.

Brissenden, Rosemary. 1996. *South East Asian Food*. Ringwood, Vic.: Penguin Books.

Chantiles, Vilma Liacouras. 1984. *The New York Ethnic Food Market Guide and Cookbook*. New York: Dodd, Mead & Co.

Chua Beng Huat. 1995. "That Imagined Space: Nostalgia for Kampungs." In *Portraits of Places: History, Community and Identity in Singapore*, ed. Brenda Yeoh and Lily Kong. Singapore: Times Editions, pp. 222–41.

Cook, Ian and Phil Crang. 1996. "The World on a Plate: Culinary Culture, Displacement and Geographical Knowledges." *Journal of Material Culture* 1 (2): 131–53.

Cook, Ian, Phil Crang, and Mark Thorpe. 1999. "Eating into Britishness: Multicultural imaginaries and the Identity Politics of Food." In *Practising Identities: Power and Resistance*, ed. Sasha Roseneil and Julie Seymour. Basingstoke, Hants: Macmillan, pp. 223–45.

de Certeau, Michel. 1984. *The Practice of Everyday Life*. Berkeley: University of California Press.

De la Pradelle, Michèle. 1996. *Market Day in Provence*. Chicago: University of Chicago Press.

Downes, Stephen. 2002a. *Advanced Australian Fare: How Australian Cooking Became the World's Best*. Crows Nest, NSW: Allen & Unwin.

―――. 2002b. "Samos in the Antipodes." *The Weekend Australian* (23–24 Mar.): R29.

Dunstan, Don. 1976. *Don Dunstan's Cookbook*. Adelaide: Rigby.

Duruz, Jean. 1994. "Suburban Gardens: Cultural Notes." In *Beasts of Suburbia: Reinterpreting Cultures in Australian Suburbs*, ed. Sarah Ferber, Chris Healy and Chris McAuliffe. Carlton, Vic.: Melbourne University Press, pp. 198–213.

―――. 2004. "Adventuring and belonging: An appetite for markets". *Space and Culture* 7 (4): 427–45.

―――. 2007. "From Malacca to Adelaide …: Fragments Towards a Biography of Cooking, Yearning and *Laksa*." In *Food and Foodways in Asia: Resource,*

Tradition and Cooking, ed. Sidney Cheung and Tan Chee-Beng. London: Routledge, pp. 183–200.

Fleming, Kylie. 2008. "Family ties." *Adelaide Matters* 95: 14–5.

Gabaccia, Donna. 1998. *We Are What We Eat: Ethnic Food and the Making of Americans*. Cambridge, Mass.: Harvard University Press.

Gerard, Pia. 2004. "To the Markets We Go." *SA Life* 1 (2): 48–54.

Giroux, Henry. 1998. "The Politics of National Identity and the Pedagogy of Multiculturalism in the USA." In *Multicultural States: Rethinking Difference and Identity*, ed. David Bennett. London: Routledge, pp. 178–94.

Goldstein, Darra. 2005. "Fusing Culture, Fusing Cuisine." *Gastronomica* 5 (4): iii–iv.

Good Living. 2007. "Bye Big Smoke, Hello Bowlo." *Good Living* (16 Jan.): 3.

Gunders, John. 2009. "Professionalism, Place, and Authenticity in the Cook and the Chef." *Emotion, Space and Society* 1 (2): 119–26.

Hage, Ghassan. 1997. "At Home in the Entrails of the West: Multiculturalism, 'Ethnic Food' and Migrant Home-building." In *Home/World: Space, Community and Marginality in Sydney's West*, ed. Helen Grace, Ghassan Hage, Lesley Johnson, Julie Langsworth, and Michael Symonds. Annandale, NSW: Pluto Press, pp. 99–153.

Heldke, Lisa. 2003. *Exotic Appetites: Ruminations of a Food Adventuer*. New York: Routledge.

Highmore, Ben. 2002. *Everyday Life and Cultural Theory: An Introduction*. London: Routledge.

Holuigue, Diane. 1999. *Postcards from Kitchens Abroad*. Sydney: New Holland.

Jacobs, Jane M. 1996. *Edge of Empire: Postcolonialism and the City*. London: Routledge.

Jory, Rex. 2008. "Talk: Falling in Love with Our Piece of Paradise." *The Advertiser* (22 Jan.): 18.

Kahn, Joel. 2006. *Other Malays: Nationalism and Cosmopolitanism in the Modern Malay World*. Copenhagen: Nordic Institute of Asian Studies Press.

Liddle, Rod. 2003. "Roasting Matilda over Taste of Asia." *The Advertiser* (2 Dec.): 23.

Liew, Cheong with Elizabeth Ho, 1995. *My Food*. St. Leonards, NSW: Allen & Unwin.

Liew, Cheong. 2001. "Cheong Liew." In Nexus Multicultural Arts Centre *Cardinal Points: Mapping Adelaide's Diversity — People, Places, Points of View*, ed. Malcolm Walker. Adelaide: Wakefield Press, pp. 5–7.

———. 2006a. "New Fusion from Warm Salad Days." *The Adelaide Review* (2–15 June): 19.

———. 2006b. "Talking Turkey." *The Adelaide Review* (1–14 Dec.): 22.

———. 2007a. "My Barbie Fetish." *The Adelaide Review* (16–29 Mar.): 25.

———. 2007b. "The Spoilt for Choice Breakfast." *The Adelaide Review* (25 May–7 June): 24.

Cooking "Asian" As Embedded Australian Cosmopolitanism   217

————. 2007c. "Duck Walk." *The Adelaide Review* (8–21 June): 24.

————. 2008a. "Chiew Chao Feast Tour." *The Adelaide Review* (April): 27.

————. 2008b. "In Praise of Goat." *The Adelaide Review* (July): 35.

McCabe, Christine. 2004. "Fearless Finesse." *The Weekend Australian* (4–5 Dec.): 8.

Moreton-Robinson, Aileen. 2003. "I Still Call Australia Home: Indigenous Belonging and Place in a White Colonizing Society." In *Uprootings/Regroundings: Questions of Home and Migration*, ed. Sara Ahmed, Claudia Castañeda, Anne-Marie Fortier, and Mimi Sheller. Oxford: Berg, pp. 23–40.

Murphy, Catherine. 2003. *The Market: Stories, History and Recipes from the Adelaide Central Market*. Adelaide: Wakefield Press.

Parham, Susan. 1990. "The Table in Space: A Planning Perspective." *Meanjin* 49 (2): 213–9.

Parker, Suzanne. 2005. *Eating Like Queens: A Guide to Ethnic Dining in America's Melting Pot, Queens, New York*. Madison, Wisconsin: Jones Books.

Probyn, Elspeth. 2000. *Carnal Appetites: FoodSexIdentities*. London: Routledge.

Ripe, Cherry. 1993. *Goodbye Culinary Cringe*. St. Leonards, NSW: Allen & Unwin.

Santich, Barbara. 1995. "Foreword." In *My Food*, by Cheong Liew with Elizabeth Ho. St. Leonards, NSW: Allen & Unwin, pp. x–xii.

————. 1996. *Looking for Flavour*. Adelaide: Wakefield Press.

Scarpato, Rosario, 2000. "Cheong Liew." *Divine* 21: 46–8.

Shun Wah, Annette and Greg Aitkin. 1999. *Banquet: Ten Courses to Harmony*. Sydney: Doubleday.

Symons, Michael. 2003. *The Shared Table: Ideas for Australian Cuisine*. Canberra: Australian Government Publishing Service.

————. 2007. *One Continuous Picnic: A Gastronomic History of Australia*. Carlton, Vic.: Melbourne University Press.

Tan Chee-Beng. 2001. "Food and Ethnicity with reference to the Chinese in Malaysia." In *Changing Chinese Foodways in Asia*, ed. David Wu and Tan Chee-Beng. Hong Kong: The Chinese University Press, pp. 125–60.

Werbner, Pnina. 2006. "Vernacular Cosmopolitanism." *Theory, Culture and Society* 23 (2–3): 496–8.

Werbner, Pnina, ed. 2008. *Anthropology and the New Cosmopolitanism: Rooted, Feminist and Vernacular Perspectives*. Oxford: Berg.

Whitelock, Derek. 1985. *Adelaide: From Colony to Jubilee — A Sense of Difference*. Adelaide: Savvas Publishing.

Non-print/Manuscript Materials

Two Fat Ladies: A Gastronomical Adventure. 1997. "Episode 2: Meat." British Broadcasting Corporation.

Liew, Cheong. 2008. Interview Transcript, 8 Dec. Copies in Chef Liew's and in author's possession.

CHAPTER

10

Southeast Asian Chinese Food in Tea Café and Noodle Shops in Hong Kong

Veronica Mak Sau Wa

TV programs such as "Travellicious,"[1] "Where the TV Stars Eat and Drink?", "The Starry Kitchen"[2] and "Chua Lam Brings You to the Vegetable Wholesales Market"[3] are very popular in Hong Kong, attracting huge audience from all walks of life. Millions of viewers, men and women, young and old are all fascinated by these food and travel stories from an "insider" perspective, going backstage or into the private kitchen with the host, visiting the wet market with the chef, exploring "authentic" cooking and eating experience.

Among the various cuisines introduced in these TV programs, Southeast Asian Chinese cuisine is most popular.[4] The growing popularity of Southeast Asian Chinese food is reflected both in the local media and in Hong Kong's food scene. Although there are plenty of choices for eating out in Hong Kong, with a wide range of cuisines and flavours from all over the world, the popularity of Southeast Asian Chinese food has grown rapidly in recent years. Southeast Asian Chinese delicacies, such as Char Kway Teow (fried *kway teow*), noodles with beef in satay sauce and Hoi Nam Chicken Rice (Hainanese Chicken Rice), have long been popular in the Hong Kong style cafe called *cha chaan teng*.[5] A recent example is the growth in popularity of *laksa* in the local food scene. Before the 1970s, this Southeast Asian noodle dish was only available in a few Southeast Asian restaurants and five-star hotels. But since the turn of the twenty-first century, there has been a growing number of *laksa* noodle shops, offering Malaysian and Singaporean *laksa*. More noticeable is a franchise-base Thai restaurant chain offering "Koon Thai Hai Nam Chicken" at HK$38 (US$4.5). This restaurant chain has opened 19 chain stores between 2007 and 2008, covering both the central and peripheral areas of the city. Nowadays, Southeast Asian Chinese food has become so popular that it is available in both casual and fine dining restaurants. One may spend as much as HK$198 (US$25) for a dish of Hainanese Chicken Rice at the Grand Café in Grand Hyatt Hotel, or as low as HK$24 (US$3) for a set meal at Fairwood, a fast food chain. If the price is still too high for the cost-cautious eaters, there is a cheaper choice of HK$16 (US$2) for a dish of freshly made Char Kway Teow at a local *cha chaan teng* or *dai pai dong*.[6]

The growth in popularity of the Southeast Asian Chinese food in Hong Kong can be seen not only in the local food scene but also in the retail sector. Since the 1990s, a few small Southeast Asian grocery shops were opened, usually near the wet markets. They provide essential daily Southeast Asian grocery products and food to the Indonesian and the Filipino household helpers. In addition, many exotic taste seekers, having experienced the distinct local flavours in the Southeast Asian countries while travelling or doing business abroad, are attracted to these shops. Apart from these small grocery shops, a new range of "ready-to-cook meal kit" with more than five "authentic" and "classic" recipes from Singapore was introduced in some high-end supermarkets in the beginning of 2008.[7] This new range of Southeast Asian Chinese foods targets the middle-class customers, who after a long-day's work may want to fix a quick meal with a taste of Singapore or Malaysia, such as a bowl of mouth-watering *laksa*.

In this chapter, I shall give a historical overview of the process of globalization of the Southeast Asian Chinese food and explain how under the interweaving global and local forces these foods are localized and adopted in Hong Kong. In particular, I am going to argue that mass media and the creation of authenticity are important to understanding this social and cultural change. Furthermore, I will also pay attention to agency and the market economy.[8]

Tracing the Process of Globalization of Southeast Asian Chinese Cuisine in Hong Kong

The globalization of Southeast Asian Chinese food is not something that just happens recently. Rice, noodles, tea, soybeans, bean curds and soy sauces have been travelling from China to Southeast Asia and around the world for a long time (Mintz 2007). Noodles, for example, under the Hokkien name *mi*, were introduced by the Chinese to Southeast Asia, while such Malaysian dishes like *laksa* were imported back to Hong Kong and mainland China in the 1960s via Fujianese restaurants (Anderson 2007: 210). In the following sections I shall first discuss the diffusion of Southeast Asian Chinese food to Hong Kong and then describe the development of the popularity of some of these foods.

Diffusion of Southeast Asian Chinese Food to Hong Kong

Back in the 1900s, Hong Kong was already well known for her strategic position in the trade route between the north and the south. There were two major trade routes linking Swatow (Shantou) in Guangdong with the rest of Asia. One went to Amoy (Xiamen), Fuzhou, Shanghai, Qingdao, Tianjin, Dalian, Taiwan and Japan. The other was directed southwards, passing though Hong Kong, Canton and Hainan and to Southeast Asia (Sparks 1978).

As the gateway to Southeast Asia, Hong Kong was the ideal place to set up trading companies and this had laid the foundation for the establishment of Nam Pak Hong (南北行), which was the working and living place for many Chinese immigrants. Nam Pak Hong was formed by a group of Chinese import/export trading firms in the early days, occupying a triangular area of several blocks in what is now the Western District on the Hong Kong Island, after the establishment of the Colony in 1842 (Sparks 1978). Most of these trading firms were owned and run by Teochius who had family connections with Southeast Asian countries, particularly Thailand. They lived and worked in Nam Pak Hong. During the early period, in March and April every year, Teochiu merchants would take advantage of the south wind to ship commodities, predominantly brown sugar from Southeast Asian countries, to the northern parts of China, such as Tianjin. In return, after selling the brown sugar, they would buy commodities such as soybean, cotton and clothing and ship them to the South during autumn (Feng 1997).

Prior to World War II, Nam Pak Hong was the commercial centre for import and export trading as well as for wholesale. Products received from and sent to Southeast Asia included rice, rubber, seafood, oil, coconut oil, sugar, leather, Chinese herbs and medicines. Products obtained from China included oil, beans, sugar, seafood, dried fruits and other foods, etc. (Sparks 1978: 29).

From the above discussion, we note that the diffusion of Southeast Asian food ingredients through Hong Kong can be traced to the pre-war period. In the next section, we shall discuss how the post-war influx of immigrants helped to introduce exotic Southeast Asian cuisine into Hong Kong and how the Southeast Asian food has transformed itself to become a symbol for an international city.

1950–69: Novel Taste of Southeast Asian Cuisine

The 1950s saw the influx of Chinese immigrants from different parts of China and Southeast Asia to Hong Kong. These immigrants brought with them capital as well as a diversity of knowledge and skills as well as culinary style, sowing the seeds for the growth of Southeast Asian cuisines in Hong Kong. The most well-known Southeast Asian restaurants opened in the 1940s and 1950s included Malaya Café (41 Des Voeux Road Central), Wah Yan Restaurant (153 Connaught Road Central) and Singapore Restaurant (Nathan Road, Kowloon). Specializing in Southeast Asian cuisines, these Southeast Asian restaurants were noted for their Hainanese Chicken Rice, Singapore-style fried vermicelli, and fried rice noodle with spicy sauce (Cheng 2003). These cafes and restaurants were popular among office workers. The different Asian foods not only broadened people's dining choices, they were also instrumental to the syncretization of the Cantonese cuisine in Hong Kong (Cheng 2002). Dishes like Char Kway Teow, Curry Mee and Hainanese Chicken Rice were popular in Southeast Asian restaurants. The highlighting of "foreign-style dishes" in the first gourmet column in *Sing Tao Daily News*, together with the advertisement of the Dairy Farm chain restaurants in the 1950 food guide, showed that there was an emerging leisure class in Hong Kong. The colonial government also played an active role in building up Hong Kong as an international city, promoting a notion of citizenship that was passive, depoliticized and economically oriented. This came at the time, as pointed out by See-Ling Cheng, when Hong Kong seemed to have suddenly taken over the role of Shanghai as the "nerve-

222

1970–97: Localization of Southeast Asian Chinese Food

The 1970s and the 1980s was the time when the first generation of locally born Chinese began to participate in the economic boom, searching for a modern cosmopolitan Hong Kong identity by drawing a line against the mainland Chinese and Taiwanese, manifested in an increasing diversification of the eating out culture of Hong Kong people. This was also the time when Hong Kong has been experiencing what Ritzer (1993: 1) calls McDonaldization of the society, which was marked by five dominant themes of efficiency, calculability, predictability, increased control and the replacement of human by non-human technology. The opening of the fast food shop, the Café de Coral, in 1969, was an icon of modernity, signifying Hong Kong as a modern metropolis, serving both Chinese (e.g. soy sauce chicken wings and thighs) and western snacks (e.g. sandwiches) (Cheng 2002).

When encountering the new wave of competition brought by the fast food chain, *cha chaan teng* strived to survive by embracing the principles of McDonaldization. On the other hand, they built up a unique identity by highlighting new varieties of non-western food, such as the Southeast Asian food, that were not available in fast food chain. To increase efficiency in production, and the demand of customers for exotic flavours, local tea cafés modernized their way of cooking, by homogenizing the food ingredients and heterogenizing the representation of dishes in a way to bring more choices for customers. The Southeast Asian Chinese food, which was once playing the role of nostalgic comfort food for the Chinese immigrants who had once worked and lived in Malaysia, Singapore and Indonesia, was gradually localized and (re)invented to meet the modern need for a more diversified choice of international cuisines.

Unlike those locally invented western-styled foods at *cha chaan teng*, which can be prepared in a few minutes, the Southeast Asian foods, such as the chilli paste with *belachan* in Malaysian dishes and the spices in Thai dishes, are usually made with many different ingredients and long labouring hour. Most of the foods served at *cha chaan teng* are usually grouped into a standard menu, including foods which can be prepared in minutes, such as Hong Kong-styled French toast, macaroni with hams, rice with canned creamed corn, deep-fried filet of Garoupa

Southeast Asian Chinese Food in Hong Kong

and local milk tea. Southeast Asian foods are subject to modification, so that they can be prepared and served quickly. I am going to illustrate this with three examples of the Southeast Asian style noodles — Char Kway Teow, Curry Mee and Beef in Satay. As pointed out by Tan Chee-Beng (2001), noodles are particularly adaptable and easily indigenized to form a new style of cooking and thus are exemplars to illustrate how these exotic food is globalized and adapted to the local needs. As the recipes of these Southeast Asian Chinese food differ among regions, it is beyond the scope of this chapter to explain the discrepancies one by one. Instead, I shall illustrate how these foods are mostly prepared in Malaysia. The reason is that the Malaysian-styled Char Kway Teow and Curry Mee are particularly popular among the local tea cafés.[9] Then, we shall discuss how they are being localized to fit into the contemporary environment in Hong Kong.

I. *Char Kway Teow: The Fried Kway Teow in Malaysian Style* (马来炒贵刁)

One example of the local invention of a Southeast Asian food is the Malaysian-style Char Kway Teow (*chao guotiao*). This is a kind of Chinese fried rice noodles introduced to Southeast Asia by the Chinese immigrants who earned their living by selling hawker food. The Chinese hawkers stir-fried the Chinese rice noodles with local ingredients, usually including shredded chicken, peeled prawns, cockles (*seehum*) or mussels, bean sprouts, and beaten egg, adding chopped garlic and blended dried chillies paste. Finally, they seasoned the noodles with salt, black and light soy sauce (Hutton 1999). Some chefs may insist on using pork lard for added aroma. Some traditional restaurants serve Char Kway Teow on banana leaves to give a peculiar fragrance and to enhance the flavour (Soo 2007).

The Char Kway Teow in Hong Kong is a localized version. To shorten the preparation time and lower the cost of employing a chef who has the knowledge of making *belachan*, ready-made curry powder is used instead of the lengthy process of soaking the dried chillies and blending them into a paste. Expensive seafood, such as cockles and mussels are replaced by popular but lower-cost roasted honey stewed pork (*char siew*). Small shrimps and local vegetables, such as onion, red and green peppers are used. Bean sprouts and eggs seem to be the only ingredients retained when compared to the similar dish from Malaysia.

II. *Curry Mee* (咖哩麵)

In addition to Char Kway Teow, Curry Mee is another "must-have" locally invented Southeast Asian dish in the *cha chaan teng* in Hong Kong. The curry from Malaysia is highlighted prominently in both the menu and advertising materials. It is time consuming to prepare the ingredients for the Curry Mee. The spice ingredients have to be grounded and blended finely, and the spice paste is then gently stir-fried. Water is added to bring to a boil, followed by coconut milk, sugar and salt.

Similar to Char Kway Teow, the Hong Kong version of Curry Mee in *cha chaan teng* is re-invented in such a way as to meet the modern demand for fast service on one hand, and the market demand for an exotic taste on the other hand. It is prepared simply by using the curry gravy from ready-made curry powder, with free combination of meat, such as chicken or beef, to the noodles. Nevertheless, the Malaysian curry, in contrast to those of India and Thailand, are particularly popular in Hong Kong. Many local tea cafés offer six to eight dishes made with Malaysian-styled curry.[10] My informants comprising chefs and customers said that from their experience, Malaysian curry is "less spicy and more aromatic. It is because more coconut milk is added to the Malaysian curry, thus making it less spicy, more pungent and more suitable to the taste of Hong Kong people." Curry for the people in Hong Kong provides a geo-typological classification of Southeast Asian cuisines. They divide various types of curries into two groups: the more spicy one from India or Thailand, and the less spicy one from Malaysia. In addition, eating chilli distinguishes Southeast Asian Chinese from the local Chinese community. People in Hong Kong draw the line simply by distinguishing the spicy food lovers (i.e. those who eat spicy foods, such as Mainland Chinese from Sichuan and Hunan and people from Southeast Asian countries) from the non-spicy food eaters, including most people in Hong Kong.

III. *Beef Satay in Nissan Instant Noodle Soup* (沙爹牛肉公仔麵)

Beef Satay in instant noodle soup is another locally invented food, and it is probably one of the most favourite dishes in *cha chaan teng* in Hong Kong. It is usually served with Japanese Nissan instant noodles or Italian spaghetti. At the same time, it can also become a wonderful snack as fillings of a sweet butter bun. Both are the highlight of the breakfast set served in *cha chaan teng* and one can hardly find a breakfast menu without this beef satay dish. Beef satay in noodle soup and the soft golden

Southeast Asian Chinese Food in Hong Kong 225

bun are even considered as a benchmark to judge the culinary skills of the chef.[11]

However, one will be disappointed to look for the same dish in Indonesia or Malaysia, where the beef is seasoned with turmeric and chilli powder, cooked over a charcoal fire, and anointed from time to time with a "brush" of fragrant lemon grass. In Hong Kong's tea cafes, beef is sliced instead of cutting into chunks, marinated by both light and dark soy sauce, salt, sugar, pepper, sesame oil to give the brownish colour instead of using turmeric which gives the characteristic yellow colour. Ready-made *satay* sauces mixed with flour water replaces those chef-made sauces with roasted peanuts used in Indonesia and Malaysia. Beef slices are stir-fried and served on top of the instant noodles instead of putting on bamboo or coconut-leaf-spine skewers to be grilled over a wood or charcoal fire. The spicy peanut sauce dip, or peanut gravy, slivers of onions and cucumbers, and *ketupat* (rice dumpling wrapped in coconut leaves) are usually not available in *cha chaan teng*.

What are the forces that shape how these dishes are localized? Both food production and marketing are involved. A chef told me about the reasons for these modes of localization. First, the menu is designed as a tactic to meet the diversified needs of the modern market. Each Southeast Asian Chinese dish is a component of the menu system in a *cha chaan teng*. These dishes complement and orchestrate with other kinds of dishes like the different kinds of musical instruments which work together to create a symphony. The local version of Malaysian-style Char Kway Teow, with ingredients like seafood, onion and green pepper, is a healthy and "lighter" alternative to the otherwise meat-heavy dishes. Secondly, there are another two locally invented dishes bearing almost the same ingredients, namely Singaporean fried rice vermicelli (星洲炒米粉) and Xiamen fried rice vermicelli (廈門炒米粉). These two dishes are local invention having the same ingredients with the exception of the tomato sauce as the base for the latter. This is a way to enhance the predictability of the ingredient quantity needed. Thirdly, because of the strong taste of curry powder, chilli and *satay*, which can mask the original taste of the ingredients, some of the left-over meat and vegetables can be used. Fourthly, the cooking time for the localized versions are dramatically shortened, so the food can be prepared and served in a minute. The short preparation time and the wide range of choices are highly appreciated by the modern working-class people who have a short lunch time but would look for "exotic" Southeast Asian foods which can spice up their appetite, especially during the hot summer. Thus the reasons for including Southeast Asian Chinese dishes on the menu of modern *cha chaan teng* have more to do with the economy of scale in food preparation and the market needs of diversification of food that can be prepared and consumed within a short time.

1998 and Beyond: Laksa in the Post-colonial Society

The growing popularity of *laksa* in Hong Kong is caused and reinforced by the phenomenon of globalization, especially the lowering cost of airfreight, booming tourist industries in Southeast Asian countries, rapid circulation of images and texts about *laksa* in international and local TV programs, magazines, newspapers, internet and menus in restaurants. What exactly is *laksa* and why does it globalize and penetrate so rapidly in post-colonial Hong Kong? Duruz (2007) describes *laksa* as a popular rice noodle in gravy made by the Chinese in Malaysia and Singapore. Tan Chee-Beng (2001: 133) explains in more detail: there are three main kinds of *laksa*, namely Thai (Siamese) *laksa* and "the curry *laksa* of Melaka and Johor," both of which use coconut milk, and the "Penang Laksa" which does not include coconut milk. The globalization of *laksa* is largely due to its high flexibility and adaptability, enabling it to be consumed by different groups of people in different social contexts. This flexibility is empowered by the metaphorical name "*laksa*." The word originates from the Sanskrit term *lakh* (meaning ten thousand);[12] this refers to a large variety of ingredients used in order to make the dish. This characteristic of high plasticity, in terms of ingredients and meanings, is of particular importance in global cities like London and Hong Kong where highly mobile people need flexibility in terms of time and space. This metaphorical name of "noodle with thousands ingredients" cooks up with a wide diversity of meanings to different food writers, from the eco-friendly vegetarian sweet potato *laksa*, to the "traditional" noodle stalls in Malaysia and the *chic* one in Australia restaurants.[13]

The successful story of *laksa* challenges the idea that people always like to eat familiar food (Fischler 1988: 275). *Laksa* was not widely accepted when it was first introduced to Hong Kong in the 1960s but it burst into fame in the 2000s as a kind of unusual, exotic Southeast Asian food. From 1970s to 1990s, those who like the exotic taste of *laksa* had to go to five-star hotels where *laksa* was categorized as a kind of Southeast Asian delicacies, or "international" food served on the buffet tables. In the year 2000, Penang Prawn Noodle Shop, the first restaurant which specialized in Penang noodles and *laksa*, opened in Wanchai, an entertainment-cum-business district on Hong Kong Island. As suggested by the restaurant name, the uniqueness of Penang Prawn Noodle Shop lays in her originality — the "authentic" recipe of prawn noodles from Penang, giving an aura of Malaysian-ness that is leveraged by other dishes, especially *laksa*. Tan (2001) tells us that Penang is a predominantly Hokkien city where the Penang Prawn Noodle is also called Hokkien Mee. This is a kind of soup noodle usually served with a vegetable called *kangkong* (water spinach) in Malay or *wengcai* in Chinese, topped with a few slices of blanched lean pork or precooked prawns. "Many people in Hong Kong have their first taste of *laksa* and *xiamian* (prawn noodle) in my shop," Mrs Shum told me proudly during an interview.

The eminence of Penang Prawn Noodle Shop points to the possibility of a high-profit margin business model desired by many entrepreneurs in the catering sector. With a small investment and low operating costs, such as food ingredients, rental fee store decoration, and high selling prices, which can double that of the average Cantonese-style noodles, these *laksa boutiques* created a new lucrative market which attracted many newcomers.

A Chinese Singaporean food restaurant in Hong Kong. (Photograph by Tan Chee-Beng, January 2011)

A Chinese Malaysian food restaurant in Hong Kong. (Photograph by Tan Chee-Beng, January 2011)

In 2005, two *laksa* noodle shops, namely Malaymama and Katong Laksa, were opened on the same street — the Mercer Street in Sheung Wan.[14] In 2006, the Penang Prawn Noodle Shop opened her second shop in Central. This sudden clustering of *laksa* noodle shops in business districts pushed up the rental costs as a result (*HK Economic Times* 工商透視, 21 Nov. 2005, D17). In recent years, *laksa* has penetrated into almost every corner in Hong Kong, from five-star hotels to specialized *laksa* noodle shops, from food courts to local tea cafes, from fast food shops to even canteens.

Media and the Signs of "Authenticity"

Five young women, elegantly dressed in black suits and white shirts and wearing high heels, stuck at the doorway of the Penang Prawn Noodle Shop, followed by a long queue during the busy lunch hour in Wanchai. They were reading a few food articles, cut from the top-selling leisure magazines and newspapers[15] and displayed at the storefront. Since the 1990s, there has been a common practice among restaurants to display food articles at prominent positions at the storefront. When I interviewed them and asked why they come to eat at this small shop, a young woman, wearing bright-blue eye shadow, said,

Southeast Asian Chinese Food in Hong Kong

We enjoy trying different cuisines for lunch everyday. An hour ago, we started exchanging emails to decide where to eat today. This is the most enjoyable break in the midst of a hard day's work. Today, Amy[16] has a sudden craving for a bowl of "authentic" *laksa*. So, here we are.

"We have decided to eat the 'Prawn soup base noodle' and the 'curry *laksa* base noodle' which are the two most 'authentic' dishes as recommended by Chua Lam[17]," another woman with her Prada handbag told me. "I have also checked Openrice.com.[18] Penang Prawn Noodle Shop has the high ranking among all *laksa* noodle shops on the Hong Kong Island. These two dishes are the most popular," The one in long skirt said.

"Authenticity," "Nostalgic" and "Traditional" are three magic words, appearing in almost every food article and every episode of TV food program which reports about the gourmet's choices and lectures on the etiquette of eating in Hong Kong since the 1997 handover. Molz's (2004: 56) study of Thai restaurants reminds us that the restaurant owners and designers usually attempt to cater to their customers' desire for an authentic experience. The cultural markers include the menu (showing the originality of the style of cooking), the ingredients, as well as the décor, which is "created to engender a sense of authenticity." Interestingly, based on the list of cultural markers proposed by Molz, the performance of Penang Prawn Noodle Shop is hardly "authentic." First, the name of the shop does not tell the actual name of the noodle dish in Penang. In Penang, prawn noodle is called "Hokkien Mee." It is only outsiders, like those in Kuala Lumpur who call the prawn noodle *xiamian* (Soo 2007). Second, the unique kind of *laksa* from Penang, called Penang Asam Laksa, was not available in the Wanchai store.[19] Third, the way of presentation is a deep borrowing from local food culture. Mrs Shum provides choices of mixing-and-matching on toppings, soups and noodles, borrowing the logic of a kind of Hong Kong-styled "cart noodle" (車仔麵). Fourth, as shown in the menu, the food ingredients of the *laksa* and Penang prawn noodles are highly localized. It is true that the recipe of the savoury soup for the prawn noodle at Penang Prawn Noodle Shop resembles those in the Malaysian cookbook: long-hour boiling with pork bones along with heaps of shrimp heads. Yet, to enhance the image of Penang Prawn Noodle Shop as a place for premium noodles, Mrs Shum adds an additional ingredient, namely "old chicken," which is widely believed to be expensive and highly nourishing, especially good for women. Customers can choose from a wide range of toppings, including common ones in Malaysia, such as shrimps, squids and mussels, egg, bean sprouts and bean curds. Nevertheless, the shrimps and meat are sliced, while in Penang more common do we find whole shrimp and minced meat. Customers can also mix the toppings with local ingredients, like the Japanese-styled fishcake and fake crabmeat, local fish-ball, meatball, squid-ball, local vegetables and mushrooms. Cockle, which is a common ingredient for *laksa* in Malaysia and Singapore, is dropped because of the unstable supply and high cost in Hong Kong. In addition, there are three choices of soups which are local inventions, namely, "spicy prawn soup base" (ingredients including shrimp shells and heads, boiled pork bones and old chicken), "curry *laksa* base" and "pork with chicken soup base."[20] Lastly, three different kinds of local dried noodles are available for choice, including the flat rice noodle, vermicelli and egg noodle.

The mix-and-match type of menu and the ingredients can hardly be associated with "authenticity," and the décors of the shop express no sense of "Malaysian-ness." The modern stainless steel-framed door, enclosed kitchen, clean and well-aligned shop layout, modern minimal styled lamp in black metal frame and white cover, the slow-moving black vintage ceiling fans all match perfectly with the light coloured wooden long bench tables, ladder-back chairs, and the black chopstick holders with black chopsticks and spoons, making the shop looks more like a modern Cantonese noodle-shop. The strategic choice of shop location in business district and the premium pricing strategy[21] reflect clear targeting of middle-class people, in contrast to those in Malaysia and Singapore where the best ones are found at the hawker stalls.

The case of Penang Prawn Noodle Shop challenges the set of cultural markers or symbols of the "staged authenticity" proposed by Molz, indicating that mass media is a factor that is too essential to be ignored. Instead, from the observations of the store, the cultural markers of the "staged authenticity" in Penang Prawn Noodle Shop include firstly, the six pieces of food articles stuck at the storefront, written in different languages (Chinese, Japanese and Korean), in both local and foreign newspapers and magazines. Through reading these food writings before consuming the noodles, the customers can imagine the history of the store, contour their articulation about the marker of authenticity and shape their experience during consumption. Second, there is a poster showing the endorsement of the shop by Chua Lam, being one of the 150 shops chosen by him in his food guide, and significantly with a big signature of him. The last cultural marker of authenticity is the Chinese auspicious calligraphy by

Chua Lam with the characters 客似云来, denoting "Customers fly in like clouds." In other words, what we witness in Penang Prawn Noodle Shop is a different kind of "staged authenticity" that mediated through mass media, which produced TV food hosts and celebrity chefs, who construct the popular collective representation.

However, as pointed out by Herzfeld (2001: 301), the mass media does not obliterate the importance of individual agency, it is actually "central to our understanding of social and cultural change." The production of the TV food stars' public images is part of public cultural knowledge. Hall and Mitchell (2002) remark that in Britain, the popularity of certain foods and cooking styles are greatly influenced by a few key food writers and TV chefs. What is different in Hong Kong is that we do not have food writers but TV hosts who happen to write something, which turns out to be the "expert knowledge" of food culture. Giddens (1991) rightly reminds us that this system of expert knowledge (food knowledge as a kind) is one of the developments of dynamism and globalizing scope that modernity built upon. More and more people rely on the experts to tell them what they need and how they choose. Hong Kong is one of the places in the world where the customers rely on the celebrities, such as the TV stars in the advertisements, to tell them what to buy (Nielsen 2006). I see these "entextualization" (Herzfeld 2001: 303) — the intertwined forms of representations (public images of TV food stars, TV programs, food articles, posters, auspicious calligraphy by TV host) as firstly a function of capitalism, and, secondly a social strategy deployed in pursuing particular interests within the embrace of a popular collective representation. It is true that this collective representation feed a global network of ravenous and highly profitable industries — food, travel, entertainment, films, TV, internets, news, etc.

Conclusion

Chinese food heritage reflects Chinese creativity and adaptation to the ecology in China and global influences (Tan 2001). For the Chinese society in Hong Kong, there has been additional access to new ingredients and non-Chinese foodways, resulting in the creation of diverse versions of local Chinese food. I would like to adopt Tan's model (2001) on the three types of cultural transformation, that is, changing continuity, direct borrowing and creative innovation to summarize my study of the Southeast Asian Chinese food in Hong Kong.

First, there is cultural continuity of the underlying Chinese principles of cooking and consuming food. The *fan-cai* (rice and dishes) principle (Chang 1977) forms the underlying structure in the meal-set formulation in *cha chaan teng*, as well as of the free noodles (fan)-toppings (*cai*) in Penang Prawn Noodle Shop. Second, there is change because of direct borrowing of the "recipes" from other groups, as it is manifested in the diversified Southeast Asian Chinese food in Hong Kong, ranging from Char Kway Teow, to different kinds of *laksa*, satay sauces, various kinds of noodles including Curry Mee. Third, there is change arising from innovation, as Southeast Asian Chinese foods are McDonaldized and localized, from complete innovation as in the case of Char Kway Teow, Curry Mee and beef in satay sauces, to the more "traditional" *laksa* in some *laksa* noodle shops.

Finally, the adaptation and innovation of the Southeast Asian Chinese food connote the problem of "authenticity." What is "authentic" Southeast Asian Chinese food? The consumption of "constructed authentic" *laksa* by the middle-class points to their cosmopolitan imagination and cultural identity mediated through the TV food critics produced by the mass media.[22] In addition, the juxtaposition of beef *satay* in Nissan noodle soup and baked bread commonly found in a breakfast meal set in *cha chaan teng* may be regarded as a fusion cuisine, with east-meets-west. However, the older generation takes it with ease because at the deeper structure, it is fundamentally Chinese, following the familiar Chinese *fan-cai principle* (bread as part of the *fan*). Southeast Asian Chinese food comes into Hong Kong with a novel taste; it localizes and becomes part of the components with the underlining Chinese cooking and culinary culture which is still *Chinese*.

Notes

1. TVB program, titled 《食盡東西》on air period: 15 Oct. 2006 to 24 Dec. 2006.
2. TVB program, titled《星級廚房》, 2008.
3. TVB program, titled《蔡瀾逛菜欄》, 2007.
4. In "Chua Lam Brings You to the Vegetable Wholesales Market," more than half of the content is on Southeast Asian food.
5. The Hong Kong *cha chaan teng* 茶餐廳 is a 1950s–60s style coffee shop, serving low-cost localized "western" foods. Based on the survey conducted in 1996, Wu (2001: 72) points out that "it was almost impossible for the researcher to identify a typical *cha chaan ting* on the basis of some objective criteria such

Southeast Asian Chinese Food in Hong Kong   233

as the exterior or interior decorations, or on the types of food and the way they were served, as this was constantly changing." Nowadays, the questions of "What is *cha chaan teng*?" is getting more complicated, with new types emerging, such as modern-styled local chain-store (e.g. Tsui Wah Restaurant), international modern-chic-nostalgic-type (e.g. Starbucks' *cha chaan teng*), milk dessert stores (e.g. Australia Dairy Company) and Macanese-styled tea café.

6. *Dai pai dong* 大牌檔 is a kind of open-air food stall.

7. In 2008, a new series of ready-to-cook meal-kit products from Singapore, branded Prima Taste, was launched in ParknShop. These included the most "authentic" and famed Singapore cuisines popular among Hong Kong people. They comprised: (1) Laksa meal-kit, which included *laksa* paste, coconut powder, *sambal chili*, dried *laksa* leaves; (2) Hainanese Chicken Rice meal-kit, including Hainanese chicken rice premix for chicken, fragrance oil for the rice, three kinds of sauces for dipping made up of ginger sauce, chilli sauce and dark soy sauce; (3) Bak Kut Teh, including the stock mix and soy sauce; (4) Rendang, composed of *rendang* paste and coconut premix; and (5) Singapore Chilli Crab, comprising chilli crab paste, premix and extra hot chilli mix. At a price more than a meal set at fast food shops (from HK$25 to HK$35 per pack), they are not for the poor but for the busy middle-class women who like to prepare exotic and health cuisines, free of preservatives, artificial colourings, in minutes with no culinary skills required.

8. This chapter is in every sense the result of a collective endeavour. In particular, I am deeply indebted to Professor Tan Chee-Beng for his inspiring lectures and papers, which I could not have asked for better stimulation. The manuscript could not have been able to materialize without his substantive input, which includes introducing me to some Southeast Asian Chinese food outlets. Beyond academia, his personal qualities of enthusiasm and generosity have transformed this research project into a particular delight.

9. This point will be explained further in the section on Curry Mee.

10. See menu of Cheung Wing Café which was established in the 1960s and Yam Lam Kwok tea café chain.

11. Data collected through openrice.com

12. "lakh" Merriam-Webster 2008: <http://search.eb.com.easyaccess1.lib.cuhk.edu.hk/dictionary?va=lakh&query=lakh> [accessed 10 June 2008].

13. Survey on the *Food and Drink* section of *Times Online*: <http://www.timesonline.co.uk/tol/life_and_style/food_and_drink/>.

14. Sheung Wan is also a business district, a five-minute driving distance from Wanchai, and a ten-minute walk from Central.

15. Food columns and features on food and travel have appeared in Hong Kong since the 1960s. By year 2008, the top selling magazines and newspapers include *Eat and Travel Weekly*, *Oriental Daily* and *Apple Daily*.

16. Pseudo-name.

234   *Veronica Mak Sau Wa*

17. Chua Lam is voted as the most influential person in the food culture in Hong Kong in year 2000, as summarized by the top selling life-style magazine, *Eat and Travel Weekly*. In particular, he is well known for his hedonistic personality. His reputation as the expert of Southeast Asian cuisine rested on his cultural root. Being a Teochiu Chinese born in Singapore, Chua Lam has been writing as a food critics in top-selling press, such as *Oriental Daily*, *Apple Daily*, *Eat and Travel Weekly*. He also published books on food and travel, including *The City Guidebook for Food*, for Hong Kong and Southeast Asia countries since the 1980s. Moreover, he is a popular host in TV food program in Hong Kong and Japan, nicknamed as one of the four most talented men in Hong Kong.

18. "Openrice.com" is the most popular online food search engine in Hong Kong, with food and restaurants pictures, rankings and food reviews.

19. In 2006, Penang Asam Laksa started to be available in the Central store.

20. This pork-and-chicken soup is probably a borrowing from the popular *Tonkotsu* from Kyushu of Japan. Because of the multi-ethnicity in Malaysia, pork meat and bones are usually not used to make the soup as pork is taboo for Muslims. However, in Hong Kong and Japan, there is no such food taboo.

21. The market price of a Cantonese-style wonton noodle is HK$20 while *laksa* in *laksa* noodle shops is sold at HK$40 or above, depending on the ingredients.

22. The term "constructed authenticity" was borrowed from Hsu (2009).

References

Anderson, E.N. 2007. "Malaysian Foodways: Confluence and Separation." *Ecology of Food and Nutrition* 46 (3): 205–19.

Chang K.C. 1977. "Introduction." In *Food in Chinese Culture: Anthropological and Historical Perspectives*, ed. K.C. Chang. New Haven: Yale University Press, pp. 3–21.

Cheng P. 2003. *Early Hong Kong Eateries*. Hong Kong: University Museum and Art Gallery, The University of Hong Kong.

Cheng Sea-ling. 2002. "Eating Hong Kong's way out." In *Asian Food: The Global and the Local*, ed. Katarzyna Cwiertka and Boudewijn Walraven. Richmond, Surrey: Curzon Press, pp. 16–33.

Duruz, Jean. 2007. "From Malacca to Adelaide…: Fragments towards a Biography of Cooking, Yearning and *Laksa*." In *Food and Foodways in Asia: Resource, Tradition and Cooking*, ed. Sidney C.H. Cheung and Tan Chee-Beng. London and NY: Routledge, pp. 183–97.

Feng Bangyan (馮邦彥). 1997. *Xianggang huazi caituan: 1841–1997* 香港华资财团 (Hong Kong Chinese Financial Institutions: 1841–1997). Hong Kong: Salian Shudian.

Fischler, C. 1988. "Food, Self, and Identity." *Social Science Information* 27: 275–92.

Giddens, Anthony. 1991. *Modernity and Self-identity: Self and Society in the Late Modern Age*. Cambridge: Polity Press.

Hall, Michael and Mitchell, Richard. 2002. "Tourism as a Force for Gastronomic Globalization and Localization." In *Tourism and Gastronomy*, ed. Anne-Mette Hjalager and Greg Richards. London and NY: Routledge, pp. 71–87.

Herzfeld, Michael. 2001. *Anthropology: Theoretical Practice in Culture and Society*. Malden, Mass.: Blackwell Publishers.

Hsu Ching-Wen. 2009. "Authentic Tofu, Cosmopolitan Taiwan." *Taiwan Journal of Anthropology* 7 (1): 3–34.

Hutton, Wendy, ed. 1999. *The Food of Malaysia: Authentic Recipes from the Crossroads of Asia*. Recipes by the cooks of Bon Ton Restaurant, Kuala Lumpur and Jonkers Restaurant, Malacca. Hong Kong: Periplus Editions (HK) Ltd.

Mintz, Sidney W. 2007. "Asia's Contribution to World Cuisine." In *Food and Foodways in Asia: Resource, Tradition and Cooking*, ed. Sidney C.H. Cheung and Tan Chee-Beng. London and NY: Routledge, pp. 201–10.

Molz, Jennie Germann. 2004. "Tasting an Imagined Thailand: Authenticity and Culinary Tourism in Thai Restaurants." In *Culinary Tourism*, ed. Lucy M. Long Lexington: University Press of Kentucky, pp. 54–75.

Nielsen, A.C. 2006. "Designer Brands:A Global ACNielsen Report": <http://pl.nielsen.com/trends/documents/GlobalDesignerBrandsReport.pdf> [accessed 5 Jan. 2010].

Ritzer, G. 1993. *The McDonaldization of Society*. Newbury Park: Pine Forge Press.

Soo Khin Wah. 2007. "Chinese Street Food: A Legacy of Unique food Culture in Penang." Paper presented at The 10th Symposium on Chinese Dietary Culture, Penang, Malaysia.

Sparks, Douglas Wesley. 1978. "Unity is Power: The Teochiu of Hong Kong." Ph.D. thesis, University of Texas at Austin.

Tan Chee-Beng. 2001. "Food and Ethnicity with Reference to the Chinese in Malaysia." In *Changing Chinese Foodways in Asia*, ed. David Y.H. Wu and Tan Chee-Beng. Hong Kong: The Chinese University Press, pp. 125–60.

Wu, David Y.H. 2001. "Chinese Cafe in Hong Kong." In *Changing Chinese Foodways in Asia*, ed. David Y.H. Wu and Tan Chee-Beng. Hong Kong: The Chinese University Press, pp. 71–80.

Contributors

Carmelea Ang See (施吟青) (Masters in Education, Lesley University) is the Director of Bahay Tsinoy, museum of Chinese in Philippine life and a volunteer for Kaisa Para sa Kaunlaran (Unity for Progress), a leading resource organization that advocates for the proactive and sustainable participation of the Chinese-Filipino community in local and national development. She also conducts literacy training for preschool and grade school teachers.

Jiemin Bao (包洁敏) is Professor of anthropology at the University of Nevada, Las Vegas. She received her Ph.D. from the University of California, Berkeley. Her book, *Marital Acts: Gender, Sexuality, and Identity among the Chinese Thai Diaspora*, was published by the University of Hawaii Press in 2005. Since then she has conducted research and published essays on Thai Americans and Buddhism, and co-edited a special issue on polygyny for the journal *Ethnology*.

Chan Yuk Wah (陈玉华) is Assistant Professor at the Department of Asian and International Studies, City University of Hong Kong. She obtained her Ph.D. in anthropology at the Chinese University of Hong Kong. Her publications cover China–Vietnam relationships, Vietnamese diaspora, and outbound Chinese tourism. Her current research projects include Vietnamese minority in Hong Kong, ethnic Chinese in Vietnam and Chinese tourists in Macau and Hong Kong.

Contributors 237

Duan Ying (段颖) (Ph.D., The Chinese University of Hong Kong) is Assistant Professor in the Department of Anthropology at the Sun Yatsen University. He works on ethnicity, transnational network, globalization, Chinese communities in Burma and Thailand, and Chinese Overseas and China.

Jean Duruz (Ph.D., Flinders University) is Adjunct Senior Research Fellow in the Hawke Research Institute at the University of South Australia. Her current research focuses on street food, markets, small businesses and ethnic neighbourhoods within contexts of global cities, such as Singapore, Mexico City and New York City. Publishing includes articles in *Space and Culture, Society and Space, Cultural Geographies, Emotion, Space and Society* and *Gastronomica*, and chapters in edited collections, such as Cheung and Tan, *Food and Foodways in Asia* (2007), Anderson and Schlunke, *Cultural Theory in Everyday Practice* (2008), and Wise and Velayutham, *Everyday Multiculturalism* (2009).

Mak Sau Wa, Veronica (麥秀華) is Ph.D. Candidate at the Department of Anthropology, The Chinese University of Hong Kong. Her major papers presented in international conferences include "National Milk, Foreign Milk, or Local Milk? A Study of Milk Supply and Consumption in Hong Kong," "Food, Space and Power: A Study of Dai Pai Dongs in Hong Kong," "A Study of Potato in Local Tea Café in Hong Kong."

Nancy J. Pollock (Ph.D., University of Hawai'i) is retired from the Departments of Anthropology and Development Studies, Victoria University, New Zealand. She has many publications related to food security and health issues in the Pacific and beyond, including *These Roots Remain* (1995), *Social Aspects of Obesity* (co-editor 1995), and *The Power of Kava* (editor, 1995). Recent articles include "Food and Transnationalism — Reassertions of Pacific Identity," in *Migration and Transnationalism*, ed. Helen Lee and Steve Francis (ANUepress, 2009), "Sustainability of the Kava Trade," *The Contemporary Pacific* 21 (2): 263–97 (2009), and "Nutrition and Anthropology: Cooperation and Convergences," *Ecology of Food and Nutrition* 46 (3): 245–62 (2007).

Myra Sidharta (欧杨春梅) (Drs. in Psychology, Leyden University, Netherlands), retired from the Faculty of Letters, Universitas Indonesia, Jakarta. She has been doing research on the culture of the Chinese in

238   *Contributors*

Indonesia, mainly on women, culinary culture, literature and religion. Her essays are published in *Indonesian Women in Focus* (ed. Elspeth Locher-Scholten), *The World of Soy* (ed. Christine M. du Bois, Chee-Beng Tan and Sydney Mintz), *Southeast Asian Chinese: The Socio-Cultural Dimension* (ed. Leo Suryadinata).

Tan Chee-Beng (陈志明) (Ph.D., Cornell University) is Professor at the Department of Anthropology, The Chinese University of Hong Kong. His major publications include *The Baba of Melaka* (1988) and *Chinese Overseas: Comparative Cultural Issues* (2004), as co-editor, *The Chinese in Malaysia* (2000), *Changing Chinese Foodways in Asia* (2001), *Food and Foodways in Asia* (2007), *The World of Soy* (2008), and as editor, *Southern Fujian: Reproduction of Traditions in Post-Mao China* (2006) and *Chinese Transnational Networks* (2007).

David Y.H. Wu (吴燕和) (Ph.D., Australian National University) is an affiliate Professor of Anthropology, University of Hawaii and Adjunct Fellow at the East-West Center, Honolulu, and Academia Sinica, Taipei. His major publications include books on *The Chinese in Papua New Guinea* (1982), *Ethnicity and Interpersonal Interaction* (editor, 1985), *Preschool in Three Cultures* (co-author, 1989, in Chinese, Korean, English, Italian and Portuguese) and he co-edited *Chinese Culture and Mental Health* (1985), *From Beijing to Port Moresby* (1998), *Changing Chinese Foodways in East Asia* (2001), and *The Globalization of Chinese Food* (2002).

Index

acar, 33
acculturation, 16, 83, 87, 98, 124–5, 164
ang ku kueh, 28
Asam Fish Head, 33
authenticity, 5, 11–2, 176, 181, 185, 219, 228–30

Baba, 11–2, 16, 28–30, 32, 34–5, 40–1, 178
Baba restaurant, 36, 121
Bah Kut Teh, 31, 36, 39, 43, 233
bamboo shoots, 127
Ban Chian Ke (*banjiandeh*) (peanut crumpets), 29
banh cuon (rice-sheet rolls), 6, 13, 156–69
banquet, 2, 100, 113, 145–6
bao (Chinese bun), 113
  siaopao (in the Philippines), 127, 132–3
barbecued pork, 151
bean sprouts, 177, 223
  toge, 132
Beijing cuisine, 16

belacan dishes, 32–3, 221–3
bird's nest, 107, 180
birthday, 28, 136
Borubudur, 111
breadfruit, 52, 54, 57, 60, 65, 69
bu (health enhancing), 25
bubur chacha, 36, 42
buffetization, 83, 85

Cantonese cuisine, 1, 13, 84, 143, 146–7
Capgomeh, 114
cha chaan teng (tea café), 7, 9, 15, 78, 218–34
Che Hu (Bosomboh), 35
chefs, 3, 7, 10–2, 14, 25, 29, 40, 50, 55, 68, 83, 85–8, 91–5, 99, 117, 176, 179, 181, 184, 188, 194, 208, 210–1, 218, 223–5, *see also* Hainanese cooks
cheong fan, 6, 13
Cheong Liew, 7, 10, 192–214
cheung fan (rice-flour rolls), 113, 122, 156–69
chilli dip, 29, 119

240   *Index*

Chinatown, 67, 117–8, 184, 194,
   205
Chinese
   American food, 8, 110
   condiments/ingredients, 125
   confinement food, 42
   cooking methods, 108
   festivals, 28
   Filipino food, 3, 6, 8–9, 124–40
   food in Burma, 9, 141–54
   food in Cambodia, 13, 18
   fusion cuisine, 85–7, 97
   Indonesian food, 3–4, 8–9, 107–22
   Malayan food, 4, 9, 24, 39
   Malaysian food, 3, 10, 15, 24, 35,
      see Chinese Malayan food
   Malaysian restaurant, 14, 18, 44
   New Year, 35, 122, 151, 180
   regional cuisines, 2–3, 55, 66, 83–4,
      121, 167
   Singaporean food, 3, 10, 24
   Singaporean restaurant, 14, 18, 44
   speech groups and food, 3, 26, 28
   Vietnamese foodways, 18
chopsuey, 10, 40, 68–9, 78, 82–3, 88,
   93, 95–7, 101
chow mein (*chow mein*), 40, 81, 83, 93,
   95, 180, 185
coffee shops, 12, 15, 35, 207
cooks, *see* chefs
culinary
   globalization, 3–5, 13, 15, 29, 85
   heritage, 6, 16
   innovation, 6, 8–10
   invention, 1, 4, 15–6
   localization, 4, 6, 8, 15–6, 30, 32,
      91–2, 124, 128, 143, 145–7,
      156, 222–3, 225
   reproduction, 4, 15–6, 24
curry, 68, 145
curry dishes, 33, 183
Curry Mee, 9, 18, 232–3

Dabogong, 148
dai pai dong (open-air food stalls), 219
daosa bnia (Tao Sar Pia), 9, 137
diasporic Chinese food defined, 4,
   5, 8, 11, 15–6, 24, 40, 75–101
   passim
diffusion of food, 3–4, 7
dim sum, 120, 128, 132, 151, 162,
   180–1
domestic workers, 10–1, 144
   Cantonese domestic helpers (Ah
      Sum), 11, 17
dosai, 207
duck cuisines, 84, *see* Peking Duck

eating out, 81, 98
ethnic food, 7, 12–3, 81, 176, 187, 193

feasts/feasting, 61–4, 67
fengshui, 180
fern shoots, 33
festivals, 12
festive food, 28
Fish Head Curry, 33
fish sauce, 166
food
   and distinction, 152
   and ethnicity, 88–9, 158, 176
   and gender, 11, 168
   and memory, 82, 118, 156, 158–9,
      196–200
   fermentation, 54
   for offering, 147–51
foodscape, 48–50, 54, 58, 65, 71
foodways explained, 188
fortune cookies, 81
fusion cuisine, 176
Fuzhou food, 1

Ghost festival, 151
globalization, *see* culinary globalization
Gongbao Chicken, 95

Index 241

Hainanese Chicken Rice, 10, 14, 17–8, 36–7, 39, 42–4, 177–8, 182, 203, 218–9, 221–3
   recipe, 17
Hainanese
   cooks, 10–1
   food, 1
Hakka
   food, 1, 2, 116–7
   restaurant, 13, 118
halal, 6, 16, 32, 118
hawkers, hawker centers, hawker stalls, hawker food, 31, 35, 126, 197, 207, 223, 230
hofan, 13–4
Hokkien (minnan) food, 1
Hokkien Mee, 8, 36, 43–4, 181, 227
hopia, 9, 137–9, *see also daosa bnia*
hybridity, hybridization, 40–1, 92, 194

Inche Kabin, 35
Indonesian
   Chinese returnees, 35
   restaurant, 36
innovation, *see* culinary innovation
intermarriage, 145
Ipoh Hofan, 31, 43
Islam 108, 111–2

jicama, 26

kerabu dishes, 33–4
kuih (*ge*), 37, 43
Kuih bangkit, 43
Kuih Pie Tee, 35
Kung Pao Chicken, 40
kway teow, 13–4, 18, 176–8, 182, 185–7, 218–9, 221–5, 232
   Fried Kway Teow, 9, 14, 18, 39, 43
   Penang Fried Kway Teow, 31, 180

Laksa, 7, 8, 11–2, 14, 34, 36, 39, 42–3, 197, 207, 219–20, 226–33
   Curry Laksa, 14, 34, 44
   laksa asam, 36, 43
   Penang (Asam) Laksa, 33, 226, 229
Lamian, 90
   Lanzhou Lamian, 29, 120, 128
   ramen, 90
Lapita culture/cuisine, 53–4, 59
localization defined, 8, *see* culinary localization
lomi, 135
low and high cuisines, 97–8
lumpia (spring rolls), 9, 21, 26–8, 128–32, 140, 176–8, 180–2
lumbnia, 26, 130

Mami (pork noodle), 133, 135
Mapo tofu, 25, 90
market gardening, 49, 65
Mawangdui, 55
Mee Siam, 36
Meicai kourou, 13
millet, 51, 56
misua (thin vermicelli), 136
moon cakes, 28
mungbean noodle, 135, 140
Muslims, 5–6, 183

nasi lemak, 34, 39, 44, 207
New Chinese migrants, 60
Nyonya cuisine, 16, 32–3, 40–1, 178, 180, 197, 204, 207
   Northern Nyonya Tradition, 33
   nyonya cooking, 77
   Nyonya curry, 180
   Nyonya tofu, 182
   Southern Nyonya Tradition, 33

Oh Chian (oyster omelette), 26
otak-otak, 36, 44, 204

242 *Index*

pad Thai, 180–1, 185
Pan-Chinese cuisine, 83, 94–7
Pancit (noodle dish), 124–5, 128, 130,
    133–4, 177
pearl milk tea, 42
Peking Duck, 11, 84, 95
Penang Chinese food, 36, 43
Penang restaurant, 121
Peranakan, 16, 32, 41, 79, 110
petai, 33
PNG Chinese food, 77–80, 117
Poh Pia, 9, 26, 28, 42, *see lumpia*

Qingming, 147–50

rendang dishes, 34, 43, 233
reproduction, *see* cultural reproduction
reterritorization, 11, 23, 36, 176–8,
    181
rice, 48–9, 51–3, 60, 69–70, 111, 129,
    167
    cultivation, 55, 66
    porridge, 30–1
        sweet potato congee, 127
Rijsttafel, 111, 117
roast
    duck, 84, 89
    meat, 29
Rojak, 36, 42, 197
roti canai, 44, 181
roti kaya, 36

sambal, 32–3, 41, 115–6
    dishes, 33
sari-sari stores, 127
satay 36, 39
    Beef Satay, 9, 223–5
sea cucumber, 66, 107, 113, 145–6
Shanghai cuisine, 16
Sharing food, 49–50, 60–1, 63, 65,
    70
Shark Fin's Soup, 66

shuan yangruo, 90
Shunde cuisine, 2, 13
siaomai (in the Philippines), 127,
    132–3
Sichuan restaurant, 30
siomay (Indonesia), 113
siumai, 151
snack, 132
Southeast Asian food, 9, 12
    ingredients, 33
soy products, 112–3, 115, 118, 127,
    136–7, 177, 220
spring rolls, *see lumpia*
standardization, 83, 92
Straits Chinese, Straits-born Chinese,
    11, 32
swike (frog legs), 120

tapai, 34
taro, 51, 54, 56–7, 62, 69–70, 77
taste, 41, 48, 50–2, 112
teahouses, teashops, 6, 109–10, 152–3,
    161
Teochiu
    cuisine, 1, 13
    porridge, 13
    restaurant, 13, 184
Teochius and Nam Pak Hong, 220
Thai restaurants, 178, 183–7
Thosai, 44
tikoy (sweet rice cake), 124, 138
tofu, 9, 17, 26, 31, 88, 108, 112–3,
    121–2, 185
    curry, 181
Totok, 32, 110
tourism, 3
tow suan, 36
transnational cuisine, 7, 175–6,
    179–80, 187–8
trepang, *see* sea cucumber

umu (earth oven), 53, 59

Index

waishengcai, see Pan-China cuisine
water spinach (*kangkong, tong-choi,*
etc.), 32, 185, 227
wedding, 136
Wenchang chicken, 17
wonton, 181

xiaoye (evening snacks), 35, 43
XO sauce, 128

Yangzhou chaofan, 25
Yi Yin, 50, 55

Yong tow fu, 207
  niang tofu, 13
Yuan Mei, 55
Yunnanese
  food, 6, 12, 143–4
  restaurant, 16

zongzi (dumpling), 28–9